521

The Story of Ted Williams' Home Runs

by Bill Nowlin

Foreword by Sam Williams

ROUNDER

521 — The Story of Ted Williams' Home Runs
By Bill Nowlin

Copyright 2013 by Bill Nowlin

Rounder Books
29 Lancaster Street
Cambridge MA 02140

ISBN-10: 1-57940-240-2
ISBN-13: 978-1-57940-240-2

Book design by Gilly Rosenthol, Rosenthol Design

Front cover photograph by Leslie Jones, courtesy of the Leslie Jones Collection at the Boston Public Library.

Back cover photograph by Bill Nowlin.

All interior photographs are also courtesy of the Leslie Jones Collection.

1. Ted Williams 1918-2002
2. Boston Red Sox (baseball team) - biography 3. Baseball - biography

First Edition

Printed in the United States of America

Table of Contents

Foreword

Maybe you can blame this book on me. I was talking with Bill Nowlin about a baseball card collection I had started of all the pitchers who gave up home runs to Ted Williams. It's a very cool collection. Bill's written several other books about my uncle, and the Red Sox. During our conversation, we decided it might make an interesting book, as well. Bill got right to work, and within what seemed like a few weeks I had a draft copy waiting in my email inbox.

Ted's career in the major leagues began in 1939, and the playing days of many of the old-timers he faced at the plate in his first year reached way back into the 1920s. When he retired at age 42 in 1960, some of the younger pitchers he faced as a seasoned but aging slugger would play for more than a decade after he hit his final home run — off Jack Fisher in his last at-bat.

As you might expect, Ted hit homers off some of the most legendary pitchers the game has ever seen — Bob Feller, Whitey Ford, Lefty Gomez, Red Ruffing, Bob Lemon, Dutch Leonard, Eddie Lopat, Schoolboy Rowe, and on and on and on. Collected here, for the first time, are the well-researched stories behind each and every one of the 521 home runs the Splendid Splinter bashed off big-league pitching. But Bill doesn't stop there. He even provides information on home runs that don't count toward his total, such as the blast he hit off the Cubs' Claude Passeau to win the All-Star Game in 1941, a homer Ted always said provided his greatest thrill in baseball. And there is even coverage of some of his home-run hitting in high school, the minor leagues, and spring training.

I'm sure I'm more than a little biased — if Ted isn't the greatest hitter who ever lived, he's right up there among the best. I remember visiting my uncle in Oakland in 1970 when he was managing the Washington Senators. Obviously, the hitters on his team frustrated him, so he came out to take a dozen or so cuts during batting practice and show them how it's done. Even though he was in his mid-50s, several of those balls soared gracefully into the seats, and most of the others came close, nearly all of them pulled straight down the right-field line. At the sound of the first mighty crack of the bat, every head in the stadium turned, and absolutely everyone stopped whatever they were doing to watch and listen as the mighty Ted Williams hit a baseball out of the park again. It ended all too soon, but everyone knew they'd witnessed history and heard a sound that had been missing from baseball for more than a decade, a sound that now has become a memory for the ages — the sound of a Ted Williams home run.

My, how the game has changed in the years that follow the decades of Ted's time in the game Bill has so ably chronicled in this book. I didn't realize only Boston's Fenway Park and Chicago's Wrigley Field remain from Ted's glory days. I'm not a baseball historian by any stretch of the imagination, so I learned many things from this book. A personal example — I discovered Ted hit a home run off Ned Garver of the St. Louis Browns on May 7, 1950, the day I was born. Wow. Reading about that homer made me smile, but I don't want to spoil your pleasure by recounting more of those stories here. I'll leave them for you to discover your own personal favorites as you read 521 — The Story of Ted Williams' Home Runs.

If you're a Ted Williams fan, a Boston Red Sox fan, or maybe just a baseball fan who loves to read stories about the greatest game ever played by the greatest athletes during what may be considered baseball's greatest era, you'll find this book a must-read for sure.

Sam Williams
The Kid's nephew

521 – The Story of Ted Williams' Home Runs

*"Hitting a baseball — I've said it a thousand times — is the single most dif-
ficult thing to do in sport."*
— *Ted Williams,* The Science of Hitting[1]

"I wanted to be the hitter who could hit every pitch out of the park."
— *Ted Williams, remembering himself at age 12* [2]

"Boy, I feel great. There ain't nothing like hittin' a home run!"
— *Ted Williams, quoted after winning the 1941 All-Star Game with a
ninth-inning come-from-behind homer.*[3]

Ted Williams was asked after he retired if there was anything he would
have done differently — and he said he'd have hit even more baseballs, taken
even more batting practice. He always said that it was the hardest thing to
do in sport — to hit a round ball with a round bat when the ball is thrown
at you something over 80 miles per hour. And to hit the ball in such a way
that it could not be adequately fielded by nine defenders, one behind you
and eight others arrayed in front of you. The pitcher isn't your friend. He
and the catcher are conspiring to deceive you — and maybe even frighten
you a little with a brushback pitch so you don't dig in too deeply or get too
comfortable at the plate.

No one can do so half the time over more than a few games. No one since Ted Williams in 1941 has been able to do so as much as 40% of the time over the course of a full season. A batter who can hit successfully 30% of the time—a .300 hitter—over a period of even just a few years in the major leagues stands a very good chance of being rewarded with millions of dollars a year. It's that difficult.

Of all the major leaguers since 1900, only four hit for a higher average than Ted Williams' career .344 mark. And none of those four combined power and average as well as Ted Williams. If one prizes both hitting for average and hitting for power, Babe Ruth and Ted Williams stand at the top of the list. Williams had a marginally-higher lifetime batting average—.344 to Ruth's .342—and he got on base more (he ranks #1 all-time with a .482 mark to Ruth's .474). Ruth hit 714 homers and Williams hit 521. Ruth showed more power, with a .690 slugging average to Williams' .634. Looking at OPS (on-base percentage plus slugging), Ruth ranks #1 with 1.1636 and Williams #2 with 1.1155.

Neither men had access to videotape, or the knowledge we have in the 21st century regarding physical conditioning. Ted Williams was always doing strengthening exercises—particularly wrist and forearm work to improve bat speed—but this was mostly squeezing a rubber ball and doing fingertip pushups rather than employing increasingly exotic strength and conditioning equipment.

He studied what he could—spending a lot of time just asking questions of other hitters ("What'd he get you out on? If I face Ruffing, and the count's 2-0, what's he going to throw me?")—to the point of annoyance, at times. He also consulted with physics professors at M.I.T. to try and learn what makes a curve ball curve, and participated in some wind tunnel studies for what he might learn.

When other players might have been more or less idle, killing time before or during a game, he kept his eyes open. "I used to watch all these opposing pitchers in the bullpen. They were always playing around and experimenting...I can think distinctly of Detroit, where I was in left field and they'd be warming up out there, and I could see them and see everything that was going on. So I had a pretty good insight as to the type of pitcher a guy was. That's what good hitters have to do if they want to stay ahead of the game."[4]

All quotations are from the *Boston Globe* unless noted. Usage has been standardized so that one newspaper which wrote "20th street" and another which wrote "20th Street" are both rendered the same. This also applied to the use of hyphens, as in "right-field bleachers" and in other respects.

The Chronology

Before the Big Leagues

We're going to jump right into it—Ted Williams' major-league career and his 521 home runs. After the completion of the big-league chronology are some remarks on his homers in high school, with the Pacific Coast League San Diego Padres, and his 1938 season in the Red Sox farm system with the Minneapolis Millers.

Ted's First Home Run

#1 April 23, 1939 at Fenway Park, Boston. Pitcher: Bud Thomas (Philadelphia A's). RH. Age 28. Thomas was coming off two full seasons of work for the A's and had 389 2/3 innings of major-league experience under his belt.

Bottom of the first inning. Two-run homer.

After all of one home run, the headline writer at the *Boston Globe* already awarded the young rookie the headline "TED WILLIAMS REVIVES FEATS OF BABE RUTH." He was 4-for-4 on the day, in just his fourth big-league game. It was a rainy and cold day.

Luther Baxter "Bud" Thomas threw the ball on April 23, 1939 that was the first home run Ted Williams hit in the majors. Thomas was pitching for the Philadelphia Athletics and Ted came up in the first inning, with Jim

Tabor on base. Ted powered it out. Contemporary reports indicate it was a fastball which Ted hit into the right-center field bleachers, where only Ruth, Gehrig, Roy Johnson, Tommy Henrich, Footsie Marcum, and Hal Trosky had ever placed one. The *Globe's* estimate had it about 400 feet, "to the right of where the higher and lower junctures of where the huge sun theater connects."

Thomas himself remembered it differently, some 58 years later; in an interview with the author on July 13, 1997, Thomas said, "He hit his first home run off me. The first one he ever hit. In Fenway Park. 1939. Spring of '39. He hit a sort of a change of pace, like it was a slow ball. He pulled it hard. It was just a fair ball way down the right-stadium line." Thomas only pitched 2/3 of an inning that day; he was pulled from the game.

In the third inning, he hit one high off the wall in left-center that missed going out by inches. He had to settle for two bases. He also singled, and in the ninth inning hit one hard enough that but for the wind might well have gone out. Though his homer had put the Red Sox in the lead, Philadelphia won the game in the end, 12-8. Thomas said he never talked about the homer with Ted, not after the game nor ever.

April 14, 1939 - Fitton Field, Worcester: Boston Red Sox rookie Ted Williams batting in front of Holy Cross catcher David Barry and hitting a grand slam.

1939

The Kid hit 31 homers in his rookie year. There was his first, the only one he hit in April. There followed 30 more. He was on his way to a season in which he drove in 145 runs, setting a major-league rookie record which has never been equaled, even with the season being extended to 162 games.

#**2** May 4 at Briggs Stadium, Detroit. Pitcher: Roxie Lawson (Detroit Tigers). RH. Age 33. Lawson had pitched off and on in the majors since 1930. He had over 600 innings' experience before throwing the fourth inning.

Top of the fourth inning. Two-run homer.

His first time up, Ted hit one out of Briggs Stadium—up and over the right-field roof, but "foul by inches." He then lined out to center. On a 3-2 count in the fourth inning, Ted's "towering smash landed atop the right-field roof, nearer center field than right, and bounded back into the playing field only because the eaves of the roof slant downward in that sector. As the crow flies, that belt was good for 360 feet without even figuring altitude."

Ted hit two homers off Lawson in 1939 (see also #29, on September 20 at Fenway.)

#3 May 4 at Briggs Stadium, Detroit. Pitcher: Bob Harris (Detroit Tigers). RH. Age 24. Harris had only 15 1/3 innings of major-league experience before throwing the fifth inning.

Top of the fifth inning. Three-run homer. GAME WINNER.

Harris had turned 24 just three days earlier. This was the first home run he'd surrendered—and it was quite a blast. If he'd been paying attention, he would have seen "Titanic Ted's" first two drives out of the park, one foul and one fair. Tigers catcher Rudy York certainly saw them. Harris, on in relief with the score 4-4, had to worry about Foxx and Cronin on base. He threw three straight balls. On the 3-0 count, John Kieran of the *New York Times* wrote that as York "signed for a fast ball, he looked up at Ted and said, 'You wouldn't think of hitting this one, would you?' 'Hit it?' says Ted, 'If it's near the plate I'll hit it outta the park.'" And so he did.

"It was a climbing liner—as much a liner as a drive could be which cleared a 120-foot barrier, straight as a string, over the whole works in right field, about a dozen feet fair. According to eye-witnesses outside the park, it landed across adjoining Trumbull av. and bounded against a taxi company garage on the other side on the first hop." Think Tigers pitchers were a little intimidated? Think the word didn't spread around baseball very quickly? "So you weren't kidding, after all?" asked York as Williams crossed home plate.[5]

The right-field grandstand was 325 feet from home plate and reached 120 feet high, the "tallest barrier in either league to clear and one that the game's greatest sluggers from Babe Ruth down had tried and never accomplished." The Detroit writers called it the longest homer ever hit at the stadium.

Detroit fans were sufficiently impressed that, the *Boston Herald* reported, "a tremendous, unanimous 'O-O-O-Oh' of amazement arose from the stands and practically all the spectators stood and applauded at Ted made the circuit and tagged the plate."

Ted hit #19 off Bob Harris, too, but he was with the St. Louis Browns at the time, traded as part of a ten-player deal on May 13.

Later homers Ted hit off Lum Harris (2), Bubba Harris, and Earl Harrist presented no family connections of which we are aware.

1939 – Boston Red Sox rookie Ted Williams leaning on the batting cage at Fenway Park.

Ted was always up for a challenge, it seemed. In spring training, as the team came north, they played two games in Atlanta, the first one on April 1. Johnny Orlando showed Ted the three parallel fences in the outfield, "one right behind the other, like a prison compound. Johnny says, 'I saw the Babe hit one out over the last one, right there.' I said, 'Oh, yeah?' Boy, I was going to do that, too. But five times up and I didn't do it, and about the eighth inning I struck out with two men on, and could hardly stand it. I went out to right field seething. The Cincinnati batter hit a little fly down the line that curved foul and I ran over, got it and dropped it, then booted it trying to pick it up. I was so mad when I finally grabbed it I threw it the hell out of the park over the last fence. The ball hit a Sears store across the street. Cronin pulled me out right away, and he didn't have to say a word because I was ashamed the moment I did it. The next day I hit one over that last fence, and I gave Johnny a hard look when I came in."[6]

#4 May 9 at Sportsman's Park, St. Louis. Pitcher: Ed Cole (St. Louis Browns). RH. Age 30. Cole had 90 2/3 innings' experience before throwing the tenth inning.

Top of the tenth inning. Three-run homer. GAME WINNER.

If you hit a three-run homer in the top of the tenth, chances are you're going to win that game for your team, and so it was in this case, though the Browns did score once in the bottom of the tenth. The Red Sox won 10-8. The Sox had almost blown in. They held a 7-3 lead after six, but let the Browns score twice in the seventh and twice in the eighth. Williams was 0-for-5 in the game before coming up with two men on in the tenth. Ed Cole was the fourth pitcher of the game for St. Louis. Vosmik singled and Foxx singled him to third base. Cronin struck out.

Burt Whitman of the *Boston Herald* wrote that Williams had been "crippled by a too-obvious home-run swinging complex." He was in a slump, one hit in his last 12 at-bats and St. Louis starter Jack Kramer had twice struck him out with the bases loaded. But facing Cole, on a full count, Ted "caught an inside pitch and lined it onto the chummy right-field roof. It barely cleared the screen."

Cole's real name was Edward Kisleauskas, but so far as we know he was un-related to Joe Krakauskas. Cole was 1-7 in his career. He only appeared in three more games, one more in May and then two in September 1939.

#5 May 27 (second game) at Fenway Park. Pitcher: Joe Krakauskas (Washington Senators). LH. Age 24.

Bottom of the third inning. Three-run homer.

Montreal native Krakauskas had 216 1/3 innings' experience before throwing the second inning. He was the first lefty off whom Williams homered. He also served up homer #100.

The Sox took both games of a Saturday afternoon doubleheader in Washington, winning 11-4 and 7-6. It was a homer-heavy day for the Red Sox, with Joe Vosmik hitting two, and Ted, Cronin, Bobby Doerr, and Jimmie Foxx each hitting one. Ted had hit a triple off the left-center field wall his first time up. He returned to bat in the third inning with Doc

1939 – Boston Red Sox Ted Williams crossing home plate and shaking hands with the batboy after hitting a home run against the New York Yankees at Fenway Park.

Cramer on second and Vosmik on first. Doerr had already homered off "Joe Crackers" into the left-field screen earlier in the inning. Ted swung on a 2-0 pitch. "It was a home run from the instant it left his light but wickedly swung bat soaring miles high and straight for the upper sector of the distant center-field bleachers. There it landed some half a dozen rows up, fully 450 feet from the dish." Gehrig, Foxx, and Hank Greenberg were among others who could be remembered to have hit any that far at Fenway "but none with the authority that Teddy displayed yesterday." Williams later slapped a double off the left-field scoreboard; he drove in six runs on the day, and lacked only a single for the cycle. The winning run came courtesy of Vosmik's second homer; Joe was the first batter up in the bottom of the ninth in a 6-6 tie.

#6 May 28 at Fenway Park. Pitcher: Walt Masterson (Washington Senators). RH. Age 19. Masterson had only 18 innings of major-league experience before throwing the fifth inning.

Bottom of the fifth inning. Two-run homer.

The *Herald* called him "Ted the Terror." His two RBIs took him to 32, in a tie for the league lead with Washington's Taft Wright after this intermittently-rainy Sunday game. Wright batted in one, while on a 1-2 pitch, Ted drove in two with his sixth home run of the year, "another landmark affair" going into one of the exit ramps fully 40 feet up in the right-center field bleachers. The Sox had already scored six times in the third inning, without the benefit of an extra-base hit (in fact, Ted's line-drive single had glanced off Foxx running from first to second, or they would have scored more.) His home run boosted the score to 10-4 in a game the Red Sox won, 12-7; while it wasn't a game-winner, it provided additional comfort for reliever Denny Galehouse later in the game when the Senators scored three times in the top of the ninth.

Masterson also was hit for homers #42, 197, 218, and 402. He was with the Senators for the first three and the Tigers for #402.

#7 May 30 (first game) at Fenway Park. Pitcher: Red Ruffing (New York Yankees). RH. Age 34. Hall of Famer.

Ruffing had 3,584 2/3 innings of major-league experience before throwing the first inning. He may have been the most experienced pitcher Williams ever faced.

Bottom of the first inning. Two-run homer.

Ruffing had broken in with the Red Sox in 1924 and was an unimpressive 39-96 for Boston into the 1930 season, when he was traded to the Yankees. Given a new start, he won 231 games for the Yankees (against 124 losses) and was ultimately voted into the Hall of Fame in 1967.

Ruffing gave up the first hit of Ted's career, a double on April 20 in Yankee Stadium. It was, Ted wrote in his autobiography, "just a foot from going into the bleachers. I'd gotten under it a little bit or it would have gone out."[7]

Young Williams was full of confidence; when he'd first seen Ruffing warming up back on April 20, he'd said to Red Sox pitcher Jack Wilson, "That's Ruffing, huh? He doesn't look that tough. After Ruffing struck him out, he said, "He throws me that pitch again and I'll hit it out of the park."[8]

Red Sox fans from northern New England parked in their cars overnight for this one, and there were 600 people in line after 7 AM. The game sold out. Those who could get in were rewarded. Ted hit one homer in each game of the Memorial Day doubleheader, and the *Boston Globe* again offered a Ruthian reference. The first home run came off Red Ruffing, who was 7-0 on the young season suffering his first defeat. The *Post*, almost in passing, called it "the longest drive ever hit in Yawkey Yard." On a 1-0 count, Ted slugged Ruffing's high fastball and "like a meteor zooming out of the heavens the ball went steaming fully 75 feet up into the right-center field stands, just to the left of the alleyway those open bleachers from the covered pavilion and just above where a sign [sic] 402 feet on the field wall. Even Ruffing couldn't conceal his amazement as Teddy loped around the bases in his usual grinning style and the crowd went completely nuts." Joe Cronin followed with a homer of his own into the left-field net.

Ruffing gave up three other homers to Ted — #47, 126, and 181.

#**8** May 30 (second game) at Fenway Park. Pitcher: Monte Pearson (New York Yankees). RH. Age 30. Pearson had 1,188 1/3 innings of major-league experience before throwing the fifth inning.

Bottom of the fifth inning. Two-run homer.

Montgomery Marcellus Pearson was on his way to a wrapping up a 56-22 record in his first four years with the Yankees, 1936-39.

For Ted Williams, this was the fourth home run in four days for "the irrepressible 20-year-old stringbean" but this one came in the fifth inning of a 17-9 pounding administered by the Yankees. It was another two-homer homer following a base on balls. This one was a "three and two slow curve sock that landed among the first pews of the right-center field sun seats." The *New York Times* saw Ted's two homers as a pair of "420-foot homers" though the one hit off Ruffing surely went further and was separately said "spectacular."

A full house took in the games. Over 10,000 fans had been turned away at the gates. Ted had now hit four homers into the rarely-reached right-field bleachers for four game in a row. Veteran *Herald* scribe Burt Whitman said the first homer was about halfway up the bleachers and deeper than anything he'd ever seen Babe Ruth hit. He thought it might have gone 500 feet on level ground.

#9 June 9 (second game) at Sportsman's Park, St. Louis. Pitcher: Harry Kimberlin (St. Louis Browns). RH. Age 30.

Top of the third inning. Three-run homer.

Kimberlin was in his fourth year in the majors, but he hadn't pitched a whole lot, just 23 games before this one.

The Red Sox won the day's first game, 6-4, but overwhelmed the Browns in the second, 18-7. They scored six times in the top of the first and three times more in the second, and were on their third reliever already—Harry Kimberlin—when Williams clouted "a smash that landed on the roof out of the right-field pavilion." In a phone call on July 7, 1997, Kimberlin told this author "I remember every bit of it. I was doing a lot of relief pitching then. The ball went halfway to the Mississippi River. Over Grand Avenue. It went over everything, son. It went over everything. I always said it went to the river, but it didn't get that far."

It was Ted's ninth homer, but he was chasing Jimmie Foxx now. Double-X had hit his 10th and 11th. Ted hit another long ball that carried 420 feet but that one went for only two bases, to straightaway center.

Kimberlin only gave up 12 homers in his big-league career, but among those who hit one were Rudy York, Hank Greenberg, Ted Williams, and Jimmie Foxx hit two.

#10 June 29 at Fenway Park. Pitcher: Nels Potter (Philadelphia Athletics). RH. Age 27.

Bottom of the fourth inning. One-run homer.

Potter had 174 innings of major-league experience before throwing the fourth inning.

This was the first solo home run Ted Williams ever hit in the big leagues. The first nine had been two-run homers (five of them) or three-run homers (four of those.) It came after a stretch of 14 homerless games; Ted was hitting, but just hadn't hit any out. On the 29th, the A's beat Boston, 8-6. Even though the Red Sox scored in five separate innings, but they only recorded one run each time, save for two in the bottom of the eighth. Ted's homer accounted for the one run in the fourth. It "went directly over second base, into the center-field stands, the ball bounding back 100 feet onto the playing field." The *Herald* account had it "a high and pretty fly to dead center… into the very front of the center-field bleachers." Ted drove in two of the other Red Sox runs, having himself a 3-for-4 day.

It was the only homer Ted hit off Potter, but obviously one well-struck.

#11 July 2 (first game) at Fenway Park. Pitcher: Lefty Gomez (New York Yankees). LH. Age 30. Hall of Famer.

Bottom of the seventh. Three-run homer. GAME WINNER.

Gomez had 2,116 2/3 innings of major-league experience before throwing the seventh inning.

Gomez was a future Hall of Famer, 181-101 with the Yankees (and 6-0 in World Series play.) He had four 20-win seasons under his belt, and had led the league twice in both wins and earned run average (26-5, 2.33 ERA in 1934 and (21-7, 2.33 ERA) in 1937.

This was Ted's third homer that counted as a game-winner. The twinbill was a hard-fought affair, with both New York's Tommy Henrich and Boston's Bobby Doerr sent to the hospital for x-rays. There were six other injuries of one sort or another before the day was over, none of them serious. There was even a hidden-ball trick executed, Cronin the victim. Ted's soaring home run gave him 61 RBIs on the season, even before the Fourth of July, tying him with Hank Greenberg for the lead. There were two outs and two on, the score tied 3-3. The ball his off Lefty Gomez carried into the right-field bleachers, "a drive that went with a favoring wind, just clearing the fence as

Henrich backed into the wall." [*New York Times*] It was Tommy hitting the wall hard (he "smacked his head against the concrete front wall as the ball carried into the bleachers and suffered a severe concussion and a lacerated scalp," wrote the *Herald*.) His injury resulted in an overnight stay at St. Elizabeth's. Ted's drive won the game for another Hall of Famer nicknamed "Lefty"—Boston's Lefty Grove.

Ted also hit #76 off Lefty Gomez.

#**12** July 4 (first game) at Shibe Park, Philadelphia. Pitcher: Cotton Pippen (Philadelphia Athletics). RH. Age 28.

Top of the first inning. Three-run homer.

Pippen had 70 innings of major-league experience before starting the first inning.

Ted had faced Pippen before, in the Pacific Coast League in 1937 when Pippen was working for Sacramento. In fact, Ted had his first at-bat as a professional against him when he pinch-hit in a game at San Diego "and just stood there too scared to swing while he poured three straight down the middle."[9]

The big story of the day was "Bad Boy Jim Tabor"—Ted's fellow rookie—who hammered two grand slams in the second game (and another homer, too, for good measure.) One of the grand slams was an inside-the-park home run. Tabor had already hit a homer in the first game. Cronin and Doerr had joined Tabor and Ted with first-game homers. There were a lot of runs scored this day, with the Red Sox prevailing, 17-7, in the opener and then winning the second game, 18-12. Ted had five RBIs on Independence Day. Where Ted's home run ball landed was lost in the stories about Tabor. Eddie Collins Jr. made his major-league debut for the A's in the first game.

Pippen surrendered 22 homers in 38 major-league appearances, and in the process served one up to each of these future Hall of Famers: Earl Averill, Joe Cronin, Bill Dickey, Joe DiMaggio, Bobby Doerr, Charlie Gehringer, Chuck Klein, and Ted Williams.

#**13** July 15 at Cleveland Stadium, Cleveland. Pitcher: Johnny Broaca (Cleveland Indians). RH. Age 29.

Top of the eighth inning. One-run homer. GAME WINNER.

Broaca had 657 innings of major-league experience before starting the eighth.

The Sox scored five runs in the top of the first inning, but the Indians got three in the third and two more in the fifth. Johnny Broaca had come into the game in the first inning and worked 6 2/3 innings of relief. With one out in the top of the eighth, Ted banged Broaca's first pitch for "a vicious clout into the far-off right-field stands" which stood as the margin of victory in Boston's 9-5 victory. The *Cleveland Plain Dealer* said it landed about six rows into the stands, not far from the foul pole. The outcome gave the Red Sox their tenth win in a row; they won the next two, too, sweeping the July 16 doubleheader.

Bay State native Broaca gave up 51 homers in 121 games. This was the only one hit by Ted, in Broaca's last season.

#**14** July 17 at Briggs Stadium, Detroit. Pitcher: Bobo Newsom (Detroit Tigers). RH. Age 31.

Top of the first inning. Two-run homer.

Newsom had 2,069 1/3 innings of major-league experience before starting the first inning.

"Thumping Theodore" followed up on a two-out Jimmie Foxx single, watching Bobo's first pitch—a slow ball—hit in the dirt. Expecting one more amped-up, Ted "leaped on a Newsom fastball and lashed it into the upper right-field deck." (*Boston Herald*) The Tiger scored six in the third inning and five in the sixth inning, on their way to a 13-6 win. The loss put an end to Boston's 12-game winning streak, though Ted's roommate Woody Rich bore the defeat. Newsom ended the year with a 20-11 record, the middle one of three years (1938-40) in which won 20 or more.

Four times, Newsom led the league in losses, but he still won 211 major-league games. This was the only homer Ted hit off him.

Players on the other clubs tried not to get Ted angry, saying, "Let him sleep, don't wake him up." In 1939 Auker saw Brownie right-hander Buck Newsom strike Williams out then laugh into his glove. Of course the Boston players made sure Ted saw it. "I thought he was going to go out and get him with a bat," Auker says. In his next time up, Williams whaled a home run off Newsom. "Laugh that off!" he yelled as he circled the bases.[10]

#15 July 18 (first game) at Comiskey Park, Chicago. Pitcher: Clint Brown (Chicago White Sox). RH. Age 35.

Top of the eighth inning. Two-run homer.

Brown had 1,283 innings of major-league experience before starting the eighth inning.

The Red Sox split a double header on the 18th, with Ted Williams collecting six hits — three in each game. He drove in three runs in the first game and one in the second, giving him 77 on the season and an eight-RBI lead over Hank Greenberg. Once again, he drove in Foxx, who'd tripled. The count was 1-0. This time "a steaming smash a good 400 feet from home plate that landed half-way up in the upper part of the right-centerfield stands." The White Sox won, 13-10. Ted's homer drove in Boston's last two runs and made the score somewhat more respectable.

It was the only homer he ever hit off anyone named Clint.

#16 July 23 (second game) at Sportsman's Park, St. Louis. Pitcher: Jack Kramer (St. Louis Browns). RH. Age 21.

Top of the sixth inning. Two-run homer.

Kramer had 127 1/3 innings of major-league experience before starting the sixth inning.

The Red Sox racked up runs and pummeled St. Louis 13-5 and 11-3. The Kid was 3-for-5 with two doubles and a single and three RBIs in the first game, but the homer was his only hit in four at-bats in the nightcap. The ball landed "on top of the right-field stands" (*Herald*) and the *Globe* agreed, saying it went "over the right-field roof." Foxx hit his 19th homer of the season in the same game, giving him the league lead.

Ted also hit homers #33, 132, 169, and 185 off Kramer.

#17 August 13 (second game) at Fenway Park. Pitcher: Alex Carrasquel (Washington Senators). RH. Age 26.

Bottom of the second inning. One-run homer.

Carrasquel had 111 2/3 innings of major-league experience before starting the second inning.

The Red Sox won seven games in a row, including the first game of the August 13 doubleheader (a 9-1 win for Fritz Ostermueller) but they dropped this one, 6-3, an eight-inning game

Ted Williams was 3-for-3 with one RBI in the first game and 3-for-3 with one RBI in the second game. He'd also walked twice in the first game, 8-for-8 in reaching base. The one RBI in game two was the leadoff homer he hit in the bottom of the second inning, off Venezuelan rookie Alejandro Carrasquel, into "the right-center field wing of the centerfield bleachers." (*Herald*) He'd been in a slump, this being the first home run in more than three weeks. It came in the final game of a 22-game homestand.

This was Carrasquel's rookie year. Ted also hit homer #86 off him.

#18 August 19 (first game) at Griffith Stadium, Washington. Pitcher: Pete Appleton (Washington Senators). RH. Age 35.

Top of the ninth inning. Four-run homer (Ted's first grand slam). GAME WINNER.

Appleton had 1,023 innings of major-league experience before pitching the inning.

The Red Sox were down to their last out when Ted hit one out. The grand slam over Griffith Stadium's 35-foot high right-field wall, clearing it by several yards, came as the climax of a five-run top of the ninth which gave the Red Sox an 8-6 win over Washington. Right fielder George Case didn't even bother to turn around. The four runs driven in brought Ted Williams to an even 100.

By the time he'd hit 18 homers, Ted had already gone deep on two pitchers who had changed their names—Ed Cole and Pete Appleton. Pete had been born Peter William Jablonowski, but changed his name in 1933, after five seasons in the majors. He'd pitched for Boston in 1932 (0-3).

A grand slam just before the season

The first grand slam Ted hit in a Red Sox uniform came during his first at-bat in New England. It was at Fitton Field in Worcester on April 14, 1939, in front of some 6,000 fans who came out in the cold. The team had just barnstormed north from spring training, playing ten exhibition games against the Cincinnati Reds in Georgia, South Carolina, North Carolina, and Virginia, then come to Massachusetts to play one against Holy Cross. In the first inning, Ted came to bat with Foxx, Cronin, and Tabor on base, facing Holy Cross pitcher Mike Klarnick. He homered, and it was "no towering, wind-blown fly. On the contrary, Ted's thump...sailed over the head of Hank Ouelette, playing a deep center field, and carried to the reaches of the football gridiron." (*Springfield Republican*) The Red Sox won, 14-2, Ted's slam a game-winner.

#19 August 22 at Sportsman's Park, St. Louis. Pitcher: Bob Harris (St. Louis Browns). RH. Age 24.

Top of the fourth inning. Three-run homer.

Harris had 114 2/3 innings of major-league experience before pitching the fourth inning.

Back in May, Williams had also hit #3 off Harris, who became the first pitcher to give up two homers to Ted. Harris was on his way to an unfortunate 4-13 season. This game wasn't one of his losses. The "L" went to starter Bill Trotter who only lasted one-third of an inning but was charged with four runs. The Red Sox won, 10-3. Ted's homer gave them an 8-0 lead. It traveled at least 455 feet, clearing the park, "landed on Grand av. and bounced so high it was visible over the top of the grandstand roof. When last seen it was traveling fast toward East St. Louis." Later in the game, he banged a triple off the 426-foot sign affixed to the center-field wall.

Ted had 19 homers now, but Foxx had 33.

This must have been the 1939 game Bobby Doerr was talking about when he told of Browns manager Fred Haney saying to Ted before the game, "Let's see how you hit sittin' on your ass." Doerr said, "When the game started, the first pitch to Ted was right near his ear and knocked the big guy down. Ted got up, didn't even dust off his uniform, took his stance and on the next pitch drove it against the right-field screen for a double. The next time up, the first pitch knocked him down and on pitch two, Ted drove it onto Grand Boulevard for a home run."[11]

#20 August 28 at League Park, Cleveland. Pitcher: Mel Harder (Cleveland Indians). RH. Age 29.

Top of the eighth inning. Three-run homer. GAME WINNER.

Harder had 2,323 innings of major-league experience before pitching the eighth inning.

Ted's home run added three more to the run scored earlier in the inning and boosted the Red Sox to a 6-5 lead over the Tribe, which held up when Cleveland was held scoreless in the eighth and ninth. Ted had swung hard and missed Harder's curveball by a foot on the previous pitch, bringing the count to 3-2. He hit the next pitch over the "chummy right-field screen" at League Park. (*Boston Herald*) The Indians had two home fields in the late 1930s — the smaller League Park and (for larger games, such as week-end affairs) the larger-capacity Cleveland Stadium. Ted had homered at Cleveland Stadium back on July 15, so he'd now homered in each of the two Indians ballparks.

Williams later hit homers #27, 73, and 113 off Harder.

The next day's *Boston Globe* quoted Joe Cronin as saying, "The Kid has lived up to his advance notice. I guess that's so even if he doesn't drive in another run for the rest of the year." After readers of the August 29 *Globe* put down their morning paper, Williams did drive in another run — five of them — that very day.

#**21** August 29 at League Park, Cleveland. Pitcher: Harry Eisenstat (Cleveland Indians). LH. Age 23.

Top of the fifth inning. Four-run homer (grand slam #2). GAME WINNER.

Eisenstat had 291 1/3 innings of major-league experience before pitching the fifth inning.

Eisenstat had begun the season with the Tigers, but was working for the Indians when Ted homered off him. The Red Sox won, 7-4. Ted drove in five of the Red Sox runs, and homer #21 was a game-winner for the second game in succession. Eisenstat had only allowed two hits over the first four, but a big six-run fifth inning did the Indians in. The first run scored on a fielder's choice, the second on a bobble, and then on a 2-1 count the "smiling stringbean rookie sensation" hit a grand slam that "traveled at least 400 feet over the right-center field wall" and, Cleveland sportswriter Eugene J. Whitney of the *Plain Dealer* explained, "ricocheted off electric light wires on the south side of Lexington Avenue and bounced into a parking lot." Ted came up with the bases loaded again in the very next inning (this time facing Floyd Stromme) and drove in the seventh run, thanks to a bases-loaded walk. Arthur Sampson of the *Boston Herald* suggested that Stromme had seen Ted hit a three-run homer and a four-run homer in back-to-back days and "apparently figured it was better to give up one run than four."

The win went to Holy Cross's Lefty Lefebvre, his first major-league decision. Lefebvre produced another notable Red Sox home run. On June 10, 1938, the pitcher had hit a Fenway Park home run in his first at-bat in the major leagues.

Williams later hit homer #97 off Eisenstat.

#**22** August 30 at Briggs Stadium, Detroit. Pitcher: Fred Hutchinson (Detroit Tigers). RH. Age 19.

Top of the third inning. Three-run homer.

Hutchinson had 47 innings of major-league experience before pitching the third inning.

Homer #22 was hit on Ted's 21st birthday—but hardly anybody knew it. He'd told everyone his birthday was October 30, so he wouldn't have the distraction of people wishing him "happy birthday" during the course of the season. Even his 1939 and other early baseball cards showed the October 30 birthdate. But he knew, and his mother May knew back in San Diego. If she'd read the A.P. story in the August 31 *San Diego Union*, she would have read that that "Boston's sensational rookie outfielder, Ted Williams, batted a home run with two mates on base to put the Sox in the lead in the third inning."

Careful scissoring for a scrapbook was in order, however. The sentence continued with the explanation that "it was his error on Birdie Tebbetts' single that permitted Pete Fox to score from first base with Detroit's winning run in the eighth." So first Ted had batted in what could have been the winning run, but then booted the ball for what became the losing run. As the *Globe* put it, "Young Ted Williams played the role of the hero and villain in the wrong order today, with the result that the Red Sox tossed away what looked like certain victory."

After Ted's home run, Jim Tabor hit one and then so did—somewhat improbably—Moe Berg. It was the last of Berg's six career home runs, spread over a 15-year career.

Ted had also made a "spectacular glove-handed catch" on one fly, but was perceived to have a "weakness on ground balls" and he "allowed the ball to roll through him" as two runs scored, including Pete Fox all the way from first base. His home run had been a "drive high into the upper tier of the right-field stands." (*Herald*)

The birthday boy had now hit homers three days in a row. And his homers had produced a lot of runs. Only three had been solo home runs. With his 22 home runs, Ted had driven in 54 runs. Foxx had 34 homers but only driven in 49 runs, since 23 of his were solo home runs.

Now it wasn't entirely a secret that the say was Ted's birthday. Lefty Grove seemed to know. A tag note after the *Globe*'s game story read: "Ol' Mose Grove started a rumor that today was also Ted Williams' natal anniversary, but Ted was so mad this evening he wouldn't even discuss it...His listed birthday is Oct. 30."

Williams later hit homers #139, 156, 163, 209, 225, 235, and 273 off Hutchinson.

In his first year or two in particular, the young Ted Williams was sometimes criticized for a lack of concentration in the field. In 1939, Joe Cronin asked Doc Cramer to give Ted a few pointers. "Cramer watched Ted field. 'He's miss one, catch one, miss one,' Doc remembered. 'Ah, hell, Doc,' Ted said. 'they don't pay off on me catching these balls. They're gonna pay me to hit.'" Responding to what Ted said about not being paid for catching balls, Cramer said, "Well, I can see that."[12]

#**23** September 3 (second game) at Fenway Park. Pitcher: Bump Hadley (New York Yankees). RH. Age 34.

Bottom of the third inning. Two-run homer.

Hadley had 2,817 2/3 innings of major-league experience before pitching the third inning.

Irving Darius "Bump" Hadley was the first pitcher to give up two homers to Ted Williams in the same game. There were 11 times he hit a pair off the same pitcher in a given game, and one time he hit three (Bob Keegan of the White Sox, on May 8, 1957).

The first game of the day's doubleheader against the Yankees was a wild one, a 12-11 win for the Red Sox (with pitcher Lefty Lefebvre pinch-hitting and driving in the go-ahead run in the bottom of the eighth). Joe Cronin had five RBIs in the game. Ted was 1-for-2 with three walks. It was the seventh win in a row for Boston over New York, a streak that started when the Sox swept every game in an unusual five-game set at Yankee Stadium in three days (July 7-9), and they'd won the Saturday, September 2 game, too, 12-7. Every one of those wins was without benefit of a Ted Williams home run. He had been a cumulative 9-for-21 with four RBIs, but nary a homer.

All in all, the day's Fenway fans had watched their team come from behind four times on the day. In the second game—the subject here—New York scored once in the first and so did the Red Sox.

Ted Williams: "Cramer was on second...and he gave me the closed fist. Curve ball coming. He'd picked up Dickey's sign. So I'm looking for a curve. Bump Hadley's pitching for the Yankees and he rears back and gives me a fastball and it's almost past when I give it one of those late little quick swings. Line drive, right center field, home run. The next day I read in the paper where Dickey said, 'Williams hit the ball right out of my glove,' which was perfect because it meant that I had waited."[13]

Ted hit a two-run homer into the right-field bleachers in the bottom of the third (#23) to make it 3-1. The Yankees took a 4-3 lead in the top of the sixth. Next came Ted's 24th homer....

#24 September 3 (second game) at Fenway Park. Pitcher: Bump Hadley (New York Yankees). RH. Age 34.

Bottom of the sixth inning. One-run homer.

Hadley had 2,819 2/3 innings of major-league experience before pitching the fifth inning.

Picking up the story in mid-game, the Yankees had scored twice in the top of the sixth to take a 4-3 lead. Ted tied it up with a solo home run in the bottom of the sixth, and Joe Cronin followed Ted back-to-back with a homer of his own to put Boston back on top. New York's Joe Gordon hit a solo homer off Elden Auker in the top of the seventh to tie it up. There it stood, 5-5, until the Yankees scored two runs in the top of the eighth. The 6:29 PM curfew was fast approaching and the Yankees wanted to speed up the game, hoping those runs would score, so deliberately began to make outs, twice trotting to home on a pitch (a nominal attempted steal of home plate) and both times being laughably caught out. The Red Sox, for their part, were trying to prolong the game by, among other things, issuing an uncalled-for intentional walk. Manager Cronin naturally came out to protest the Yankees tactics, which consumed a few more minutes. The *Globe* frowned on the "disgraceful conduct of the crowd"—fans littering the field with pop bottles and "Summer skimmers and undevoured hot dog rolls"—so many that the field were rendered unplayable. "The barrage lasted for fully three minutes," eating up more time. At 6:26, umpire Cal Hubbard forfeited the game to the Yankees, the score per rule becoming

9-0. He said he worried about the safety of the New York players and that Boston home officials were unable to control the crowd. Cronin said he would appeal on the grounds that the umpires had neglected to deal with the Yankees' actions, which is what had incited the crowd.

But the forfeiture wasn't the end of it. Five days later, American League president Will Harridge overruled Hubbard, fined each of the Yankees who'd deliberately run into outs at the plate, and also fined Babe Dahlgren for swinging on an intentional pitchout. He ruled that the game be replayed on September 26 as part of a doubleheader. Those games were rained out. They were then to be played on September 27, but those games were postponed due to rain and cold and the Red Sox had to head out on the road. The plan was then to play two double headers, albeit in New York, to make up the games lost, on September 30 and October 1. The games on the 30th were played, but "an all-day drizzle" washed out the two October 1 games. Without having replayed the game ordered to be replayed, but with the forfeit overturned, September 3's second game goes into the books as a 5-5 tie. And Ted's two homers went in the books, too.

The home runs Ted had hit both went into the right-field bleachers, and both were said to have traveled 425-440 feet.

#**25** September 10 (first game) at Shibe Park, Philadelphia. Pitcher: Chubby Dean (Philadelphia Athletics). LH. Age 23.

Top of the ninth inning. Two-run homer. GAME WINNER.

Dean had 129 innings of major-league experience, almost all in relief, before pitching the ninth inning.

This day might have been more notable as the day Ted Williams hit two triples; one was hit to right field and the other to left. He also hit a home run in each game, both over the short right-field Shibe Park wall. The Sox were ahead, 6-4, after eight innings. They collected four runs in the top of the ninth, taking a 10-4 lead, but Boston pitching surrendered three as Philadelphia rallied. Ted's homer with Lou Finney aboard, gave them an 8-4 lead and proved to provide the margin of victory.

Williams also hit homers #41 and 70 off Mr. Dean.

#**26** September 10 (second game) at Shibe Park, Philadelphia. Pitcher: Lynn Nelson (Philadelphia Athletics. RH. Age 34.

Top of the first inning. One-run homer.

Nelson had 620 1/3 innings of major-league experience before pitching the first inning.

Ted's solo homer in the first inning started the scoring; the final was 5-1, Boston, with Joe Heving going the distance and throwing a four-hitter. As noted above, Ted's drive went out over the right-field wall. He was 5-for-7 on the day (there was a simple single in the mix, too) and he drove in three, scoring five times.

#**27** September 16 at Fenway Park. Pitcher: Mel Harder (Cleveland Indians). RH. Age 29.

Bottom of the ninth inning. One-run homer.

Harder had 2,359 1/3 innings of major-league experience before pitching the ninth inning.

Mel Harder outdueled Charlie Wagner for a 2-1 win. The only run the Red Sox scored was on Ted's home run in the bottom of the ninth inning—but there was no one on base at the time. Ted's hit came with one out, a "vicious line drive…above five yards on the right side of the flagpole" and into the right-field seats.

Williams also hit homers #20, 73, and 113 off Harder.

#**28** September 17 (first game) at Fenway Park. Pitcher: Thornton Lee (Chicago White Sox). LH. Age 32.

Bottom of the fourth inning. One-run homer.

Lee had 843 2/3 innings of major-league experience before pitching the fourth inning.

More than 20 years later, Thornton Lee's son Don threw homer #517 to Ted Williams. That was also at Fenway Park. Thornton had kept the Red Sox hitless until Ted struck, a "lordly smash into the far right field pavilion." (*Boston Herald*) It was the only run he gave up in the game, a 6-1 White Sox win. It came on a 2-0 pitch with one out in the bottom of the fourth. Lee only allowed two other hits in the game. Boston got 16 hits in the second game and won, 11-7. Only one of them was a Ted hit, a single.

#29 September 20 at Fenway Park. Pitcher: Roxie Lawson (St. Louis Browns). RH. Age 33.

Bottom of the third inning. Two-run homer.

Alfred Voyle "Roxie" Lawson had pitched off and on in the majors since 1930 and had been 18-7 for the Tigers in 1937, despite a 5.26 earned run average.

Ted had 16 innings in which to hit homers, but he only hit one—"a fine high smash into the right-field bleachers." (*Herald*) It gave the Red Sox a 6-2 lead at the time, but the Browns caught up and tied the game, then won it with three unanswered runs in the top of the 16th. Ted was 1-for-3 at bat, but actually reached base six times (he drew four walks and was hit by a Lawson pitch.) He scored three runs. But the Sox lost. Ya can't win 'em all.

Earlier in the year, Ted hit homer #2 off Lawson.

#30 September 23 at Fenway Park. Pitcher: Sam Page (Philadelphia Athletics). RH. Age 23.

Bottom of the third inning. Two-run homer.

Page had only 15 2/3 innings of major-league experience before pitching the third inning.

This was Page's only year in the major leagues, and the September 23 game was just his second start. He lost the game, running his record to 0-3. It looked like the Red Sox were going to have a very comfortable win, since they took a 9-0 lead. In fact, Ted's two-run homer in the third inning could have stood as the game-winner, even after the A's got one run in the sixth. But they put a fright in the Red Sox, scoring three in the seventh, two in the eighth, and two more in the ninth. The final score was 10-8, Boston. Finney had walked leading off the third and Page recorded two outs. Ted swung at the first pitch and hit a long drive that he thought was a foul ball. "Then he realized there was a south wind of gale proportions and suddenly started to sprint as he saw the ball curving toward fair lands. It had such a high trajectory, as do so many of Ted's smacks, that it cleared the right-field pavilion front wall and dropped in there fair by a matter of only a couple of feet." (*Boston Herald*)

#**31** September 30 (second game) at Yankee Stadium, New York. Pitcher: Steve Sundra (New York Yankees). RH. Age 29.

Top of the fourth inning. One-run homer.

Sundra was 17-4 lifetime before this game.

No one knew this was the last game of the year, since there were two games scheduled for October 1, but they were rained out. It's a good thing Ted hit one out on the last day of September without waiting for the following day. Why? With this homer at Yankee Stadium, The Kid had hit a homer in every one of the American League's ballparks—and even in both of Cleveland's.

The Yankees—pennant winners in 1939—won the first game, 5-4. Ted had a double in four at-bats. Steve Sundra started the nightcap, riding a streak of 11 consecutive wins. Indeed, he hadn't lost a game all year. But his final record was 11-1, since the Red Sox won this one (4-2). Ted's home run was the first of the runs, "into the chummy right-field seats" at Yankee Stadium. Ice broken, the Sox scored once more in the fifth and added two more in the sixth. He'd admitted to his ambition early in the year, and he'd accomplished it—hitting a homer in every park. The run he drove in (himself) was #145. It was the first time a rookie had ever led the league in runs batted in, and the figure still stands as the major-league record for RBIs by a rookie, even in the days of the 162-game season.

In his rookie year, only eight of Ted's 31 homers were solo shots. He hit 12 two-run homers, nine three-run homers, and two grand slams.

With this homer at Yankee Stadium, The Kid had hit a homer in every one of the American League's ballparks—and even in both of Cleveland's parks. He hit four in Detroit and four in St. Louis.

In years to come, once or twice there was a rumor that Williams would be traded to the Yankees—maybe even a trade for Joe DiMaggio—and that Ted would wreak havoc there because of the Stadium's close right-field porch. Ted wrote: "I didn't like Yankee Stadium. A bad background in center field when the crowd is big, and all that smoke hanging in there....I always felt jacked up in Yankee Stadium because of the crowds, but I never wanted to play there."[4]

Fourteen of Ted's 31 home runs were hit at Fenway Park. No other left-handed hitter on the team hit more than one.

Nine of his homers were game-winners, tying him with 1947 and 1956 for game-winners in a single season.

1940

Except for a few games in midsummer, Ted no longer played right field for the Red Sox. After the 1939 season, he moved over to left and played there for the remainder of his days with the Red Sox.

The Red Sox installed bullpens in Fenway's right field, shortening by 20 feet the distance a ball would have to travel for a home run. It had been expected that this would help Ted Williams hit more homers at home (only 14 of his 31 homers in 1939 had been at Fenway Park.) The area enclosed by the new bullpens was known as "Williamsburg" for a period of time.

32 (**#1 in 1940**) April 23 at Fenway Park. Pitcher: Dutch Leonard (Washington Senators). RH. Age 31.

Bottom of the first inning. One-run homer.

Ted's first homer of his sophomore season came on the first anniversary of his first homer run. He hit it in the fifth game on the Red Sox schedule, a very cold April day. The homer also provided his first run batted in. It was hit at Fenway but did not land in the newly-installed bullpen. With two outs, on a 1-1 count, Williams hit the ball "half a dozen rows up in the old right-centerfield seats." Finney and Foxx hit homers, too, and the Sox won, 7-2.

This was the "other" Dutch Leonard; the first one pitched six seasons for the Red Sox, from 1913 through 1918 (90-64, with a 2.13 ERA.) He had been part of three World Championship teams, and set a still-standing major-league record for the lowest earned run average in a single season: his 0.96 ERA from his 19-5 season in 1914.

This Dutch Leonard pitched for 20 seasons, 1933-53, and was 191-181 with a career 3.25 ERA. He only allowed Ted one home run.

33 (#2) May 3 at Fenway Park. Pitcher: Jack Kramer (St. Louis Browns). RH. Age 22.

Bottom of the sixth inning. Two-run homer.

The weather was summery and it was a Ladies Day at Fenway Park. The Red Sox were down 8-5 when they came up to bat in the bottom of the eighth, but they tied the game with two that inning and another in the ninth, and won it in the tenth. Tabor hit two homers and Cronin hit one, building on Ted's two-run shot in the sixth. Ted doubled high off the left-field wall to lead off the tenth, hit so high off the wall that it looked at first that he'd hit his first homer to left. After a walk, a sacrifice bunt, and another walk, Ted was on third with the bases loaded and Jim Tabor hit one off the wall in left-center to win the game. Williams' homer was just barely fair, into the grandstand seats and the closest to the right-field foul pole (yet to be known as the Pesky Pole) he'd yet come.

Ted had hit #16 off Kramer in 1939. He later hit three more — #132, 169, and 185.

34 (#3) May 21 at Briggs Stadium, Detroit. Pitcher: Al Benton (Detroit Tigers). RH. Age 29.

Top of the ninth inning. One-run homer.

Jimmie Foxx hit grand slams on back-to-back days, this day and the game before. Only Babe Ruth and Bill Dickey had done that before. For Williams, he was hitting fine (.347 coming into this game), but it was the only his third home run of the season, coming in the 26th game. He "lined a fiery drive into the deep upper right-field barrier." (*Boston Herald*)

Foxx now had 11 homers. It's no wonder that Ted more or less idolized Foxx.

Doc Cramer hit a homer, too—which would be his only home run in 712 plate appearances during 1940.

Ted later hit five more homers off Al Benton: #83, 114, 119, 161, and 277.

35 (#4) May 26 at Fenway Park. Pitcher: Johnny Murphy (New York Yankees). RH. Age 31.

Bottom of the eighth. One-run homer.

TED LOCATES WILLIAMSBURG—*Boston Globe* headline. This was Ted's first homer into "Williamsburg" and it came late in a game the Sox dropped to New York, 7-2, just the second hit of the game off. Johnny Murphy. Catcher Gene Desautels had the only other hit, a seventh-inning triple, breaking up the no-hit bid. Ted's home run went into the Yankees' bullpen and was caught on the fly by bullpen catcher Johnny Schulte. The *Boston Herald*'s "Bob Dunbar" (the name was a pseudonym shared by rotating staff writers over the years) opined that Ted was "obsessed by the idea of homers this year, to the exclusion of other things which might be of equal value to the team. The obvious effort to get the long one is seen in his hitting up very strenuously at the ball. He's not leveling off the way he did a year ago, even if he still is hitting well over .300, a figure he was below at this time a year ago."

Murphy later gave up homer #158 to Ted, in 1946.

36 (#5) June 11 at Fenway Park. Pitcher: Joe Dobson (Detroit Tigers). RH. Age 23.

Bottom of the seventh. Three-run homer.

More than two weeks passed before Ted hit his next home run, just his fifth of the year.

Dobson only gave up the one homer to Ted Williams. Perhaps he would have given up another one or two, except that he spent nine seasons pitching for the Red Sox, and 259 of his 414 games were for Boston. He was on

1940-41 - Cleveland Indian Bob Feller and Boston Red Sox Ted Williams in the dugout at Fenway Park.

in relief of Bob Feller, who'd been driven from the game by Boston's bats. "Child Theodore" drove in four runs in all, the first of the four on his third-inning triple off the center-field wall. The homer was the second one he'd hit into the right-field seats (the other being the May 3 homer.)

In 1941, Dobson caught one of Ted's home runs — in the Red Sox bullpen. The two were then teammates.

37 (#6) June 15 at Comiskey Park, Chicago. Pitcher: Bill Dietrich (Chicago White Sox.) RH. Age 30.

Top of the fourth. One-run homer.

This was Ted's sixth home run of the season. In this same game, Jimmie Foxx hit his seventh — his seventh one against the White Sox, that is! He'd hit eight against non-White Sox pitchers. Interestingly, after Foxx homered, Williams bunted to third, reaching safely but then was thrown out when over-sliding third base a bit later on an attempted double steal. On a 1-1 pitch, Ted's slammed a "wicked drive" (*Herald*) for a home run that hit "the balustrade of the right field upper deck" (*Chicago Tribune*). The Kid must have been feeling fleet of foot, since he also scored all the way from first on a Joe Cronin double, his cap flying off as he rounded the bases.

Dietrich gave up another homer in 1940, #43, some 39 days later and also at Comiskey.

38 (#7) June 16 (first game) at Comiskey Park, Chicago. Pitcher: Ted Lyons (Chicago White Sox). RH. Age 39. Hall of Famer.

Top of the 12th inning. One-run homer. GAME WINNER.

Ted clearly began picking up the pace, hitting a homer for the second day in a row. This one won the game, beating future Hall of Famer Ted Lyons who'd gone the distance only to lose, 4-3, in the 12th inning. Lyons had pitched a great game. Only the second hit he'd allowed was the eighth-inning triple hit by Mr. Williams. Cronin singled him in. It was a two-triple day for Ted. He hit another in the second game of the Sunday double header. His home run was "a terrific drive into the upper right-field stands." (*Boston Herald*) The Red Sox won the second game, 14-5.

Perhaps partly because he encountered him early on, when Lyons was a true veteran, Williams greatly respected Ted Lyons—though admittedly, so did many others. Lyons was a Hall of Fame pitcher. He cited him as one of the least predictable pitchers, "moving the ball all the time, giving you something here, then a curve there, then a little extra on the fastball, moving the ball all the time. Much tougher to guess with. A guy like Lyons would fool you because you'd have him figured and he'd come right back and cross you up. Ninth inning, wind blowing out, you have just hit his fastball the last time up, you know he can't throw a fast ball now, and sure enough he'd throw it and then come right back and throw it again. Lyons was that exception they told me about when I first came up: Don't guess with this guy. Hit what you see. It was fun for a young hitter to face a guy like Lyons. I often wish I could do it all over again."[15]

39 (#8) June 21 at League Park, Cleveland. Pitcher: Al Milnar (Cleveland Indians). LH. Age 26.

Top of the third inning. Three-run homer.

Williams and Foxx both hit home runs but Boston lost its fifth game in a row, a 7-4 defeat. Ted's went over to deep right-center and over the fence. It gave the Sox a 3-0 lead, but the Indians came back in the bottom of the third with three of their own. Foxx's gave the Red Sox a 5-4 lead, but then Cleveland scored four in the bottom of the eighth. Williams, Tabor, and Boston pitcher Jack Wilson later "each slammed smashes to remote center which would have been homers at Fenway Park but were caught here by [Roy] Weatherly in dimly-seen stretches of the center-field terrain which goes as far as 460 feet from home plate." (*Cleveland Plain Dealer*)

This was the only homer Ted hit off Milnar.

40 (#9) June 29 at Fenway Park. Pitcher: Sid Hudson (Washington Senators). RH. Age 25.

Bottom of the seventh inning. Two-run homer.

The Senators took a 5-1 lead, but Ted's two-run homer in the seventh brought the score even at 7-7. It came down in the center-field corner of the visitors' bullpen. Promptly, Washington scored two more runs and won the game, 9-7, a game of which Arthur Sampson of the *Herald* wrote, "You'll have to do a lot of back-breaking labor to unearth one more noisily smelly." He wasn't impressed by Boston pitching. Williams had four runs batted in.

Hudson also allowed homers #116, 150, and 274. He was one of Ted's teammates in 1953 and 1954.

41 (#10) July 3 at Fenway Park. Pitcher: Chubby Dean (Philadelphia Athletics). LH. Age 24.

Bottom of the ninth. Three-run homer.

This one was a battle. The Red Sox were down 8-0 after four innings, and by 10-3 after six. The Red Sox scored three more on a Jim Tabor homer in the eighth, making it 10-6. The A's added an insurance run in the top of the ninth. In the bottom of the ninth, the Sox scored one run and had two on base. Reliever Chubby Dean was summoned in. Doc Cramer singled in another run, making the score 11-8. Ted turned on Dean's first pitch and crashed it off the back wall of the Philadelphia bullpen (another home run into "Williamsburg") to tie the game. Up next was Jimmie Foxx, who hit a walkoff just inside the left-field foul pole and into the net atop the wall.

Dean had been hit for Williams homer #25 and would later be hit for #70.

42 (#11) July 5 at Griffith Stadium, Washington. Pitcher: Walt Masterson (Washington Senators). RH. Age 20.

Top of the fifth. Two-run homer. GAME WINNER.

It was a Friday "ladies day" crowd in the Nation's Capital and the Red Sox fired off 14 hits (eight of them for extra bases) for a 9-4 win, Foxx hitting his 20th and Williams his 11th. Ted's was "bashed over the garden wall" (*Herald*) in right field and drove in the fifth and sixth runs that gave the Red Sox the edge they needed. Both Williams and Foxx had homers and doubles. On the pitch before he connected for the four-base hit, Ted swung hard at another pitch, completely missed it by "a mile and the bat slipped out of his hands, sailing clear out into right field for a new intercollegiate record for bat throwing."

Masterson's five homers were #6, 42, 197, 218, and 402.

43 (#12) July 24 at Comiskey Park, Chicago. Pitcher: Bill Dietrich (Chicago White Sox). RH. Age 30.

Top of the fourth. One-run homer.

Like homer #37, this one was also hit at Comiskey in the top of the fourth and was also a solo home run. It had been 19 days, though in between Williams went to his first All-Star Game (he was 0-for-2 with one base on balls). The game was quite a slugfest, with 34 hits and 64 total bases, but

20 of the hits were White Sox ones, and they pulled out a 12-10 win. Ted's solo home run just added the one run, and it produced his only RBI. He hit it on a 3-2 pitch, and it was "a most lordly homer into the remote upper right-field stands." (*Herald*) The loss was Boston's seventh loss in succession.

Dietrich had recently given up homer #37, the only other homer Ted hit off him.

44 (#13) July 26 at Sportsman's Park, St. Louis. Pitcher: Lefty Mills (St. Louis Browns). LH. Age 30.

Top of the fifth inning. Two-run homer.

Two in one day, one in the fifth and one in the ninth. St. Louis had held a 6-4 lead until the Red Sox put together a six-run fifth inning to take command of the game. By game's end, they had recorded 19 hits. Ted's home run sailed far over the right-field wall giving the Sox runs #9 and 10. (Earlier in the game, he'd just barely missed — by inches — a home run to left field.)

With an 0-6 record, this was Mills' last year in the major leagues. This was the only time Ted homered off him.

45 (#14) July 26 at Sportsman's Park, St. Louis. Pitcher: Bill Cox (St. Louis Browns). RH. Age 27.

Top of the ninth inning. One-run homer.

This was the only homer Ted hit off Cox, and it occasioned very little comment in the press, perhaps because it was anticlimactic in a 14-7 victory. Earlier in the day, manager Cronin had a "heart to heart talk" with Ted "whose attitude toward most of the Boston writers has been antagonistic." Cronin reportedly urged him to forget about the writer and work on his defense. Ted also favored offense, and the talking to might have given him a little extra juice. Ted's home run reportedly went 460 feet, deep into the upper grandstand and not fair by much.

Ted hit only one homer off Cox, who was 2-9 (6.56) in 50 major-league games.

46 **(#15)** August 13 (second game) at Yankee Stadium, New York. Pitcher: Atley Donald (New York Yankees). RH. Age 29.

Top of the sixth. One-run homer.

Now being referred to as Boston's "problem child" by the Associated Press, Williams was reported to have said that Boston was a "lousy town" and that he wanted to be traded to the Yankees. He denied some of it later. Team owner Tom Yawkey said he felt sorry for Ted since he was only hurting himself. He suggested to his left fielder that maybe the trouble lay within him. The Yankees won the first game 9-1 and the second game 19-8. His two-out homer went into the upper deck in right field, fair—but not fair by a lot.

Donald also gave up homer #103.

47 **(#16)** August 14 at Yankee Stadium, New York. Pitcher: Red Ruffing (New York Yankees). RH. Age 35. Hall of Famer.

Top of the first inning. One-run homer.

The Red Sox lost again (8-3), but Ted Williams hit a home run into the right-field stands (right after Lou Finney hit one in the same general location) which had provided an early 2-0 lead. Finney's was the harder hit; Ted's barely cleared the wall and was caught on the fly by a fan in the very first row. There was a lot of baseball left on the day, though, and the five runs the Yanks scored in the bottom of the seventh sort of sealed the deal. Williams, "apparently a much chastened young man, actually acted genial and slightly happy on the bench before the game, and hustled his head off." (*Boston Herald*) The Sox had six hits off Ruffing—two from Finney, two from Foxx, and two from Williams.

Ruffing also gave up homers #7, 126, and 181.

48 **(#17)** August 15 at Yankee Stadium, New York. Pitcher: Bump Hadley (New York Yankees). RH. Age 35.

Top of the fifth inning. Four-run homer. Grand slam #3.

This was the third day in a row that Ted hit a homer at the Stadium. Jimmie Foxx's 29th homer of the year was the game-winner, a three-run blow in the top of the first—since Boston's Joe Heving threw a three-hitter. The Red Sox won, 11-1, with Ted's first grand slam of the year coming in the fifth and producing runs eight through 11. The ball was hit into the lower right-field stands.

Hadley also surrendered homers #23, 60, and 84.

NOTE: Even from his earliest days, Williams paid special attention to the tools of his trade. "I always worked with my bats, boning them down, putting a shine on them, forcing the fibers together. Not just the handle, the whole bat. I treated them like babies. Weight tolerance got to be a big thing with me. The weight can change. Early in the season it's cold and damp and the bats lying around on the ground pick up moisture and get heavier. I used to take them down to the post office to have them weighed. Eventually, with the Red Sox, we got a little set of scales out in the locker room."[16]

49 (#18) August 19 at Fenway Park. Pitcher: Johnnie Humphries (Cleveland Indians). RH. Age 25.

Bottom of the seventh. Three-run homer.

Ted Williams was Boston's #3 home-run hitter. Foxx hit his 33rd in the game. Jim Tabor hit a grand slam for his 20th home run of the year. And Ted hit #18. Bobby Doerr hit #16. With all those homers, the Red Sox won handily, 16-7. Ted's home run went into the Red Sox bullpen in center field, or the bleachers in right-center (depending on the account), but "he circled the paths to the accompaniment of scattered boos from every part of the stands," observed Gordon Cobbledick of the *Cleveland Plain Dealer*. "Six months ago Williams could have had anything he wanted in Boston, up to an including the mayoralty. He was in a fair spot to become the greatest baseball hero in the town's history. But the customers are booing him now. He asked for it and he's getting it."

This was the only homer Ted hit off Humphries.

50 (#19) September 7 at Fenway Park. Pitcher: Marius Russo (New York Yankees). LH. Age 25.

Bottom of the eighth inning. One-run homer.

First-pitch swinging, Ted Williams drove in one run in the first inning (with a sacrifice fly), another in the third inning (on a single), and then homered into the right-field grandstand, just fair. But there was no one on board at the time. The final score was Yankees 4, Ted Williams 3. There was an amusing moment in the fourth when Williams and Cronin both converged on a pop fly to short left. Cronin caught it and he and the rest of the Red Sox ran in to their dugout. Ted, however, "sublimely oblivious of the fact that it was the third out, jogged back to his post in left." (*New York Times*)

Ted also hit homer #51 off Russo.

51 (#20) September 22 at Yankee Stadium, New York. Pitcher: Marius Russo (New York Yankees). LH. Age 25.

Top of the fifth inning. One-run homer.

Ted hadn't hit a home run for 15 days, but when he did, he hit it off Russo again—though, once more, the damage was limited to just one run. This and #50 were the only two he ever hit off Russo. It was the last matchup of the season between the two teams, and New York prevailed, 6-3. Ted's home run into the bottom deck in right field had tied the game, but from that point on the rest of the scoring was the Yankees'.

52 (#21) September 24 (first game) at Shibe Park, Philadelphia. Pitcher: George Caster (Philadelphia Athletics). RH. Age 32.

Top of the fourth inning. Two-run homer.

As with #50 and 51, Ted hit his next two off the same pitcher, though this time they both came in the same game. His first one "behind the right-field screen" gave the Red Sox a 7-3 lead. The day wasn't over yet, not by a long shot.

Ted hit #53 and, in 1941, #75 off Caster. In 1940, Caster's record was 4-19. It was the second year he'd led the American League in losses.

53 (#22) September 24 (first game) at Shibe Park, Philadelphia. Pitcher: George Caster (Philadelphia Athletics). RH. Age 32.

Top of the sixth inning. One-run homer.

In his next at-bat, Ted hit another homer off Caster. The following year, he hit #75 off him as well. This second homer of the game followed a Dom DiMaggio triple and a sacrifice fly, so the bases were empty. It went out "over the right-field fence." The most significant home run of the game, though, was the next one — Jimmie Foxx's 500th career home run into the left-field pavilion. Back-to-back-to-back it was, with Joe Cronin hitting one onto the roof in left field. A little later in the inning, Doerr tripled — though some thought he might have had an inside-the-park home run had he not been held up at third base. Jim Tabor then homered, the fourth of the inning. The Red Sox won the game, 16-8. And the second game, 4-3.

54 (#23) September 29 (first game) at Fenway Park. Pitcher: Les McCrabb (Philadelphia Athletics). RH. Age 25.

Bottom of the sixth inning. One-run homer.

The Red Sox won both games on the 29th (9-4 and 4-1) and finished the season tied for fourth place. Ted was 3-for-4 in the first game (driving in three) and 2-for-4 in the second (driving in two). The five RBIs brought his total for the year to 113. That would be impressive for anyone, but for Ted Williams it was the smallest number of runs he drove in from 1939 through 1949. Had he not broken his elbow in the 1950 All-Star Game, he would almost certainly have surpassed that sum once again. The Red Sox pulled off a triple steal in the nightcap. Ted's home run was hit "over the right-field barrier." (*Boston Post*)

McCrabb gave up HR #93, too.

Ted hit eight fewer home runs in 1940. Indeed, the Red Sox team hit only 98 homers, down from 124 the year before. Of Ted's homers, only nine were hit at home — five fewer than in 1939. And he'd only hit one in Detroit, but he had — once again — hit one in every major-league city.

1941

This is, of course, the year in which Ted Williams hit .406 — the last major leaguer to hit as high as .400. Just a couple of weeks into spring training, on March 19 in Sarasota, he chipped a bone in the ankle of his right foot while sliding into second base. He played all season with the ankle taped and Bobby Doerr always felt that it helped him, "that it was sensitive enough to make him stay back for as long as possible to keep the pressure off his front foot."[17]

Because of Williams' ankle injury, he couldn't put in as much time running and consequently spent more time in the batting cage. He also credited Joe Dobson for pitching batting practice to him, and bearing down when he did. "I had a chance to have more good batting practice that year probably than any time in my career. That year we got a pitcher from Cleveland, who in 1939 and '40 was tough as hell for me. Name was Joe Dobson. Had a real good curve ball, and a *good* overhand fastball. And he liked to pitch all the time, pitch to me. We'd have a game. He'd be bearing down as hard as he could to me, and I'd be bearin' down against him. I was just young and really comin', and boy, it was the greatest thing that ever happened to me."[18]

55 (**#1 of 1941**) April 29 at Briggs Stadium, Detroit. Pitcher: Johnny Gorsica (Detroit Tigers). RH. Age 26.

Top of the sixth. One-run homer.

It had been seven months to the day since Ted Williams had last hit a home run in a regular-season game. A minor injury had for the most part limited Ted to pinch-hitting duty up to this point in the young season. Lefty Grove was going for his 294th win, but the Red Sox only scored three runs to the five Detroit had racked up in the early innings. Ted's homer was "just an old time Williamsonian four-bagger, fully 440 feet right off the war club… shot into the upper deck of the right-center stands." He hit a long double later in the game.

Gorsica also gave up homers #59 and 175.

56 (**#2**) May 7 at Comiskey Park, Chicago. Pitcher: Johnny Rigney (Chicago White Sox). RH. Age 26.

Top of the third inning. One-run homer.

Ted's two homers were widely separated, coming as they did in the top of the third and then not again until the 11th. White Sox started Johnny Rigney pitched a complete game, so was tagged for the two of them. "The loose-jointed fly chaser picked off an early homer," wrote Irving Vaughan in the *Chicago Tribune*. Charlie Wagner had scored on Dom DiMaggio's single, but then Dom was picked off first. That's the reason he wasn't on board when Williams "lashed a homer well up into the seats in the upper grandstand in right-center." (*Herald*) The *Globe* said it was hit "almost dead-center."

Rigney gave up another homer later in this same game and then one at Fenway less than a week later. He also gave up homers #64, 72, 89, and 133.

57 (**#3**) May 7 at Comiskey Park, Chicago. Pitcher: Johnny Rigney (Chicago White Sox). RH. Age 26.

Top of the 11th inning. One-run homer. GAME WINNER.

Ted's second home run, of course, cost the Rigney the game. The game was tied, 3-3 (with another of the Red Sox runs having been driven in by Ted Williams on a first-inning single.) In the top of the 11th, he hit a ball to the same area as his first one, but about 50 feet higher and "onto the top of the double-deck stands...Ted's blow must have covered 450 at least and was the proverbial mile high." The *Herald* wrote, "A conservative estimate of the distance the drive would have gone, on the level, was 500 feet." It gave the Red Sox the lead, and Wagner held back Chicago for a 4-3 win. The *Globe* said, "The roof of the upper deck in right field is nearly 400 feet from the batter's box. Williams's drive was a lift far above the top of the upper grandstand roof, which in turn must be 70 feet above the playing field. When it landed on the roof the ball bounded at least 50 feet in the air, and then disappeared to parts unknown."

Ted's homers off Rigney: #57, 58, 64, 72, and 89.

58 (#4) May 13 at Fenway Park. Pitcher: Johnny Rigney (Chicago White Sox). RH. Age 26.

Bottom of the ninth inning. One-run homer.

"Hello, John," Ted may have thought, having homered off Johnny Rigney twice just six days earlier. He was back for more. This homer came in the bottom of the ninth inning, at home. Rigney again faced off against Charlie Wagner, who once more held Chicago to three runs. This time, though, the Red Sox only had one run heading into the ninth. Ted had been trying; twice he was robbed of what looked like sure home runs, due to a strong east wind blowing in from right field. The one run the Red Sox had came on their only hit through six innings — a Jimmie Foxx homer to left. Ted's one-out home run in the ninth "landed just inside the right-field foul line."

Later in the year, Rigney gave up a fourth 1941 home run to Ted Williams (#64), and a fifth (#72) — and even a sixth (#89)!

59 (#5) May 19 at Fenway Park. Pitcher: Johnny Gorsica (Detroit Tigers). RH. Age 26.

Bottom of the seventh. Two-run homer.

Bracketing Rigney's three home runs, Johnny Gorsica gave up another. Williams now had five home runs on the season, all off either Gorsica or Rigney.

Gorsica threw a four-hitter and beat Boston, 4-2, and he would have had a shutout had Ted Williams hit a seventh-inning homer with Lou Finney on board. Only two Sox had even reached first base. The homer was fairly close to the foul pole and landed in the right-field seats, though pretty far in. It was Boston's fifth loss in a row and dropped them in the standings down to fifth place.

Gorsica also gave up homers #55 and 175.

60 (#6) May 27 (first game) at Fenway Park. Pitcher: Bump Hadley (Philadelphia Athletics). RH. Age 36.

Bottom of the third inning. One-run homer. GAME WINNER.

The Red Sox achieved only ten hits in the doubleheader, seven in the first game (a 5-2 win) and three in the second game (an 11-1 loss.) Dom DiMaggio had three of the first game's seven — a single, a double, and a triple. And Ted Williams had a home run, into the center-field bleachers (*Globe*) or right-field bleachers (*Herald*.) Later researchers might surmise it landed somewhere in right-center. Wherever it came down, it scored a run. Added to the single runs the Sox had registered in the first and the second, this third run proved to be the game-winner. Ted had a single in the second game.

Hadley also was touched up for Ted's homers #23, 48, and 84.

61 (#7) May 29 at Fenway Park. Pitcher: Jack Knott (Philadelphia Athletics). RH. Age 34.

Bottom of the seventh inning. Two-run homer. GAME WINNER.

Right after the seventh-inning stretch, Boston pitcher Joe Dobson singled, moved to second on a bunt, advanced to third on an infield out, but trotted home without worry when Williams swung at a 1-0 pitch poled a long ball that landed in the break between the bleachers and the right-field grand-stand. Ted had singled twice earlier and was batting .417.

Ted notched homers #85 and 102 off Knott, too.

62 (#8) June 1 (second game) at Briggs Stadium, Detroit. Pitcher: Schoolboy Rowe (Detroit Tigers). RH. Age 31.

Top of the sixth inning. Two-run homer.

One of four major leaguers with the nickname "Schoolboy," Rowe never let Williams hit another homer off him. But Ted got this one in a game where every run counted. The Red Sox won the first game, 7-6 (Foxx homered), and the second game (Williams homered), 6-5. Ted's homer led off the sixth and was another upper-deck job ("a towering drive into the top tier") in Briggs Stadium's right field. He was 4-for-9 with four runs batted in.

63 (#9) June 5 at League Park, Cleveland. Pitcher: Joe Heving (Cleveland Indians). RH. Age 40.

Top of the fifth inning. Two-run homer.

Joe Heving had been Ted's teammate in 1939 and 1940. His brother Johnnie had been a catcher for the Boston Red Sox, but in earlier years. Toothpick Ted drove in three runs in the game, two of them on the fifth-inning homer off Heving. He hit the ball over League Park's outfield wall in right-center. Mickey Harris was the beneficiary of 16 hits and a 14-1 Boston win. Ted got on base often enough he scored four runs, as did Dominic DiMaggio. This was the only homer Ted hit off his former teammate.

64 (#10) June 6 at Comiskey Park, Chicago. Pitcher: Johnny Rigney (Chicago White Sox). RH. Age 26.

Top of the third inning. Two-run homer. GAME WINNER.

It was only June 6, but after this 400-foot two-run home run into Comiskey Park's upper-right field deck, Rigney had already been victim to four Ted Williams home run swings. Foxx and Tabor hit homers in this one, too, and the Red Sox won, 6-3. All the runs scored on homers, but Ted's was the one that provided the margin of victory.

This day was the 22nd day of Ted's consecutive-game hitting streak. June 7 was the 23rd and last game in the streak.

Rigney took responsibility for Williams home runs #56, 57, 58, 64, 72, 89, and 133.

65 (#11) June 12 (second game) at Sportsman's Park, St. Louis. Pitcher: Johnny Niggeling (St. Louis Browns). RH. Age 37.

Top of the third inning. Two-run homer. GAME WINNER.

Knuckleballer Johnny Niggeling gave up three more homers before the year was out (#71, 74, and 82) and #95 in 1942. This was the only one that won a game. The Sox split a doubleheader in St. Louis, dropping the first game, 9-4 (Ted was 1-for-5, a single), but winning the nightcap, 3-2. Boston scored once in the first, then got their second and third runs on Ted's home run. Lou Finney was on base (he'd tripled in the first and scored on a Cronin single) when—swinging at a 3-0 pitch—"Tall Ted teed off and belted the next pitch over the roof of the right-field pavilion and onto Grand." (*Herald*) It went "a mile over the roof" according to Hy Hurwitz of the *Boston Globe*.

66 (#12) June 15 (second game) at Fenway Park. Pitcher: Buck Ross (Chicago White Sox). RH. Age 26.

Bottom of the sixth inning. One-run homer.

#123 was the other home run Ross rendered unto Williams. Two future Hall of Fame pitchers—Lefty Grove and Ted Lyons—had faced off in the first game, though Grove was hit by a batter ball and had to leave the game in the fourth. He'd come into that frame with a 5-1 lead and looked on his way to his 298th win but when a line drive caromed off his leg, a five-run White Sox rally followed and it was a couple of innings more before Boston re-took the lead. This was Ross's first start for the White Sox. Ted's "lusty thump to right" (*Chicago Tribune*) helped the Red Sox take a 4-2 lead in the sixth; both teams scored a pair of runs later on. So it was Red Sox as winners, 8-6 and 6-4. Ted was 2-for-3 in each game and the *Herald* said his homer went deep, "into something like the 20th row of the right-field wing of the grandstand, not many yards fair."

67 **(#13)** June 17 (first game) at Fenway Park. Pitcher: Bud Thomas (Detroit Tigers). RH. Age 30.

Bottom of the seventh inning. Two-run homer.

Thomas had 549 innings' experience before throwing the seventh inning.

It was Evacuation Day in Boston, celebrating the victorious Battle of Bunker Hill in the Revolutionary War, after which British troops left the city. The Sox and Tigers split the holiday doubleheader, 14-6 and 8-5. The first game saw the Tigers with the edge on the Red Sox, 6-5, until a modest eight-run seventh-inning rally catapulted Boston into the lead. Ted's two-run homer produced the first two of the eight runs

This was the same Bud Thomas who had thrown the first pitch The Kid had hit for a home run, back in April 1939. This was the 50th homer of Thomas's career, but his first of 1941.

68 **(#14)** June 25 at Fenway Park. Pitcher: Jim Bagby (Cleveland Indians). RH. Age 24.

Bottom of the fourth. Two-run homer.

The Indians scored twice in the top of the fourth. Ted's two-run homer "deep into the right-field bleachers" (*Cleveland Plain Dealer*) tied the game, 2-2, in the bottom. There was no other scoring in the game except for five runs the Red Sox tallied in the seventh thanks to what the *Plain Dealer* dubbed a collection of "pop hits and errors." The *Boston Globe* was more enthusiastic about Ted's home run calling it "one of the most monstrous the stringbean slugger ever hit. The smash settled fully a dozen rows up in the open bleachers back of the Boston dugout." The final score was 7-2 and Lefty Grove won his 298th game.

Jim Bagby Jr. also gave up homer #118.

69 (#15) June 29 (first game) at Shibe Park, Philadelphia. Pitcher: Lum Harris (Philadelphia Athletics). RH. Age 26.

Top of the eighth inning. One-run homer.

Boston outscored Philadelphia 15-4, but only won one game — the 13-1 first game. (Deduction shows the Sox lost the nightcap, 3-2.) Charlie Wagner only allowed five Athletics hits in the lopsided game, and benefited greatly from Joe Cronin's grand slam in the top of the third. Ted's solo homer was "a high fly over the right-field wall…and across 20th Street" but not crucial to the game; it boosted the score from 12-1 to 13-1. He was 0-for-4 in the second game, which dropped his batting average to .404.

Homer #121 was Harris's other homer hit by Ted Williams.

70 (#16) July 3 at Shibe Park, Philadelphia. Pitcher: Chubby Dean (Philadelphia Athletics). LH. Age 25.

Top of the eighth inning. Two-run homer.

Two insurance runs were provided by "Teddy the Bear" who boosted Boston's 3-2 lead to 5-2 in the top of the eighth, with a ball hit out of Shibe Park and "into the residential section behind the right-field fence." Lefty Grove, 41, was pitching for the Red Sox and he'd been given a 3-0 lead in the top of the first. He struggled a bit in the fifth and sixth, but held the A's to two, and walked off the mound in the bottom of the ninth with win #299. The Williams home run had come on a 3-2 count and after Ted fouled off two pitches. "A stiff wind which was blowing in toward the plate from right field had shackled all other blows hit in that direction but it didn't hamper Teddy's drive one bit. When Child Theodore unloaded on that fast ball he drove it so far and so high into the teeth of the wind that there was never any doubt that its destination was the apartment house doorstep in the other side of 20th street." (*Herald*)

This was the third (of three) home runs hit off Dean. Numbers 25 and 41 were the first two.

1941 All-Star Game—July 8 at Briggs Stadium, Detroit

The National League held a 5-3 lead when Ted Williams came up to bat in the bottom of the ninth. Ken Keltner had singled and come around to score when Joe DiMaggio hit into a force play for the second out of the inning. Joe Gordon was on third base and Joe DiMaggio was on first.

"Claude Passeau of the Cubs was pitching for the National League. Passeau was a good pitcher. He had struck me out in the eighth inning on a fast tailing ball that acted like a slider (they didn't call them sliders in those days.) He would jam a left-hander with it and get it past you if you weren't quick. I was late on that one, and as I came up in the ninth I said to myself, 'You've got to be quicker, you've got to get more in front.' On a 2-1 pitch, he came in with that sliding fast ball I was anticipating, and I hit it off the facing of the third deck in right field."[19]

Dom DiMaggio was on deck and thought they'd walk Ted and pitch to him. They couldn't have done any worse. He almost hit it over the roof, DiMaggio remembered. "This was a line blast. It went off the façade on a line…this wasn't any fly ball."[20]

Ted recounted the at-bat to J. G. Taylor Spink of *The Sporting News:*

"When I got up to the plate, all the National League team except the outfielders ganged up with Passeau on the mound and I figured they were discussing how they would pitch to me. So I turned by back to them and talked to [umpire Babe] Pinelli. I asked him where that third strike was [Ted had struck out his last time up] and he said right at the knees. I told him I thought it was low, but he wouldn't agree.

"Then I stood back and sort of gave myself a fight talk. I said, 'Listen, you lug. He outguessed you last time and you got caught with your bat on your shoulder for a called third strike. You were swinging late when you fouled one off, too. Let's swing, and swing a little earlier this time, and see if we can connect.'

"Passeau pitched to me pretty careful. I did foul another one off, but he pitched two balls, so I was ahead of him—had him in the hole and the next one would be in there. I was cocked when he let go. And soon there it was—a fast one, chest high. I swung and I got the fat of my bat on it and away it sailed. I knew as soon as it was hit that it might go all the way, but I wasn't sure whether it would clear the roof until I saw it hit the front of that third deck up there in the sky."[21]

"It was the kind of thing a kid dreams about and imagines himself doing when he's playing those little playground games we used to play in San Diego. Halfway down to first, seeing that ball going out, I stopped running and started leaping and jumping and clapping my hands, and I was just so happy I laughed out loud. I've never been so happy, and I've never seen so many happy guys. They carried me off the field."[22]

It's worth keeping firmly in mind that All-Star Games were hard-fought battles in this era, rivaling the World Series in the eyes of the players themselves.

The Associated Press story quoted The Kid as saying, "I had a feeling that if I got up there in the ninth, I'd go for the Downs. Boy, I feel great. There ain't nothing like hittin' a home run."[23]

It may not have just been hyperbole when *Collier's* magazine wrote in a 1946 piece that this All-Star Game-winning home run was " a wallop which for altitude, violence, and timeliness has never been bettered by Babe Ruth, Lou Gehrig, Shoeless Joe Jackson, or anybody in the history of the world."[24]

71 (#17) July 20 (first game) at Sportsman's Park, St. Louis. Pitcher: Johnny Niggeling (St. Louis Browns). RH. Age 37.

Top of the ninth inning. Three-run homer.

Williams was nursing an injury incurred when he'd turned his right ankle in Detroit on July 12; it was the same ankle he'd hurt during spring training in Sarasota. But he was asked to pinch-hit in the top of the ninth inning at Sportsman's Park. Had he not, the Red Sox might have gone down to 6-0 and 10-0 defeats. Niggeling had held the Sox to five singles in the first game through eight. Foxx walked and Stan Spence singled, and with one out, Williams took a ball and then struck. "The first pitch almost hit his right ankle, the sore one, but he kissed the next one high up over the roof of the right-field stands, not far from the foul line, against the screen which prevents pedestrians getting hurt on Grand Boulevard." (*Boston Herald*)

Homers #65, 74, 82, and 95 all came courtesy of Johnny Niggeling.

72 (#18) July 22 at Fenway Park. Pitcher: Johnny Rigney (Chicago White Sox). RH. Age 26.

Bottom of the second inning. One-run homer.

Back in the regular lineup again, Williams walked, got hit by a pitch, and hit a home run. The homer came first and might have had something to do with the walk and the HBP. Ted was batting fifth in the lineup and he led off the bottom of the second with a "magnificent shot over the visitors' bullpen and against the right-center field bleacher front." (*Herald*) Two pitches later, Jimmie Foxx sent an even harder hit ball into the center-field bleachers.

Starting with his pinch-hit homer on the 20th, Ted launched into a 12-game hitting streak, going 19-for-35 over the streak, carrying him above .400.

This was the sixth homer hit off Rigney in 1941, six of Ted's 37 homers in 1941. The other homers were #56, 57, 58, 64, and 89. After World War II, Williams collected #133 off him as well.

73 (#19) July 25 at Fenway Park. Pitcher: Mel Harder (Cleveland Indians). RH. Age 31.

Bottom of the fourth inning. Two-run homer.

Lefty Grove won his 300th game. A 3-for-5 day brought Williams to .400 again and he stayed there again for the rest of the season—though on the next-to-last day (September 27) his average actually dipped to .3996. But that was still three months in the future. On this day, he collected his third home run off Mel Harder, who'd come in to relieve the "Lithuanian lefty," Joe Krakauskas. The Indians actually held a 4-0 lead after 3 ½, and it wasn't looking good for Lefty Grove to win his 300th game. The two in the fourth, thanks to Ted, and two more in the fifth tied the game. Ted's homer landed "a few rows out of right-fielder Jeff Heath's reach" in the "extreme left section of the right-field covered seats." The Indians added two in the top of the seventh, and the Sox came right back with two on a Jim Tabor home run. In the eighth, the Red Sox had a chance to take the lead after a walk to Doerr, a sacrifice, and an intentional walk to Cronin, Ted Williams came up — but he popped up to third base — "so disgusted with himself...that he tossed his bat for a new altitude record." (*Herald*) But Jimmie Foxx tripled to drive in two, and scored himself on a bad throw in from the outfield. Hundreds of fans mobbed Grove on the field at game's end and it took half a dozen policemen to clear the way for him to get off the field.

Harder's homers hit by Ted were #20, 27, 73, and 113.

Harder said, "I always tried to keep the ball down on Ted. If you got it too high, he'd get under it and drive it quite a distance."[25]

74 (#20) July 29 at Fenway Park. Pitcher: Johnny Niggeling (St. Louis Browns). RH. Age 37.

Bottom of the third inning. Two-run homer.

There were never that many times that the St. Louis Browns won five games in a row from the Red Sox, but the July 29 game was indeed the fifth. It was a 3-2 loss, with Ted's two-run homer producing all of Boston's runs. Niggeling was a knuckleball pitcher and Burt Whitman's *Boston Herald* game story had a most unusual lead: "If Harvard, the National Geographic Society, or the American Natural History Museum feels like adding to its butterfly specimens we suggest that it commission as collector Ted Williams, whose homer, his 20th of the year, provided the Red Sox with the only runs they made yesterday when Knuckler Johnny Niggeling of the St. Louis Browns, for the third time this year, defeated them, 3 to 2, at Fenway Park. Sometimes Johnny's knuckle ball pitch acts like a falling leaf, occasionally like a humming bird, but usually is slowly elusive, like a butterfly. And 'butterfly' is what the trade calls the pitch."

At first it seemed to some that the home run was not a home run, but a foul ball. The *Globe* explained, "For a moment it looked as if Williams' hit was not to count, for Umpire Geisel, at the plate, inadvertently made a movement with his left hand, indicating the ball was foul. [Umpire] Pipgras misunderstood what he thought was a signal to this effect and stopped Williams after he had turned and was on his way around the circuit. Geisel quickly corrected the false impression, and Pipgras told Williams to proceed about his business. Geisel said after the game he was unconscious of the movement, and that there never was any doubt in his mind it being a fair ball."

His five home runs were #65, 71, 74, 82, and 95.

75 (#21) July 31 (first game) at Fenway Park. Pitcher: George Caster (St. Louis Browns). RH. Age 33.

Bottom of the seventh inning. Four-run homer. Grand slam #4.

It was "one of the weirdest doubleheaders of all time," wrote the *Boston Globe* of the two games at "foggy Fenway" attended by a "pneumonia-risking crowd of 5210 paid and 2900 ladies." The six-run seventh inning for the Red Sox in the first game looked like it might give them the game, now that they had come from behind and built an 11-7 lead. But the Browns scored three times in the top of the eighth and six more in the top of the ninth, and won 16-11. Neither team committed an error. Ted Williams' grand slam on a two-out 3-2 count produced most of the runs in the seventh. Roy Cullenbine of the Browns also hit a grand slam. After fouling off the first pitch with the full count, Ted "smashed the next one through wind, rain, and fog into the Boston bullpen. There Joe Dobson caught the dramatic clout and jumped up and down in high glee." The Red Sox won the second game, 4-1, called after 7 1/2.

Ted had previously hit homers #52 and 53 off Caster, both in the September 24, 1940 game.

76 (#22) August 7 at Fenway Park. Pitcher: Lefty Gomez (New York Yankees). LH. Age 32. Hall of Famer.

Bottom of the second inning. One-run homer.

It was a 9-5 win for the Red Sox, Dick Newsome getting the win. Ted's solo home run off Gomez was the first of the runs. He led off the second and hit a "wickedly pulled long drive which landed 15 rows up in the right-field wing of the grandstand, well away from the foul line extended." Even though it was just a solo homer in a game that the Yankees already led 2-0,

Burt Whitman of the *Boston Herald* continued, "We sincerely believe that it marked the turning point of the contest, with the Sox thereafter treating Gomez, who had won eight in a row, as merely another flinger." And despite the fact, apparently, that Boston next scored in the fourth inning, adding just two more runs. Williams did add two more hard-hit singles, each of which was key in the three-run rallies that characterized both the sixth and seventh.

Homer #11 was also hit off Lefty Gomez.

77 **(#23)** August 14 (first game) at Shibe Park, Philadelphia. Pitcher: Tom Ferrick (Philadelphia Athletics). RH. Age 26.

Top of the eighth inning. Three-run homer.

In the top of the eighth, Williams—to that point, 0-for-4—"picked on the 2-2 pitch and lashed it miles over the right-field wall to tie the contest" at 8-8. The Red Sox scored three runs in the top of the 11th and won, on a Foxx home run. This was another double-header day; the Red Sox lost the second game, 10-8. Ted hit a single in four at-bats in the nightcap, a rare 2-for-9 day which dropped his average from .413 to .408.

Ferrick furnished homers #77, 130, 247, and 304.

78 **(#24)** August 19 (first game) at Sportsman's Park, St. Louis. Pitcher: Denny Galehouse (St. Louis Browns). RH. Age 29.

Top of the third inning. One-run homer.

One in the first game, two in the second = three homers on the day. His homer in the first game came down on top of the right-field roof and accounted for half the runs in the 3-2 loss. He went 4-for-5 in the second game.

Galehouse, who would later loom large in Red Sox history starting the single-game playoff for the pennant in 1948, also gave up homers 111 and 124, both in 1942.

79 *(#25)* August 19 (second game) at Sportsman's Park, St. Louis. Pitcher: Bob Muncrief (St. Louis Browns). RH. Age 25.

Top of the fifth inning. One-run homer.

Ted's first gave Boston a 4-2 lead, but the Browns came right back in the bottom of the fifth with four runs and led 6-4. Each team got a run and it was 7-5, St. Louis, when Ted led off—and struck again. Homer #79 was launched "onto the right-center field roof directly above the 354-foot sign. Ted's smash bounced against the back screen on the first hop and was the hardest hit of the three."

Muncrief allowed Ted six homers: #79 and 80 in the same game, and then #99, 177, 187, and 195.

80 *(#26)* August 19 (second game) at Sportsman's Park, St. Louis. Pitcher: Bob Muncrief (St. Louis Browns). RH. Age 25.

Top of the eighth inning. Two-run homer.

This was Ted's second home run off the game off Muncrief. Again, the gopher ball landed on the right-field roof—his third homer of the day to the same rooftop. It tied the game in the eighth; three more Red Sox runs, in the ninth inning, made the difference in Boston's 10-7 win.

81 *(#27)* August 20 (first game) at Sportsman's Park, St. Louis. Pitcher: Elden Auker (St. Louis Browns). RH. Age 30.

Top of the eighth inning. Two-run homer.

After hitting three homers in a doubleheader on the 19th, Ted hit two more in a back-to-back doubleheader on the 20th. This time the Red Sox lost both games, however. They dropped the first game, 11-9. The Browns jumping out to an 8-2 lead gave them a leg up, and though the Sox scored seven more time, they still couldn't catch up. Ted's homer came in the top of the eighth. He drove in two runs in each game. His first-game homer was "rifled…high onto the right-field pavilion roof." (*Boston Herald*)

Auker, a teammate of Ted's in 1939, was hit for another homer in 1942—#96.

82 (#28) August 20 (second game) at Sportsman's Park, St. Louis: Pitcher: Johnny Niggeling (St. Louis Browns). RH. Age 37.

Top of the first inning. Two-run homer.

Ted hit a home run in his last at-bat of the first game, and his first at-bat of the second. It was the fourth homer he'd hit off Niggeling in 1941 (see also #65, 71, and 74). The ball went onto the right-field roof, "almost identical with the four-master Ted hit off Niggeling last trip here, just shaving the foul post." It also landed, said the *Herald*, in the "same vicinity" as the first game's homer.

Ted later hit #95 off Niggeling, too, though that came in 1942.

83 (#29) August 28 at Briggs Stadium, Detroit. Pitcher: Al Benton (Detroit Tigers). RH. Age 30.

Top of the second inning. One-run homer.

Ted Williams got them off to a good start, with a home run "to almost the identical spot where he hit one against the upper tier in this year's All-Star game." (*Herald*) The Tigers tied it in the bottom of the second. The Sox built up a 7-2 lead, but lost the game after Detroit scored once in the sixth and five more times (including a Rudy York grand slam) in the seventh. Ted later tripled, too.

Benton's six homers: #43, 83, 114, 119, 161, and 277.

84 (#30) August 30 at Fenway Park. Pitcher: Bump Hadley (Philadelphia Athletics).

Bottom of the fourth inning. Two-run homer.

Williams had a 2-for-3 day and boosted his batting average to .409. He was doing it with power, too—witness this stretch in which he hit six home runs in five days. The homer off Hadley was the second of the six. Ted also walked twice, letting him reach base four out of five times. This home run had a bit of an assist from Athletics center-fielder Sam Chapman. Ted had belted the ball "high and far to deep center. Running back to the corner of the visitors' bullpen where the fence veers back sharply to the dead center-field wall, Chapman jumped at the last minute and reached the ball with his glove hand, only to see the pellet pop out and over the bar, a roundtripper." [The bullpen in question is the one which today is the Red Sox pen — the one more in center field.]

Hadley, when he'd been with the Yankees, had given up homers #23 and 28, and — earlier in 1941 — homer #60 against the Athletics.

85 (#31) August 31 (first game) at Fenway Park. Pitcher: Jack Knott (Philadelphia Athletics). RH. Age 34.

Bottom of the sixth inning. Three-run homer. GAME WINNER.

The Red Sox split a Sunday doubleheader, winning the first game, 5-3, but dropping the second (cut short after seven innings), 3-2. Philadelphia was pitching around Williams; he drew four bases on balls. They knew what could happen when they pitched to him. Their 3-1 lead disappeared when Ted hit a three-run homer in the sixth on a 2-1 count "right into the teeth of a nasty east wind...into the right-field wing of the grandstand...eight rows deep and yards on the fair side of the yellow foul pole." (*Herald*) Burt Whitman offered the observation that "Ted the Kid stole the show...just the way Babe Ruth used to monopolize the spotlight when he was hitting them over the horizon for the old Sox and Yankees."

True, a hitter going for .400 doesn't like outs — but was this taking things a little too far? Bob Dunbar of the *Herald* let it be known that the day before, Ted had "bored a couple of holes through the left-field fence with his new rifle...Teddy's sharp-shooting ability was attested by the absence of one of the 'out' signs in the electric scoreboard."

Ted hit homer #61 off Knott in May. In May 1942, he hit #102 off him.

86 (#32) September 1 (first game) at Fenway Park. Pitcher: Alex Carrasquel (Washington Senators). RH. Age 28.

Bottom of the fifth inning. One-run homer.

It was the first of September, the final month of the season, and Ted Williams was in hot pursuit of .400. He didn't wilt on the first day of the month; he went 3-for-5 on the day (with two walks in each game)—and each of the three hits was a home run. He drove in five runs on the day, four in the first game. His 32nd homer gave him one more than his personal best, and the 17 homers he'd hit at Fenway eclipsed the 14 he'd hit in 1939. This first homer wasn't the hardest-hit; it went "floating into the grandstand just beyond the foul line." The grandstand in right field, of course; there was no grandstand in fair territory in left.

In 1939, Ted had hit his 17th homer off Alex.

During the sixth inning, Williams hit another drive—possibly the longest ball he ever hit. It went out of Fenway Park completely over the right-field roof. The roof is around 60 feet high at that point and 400 feet from home plate. No one had ever hit a ball over the right-field roof before, and only one person has ever done so since (Carl Yastrzemski); the only problem is that both Ted's and Yaz's balls hit out were both foul balls.

87 (#33) September 1 (first game) at Fenway Park. Pitcher: Bill Zuber (Washington Senators). RH. Age 28.

Bottom of the eighth inning. Two-run homer. GAME WINNER.

It was a sweltering day, but Fenway fans were thrilled to see Ted hit a two-run homer in the seven-run bottom of the eighth which lifted the Sox from a 9-6 deficit to the 13-9 final score, a win. His second homer of the game "drove in the tying and winning runs in the eighth frame, this wallop being a 420-foot drive in the bleacher...just above the Red Sox bullpen roof in right field." It landed about five or six rows in. Not one of the three homers took advantage of the shortened distance that "Williamsburg" had added with the installation of the bullpens before the 1940 season.

Zuber was the only pitcher who ever beaned Ted Williams. It happened in 1938, when Ted was playing for the Millers and Zuber pitching for Milwaukee. Ted was knocked unconscious and in the hospital for two days. In the first five games after coming out of hospital, he hit three homers and drove in 12 runs. Zuber joined the Red Sox after the war and was 5-1 in 1946.

This was the only homer Ted hit off Zuber, who remains—to be the best of our knowledge—the only major-league pitcher born in a commune: the Community of True Inspiration (the Amana Colonies, in Iowa.)

88 (**#34**) September 1 (second game) at Fenway Park. Pitcher: Red Anderson (Washington Senators). RH. Age 29.

Bottom of the sixth inning. One-run homer.

Shooting for .400, Williams hadn't hit a single in the two games, not even a double. He didn't hit a triple—just three home runs. The walks ratcheted his on-base percentage up to .554—more than 55% of the time Ted had come up to bat, he got on base. His 34th home run gave him a one-homer edge over New York's Charlie "King Kong" Keller for the league lead in home runs. He'd homered in each of the last four days the Red Sox had played, with six homers over the span. The third homer of the day, this in the second game, came on a 3-1 pitch and was sent "into the bleacher-grandstand separation in right field." The one strike had been on a savage foul ball Williams hit *over* the right-field roof. He came up a second time in the inning and his another one over the roof—but foul. And then walked. The Sox already held a 4-2 lead over the Senators, but the six runs sparked by Ted's sixth-inning homer made it 10-2.

Arnold Revola "Red" Anderson was the second Iowan in a row to give up a homer to Ted Williams.

There was a home run that wasn't in the first inning of the September 7 game at Yankee Stadium. Ted's ball "struck the right-field foul pole and caromed into foul territory into the stands. Under a screwy local rule, it was a ground rule double. If it had caromed into fair territory, it would have been good for a homer." Although the foul pole is always deemed in fair territory, this is the way the ground rule was at Yankee Stadium at the time. Though homerless, The Kid was 3-for-4 on the day.

89 (#35) September 15 at Fenway Park. Pitcher: Johnny Rigney (Chicago White Sox). RH. Age 26.

Bottom of the seventh inning. Three-run homer.

It had been two weeks since Ted hit a home run. This one was his only hit of the day, but any ballplayer will welcome a three-run homer any day of the year. Hit into the center-field bleachers on a 1-0 count, this was the sixth homer he'd hit off Johnny Rigney just this year. "The ball soared high and far, over the end of the Chisox bullpen and into the bleachers on a carry of more than 450 feet from home plate." The Red Sox had been leading Chicago 2-0 through six innings; this homer helped put the game on ice. The final was 6-1.

Williams was hitting .409. Unsurprisingly, Ted was getting national attention. September 16 was an off-day and he agreed to fly to New York to do some "radioing over an extensive hookup" which apparently could not be done from Boston.

This was the sixth of the seven homers Williams whacked off Rigney. See also #56, 57, 57, 64, 72, and 133.

90 (#36) September 21 at Fenway Park. Pitcher: Tiny Bonham (New York Yankees). RH. Age 27.

Bottom of the sixth inning. Two-run homer.

It was the last home game of the 1941 season. The *Boston Herald* head-lined "Williams Drives 36th As Sox Blast Yankees in Homeric Adieu, 4-1." Nineteen years later, John Updike's famous *New Yorker* article on Ted's 521st homer was titled "Hub Bids Kid Adieu." The three homers hit by the Sox (Cronin and Finney each had one) scored all four runs and clinched second place for the Red Sox, though well behind the Yankees in the standings. Both Finney's and Williams' home runs landed in the Red Sox bullpen, both of them "splashed against the front wall of the bleachers" behind the Boston pen. (*Herald*)

Ted hit four homers off Tiny: #90, 109, 157, and 159.

91 (#37) September 28 (first game) at Shibe Park, Philadelphia. Pitcher: Dick Fowler (Philadelphia Athletics). RH. Age 20.

Top of the fifth inning. One-run homer.

This time the focus was more on the hit than the fact it was a homer. Ted entered the final game of the 1941 batting .39955. There were suggestions that he might want to sit on the mark, knowing it would round up to .400—but many newspapers made it clear that was not really an option, running headlines after the previous day's game proclaiming that he'd fallen below .400. After all, .39955 was not really .400. And he'd been in something of a relative slump, dropping from .413 on September 10 to the hair under .400. Cronin ordered other players on the Red Sox not to be giving Ted tips, to help him keep his mind less cluttered.

So Ted stepped into the batter's box in the second inning in Philadelphia with a great deal of weight on his shoulders. On a 2-0 count, he "sent a sizzling single past first baseman Bob Johnson's right" That hit put him comfortably over the .400 mark, enough so that even if he'd been inclined to come out of the game to preserve his mark, he could have risked one more at-bat first. That second at-bat rolled around in the fifth inning, and he homered over the right-center-field wall "out onto 20th street, a smash good for at least 440 feet on the level." (*Herald*)

Earlier in the day, rain had threatened. Imagine if Williams had gotten his single and a home run and then the game had been washed out before it was official. But the skies had cleared before the game got underway and Ted added two more singles before the game was over—then hit two more hits in the second game. And the double he hit in the fourth inning of the second game was "one of the most wicked liners we've seen Ted make," wrote the *Herald*'s Burt Whitman—hit so hard it broke a speaker affixed just below the top of the right-field wall, punching a hole through the speaker horn. A few inches higher and it would have been an even longer home run than the one in the first game. It was a 6-for-8 final day. He wound up, of course, with a .406 average—and an astounding .553 on-base percentage record. His 37 homers gave him the league lead, too.

For the season, Ted had hit 37 homers, but only struck out 27 times. It wasn't the only year he did that.

This was a hugely significant home run; Ted later hit five more off Fowler: #105, 242, 252, 267, and 295.

Just a week later, both Ted Williams and Jimmie Foxx played in an exhibition game at San Diego's Lane Field against Pirrone's All-Star on October 5. It was the park where Ted had played with the Padres in 1936 and 1937. There was a home-run hitting event before the game. The *San Diego Union* said that Williams played "Santa Claus to the kids on Pacific Highway" where he "rained baseballs over the Lane Field fence in a convincing demonstration of batting power." Four of them were hit completely out of the park. As Tom Larwin wrote in his article about Ted's 1941 visit to San Diego, there were more than 3,000 fans who packed Lane Field. In the game itself, "Fans got to see what they hoped to see—both Foxx and Williams hit home runs."[26] Hitting against Jesse Flores in the third inning, Ted "pasted a fast ball over the right-field wall…a whistling homer over the fence, clearing it somewhere along the 275-foot marker."[27]

Ten weeks to the day after Ted's final home run for Boston—after he became the last man to hit .400 in the major leagues—Japanese warplanes attacked Pearl Harbor and the nation was suddenly plunged into war.

1942

There was no way to know how the war would affect any given player. Ted might have ended his career with 91 home runs, and never played another game. Major League Baseball was prepared to cancel the season, but President Franklin Roosevelt gave them the "green light" and encouraged teams to play as a morale boost to those who would need to fight. Ted Williams was granted an exemption from service, since he was the sole support of his mother. Some howls of protest came from some quarters about an obviously fit young man being exempt. Ted was torn. This isn't the place to recount the story in detail but interested readers are referred to *Ted Williams at War*, a full book devoted to the subject of Ted and his military service. He stood up to his critics, got enthusiastic cheers from servicemen during spring training games, and played out the year—though early in the season he enlisted in the Navy, for induction after the season was over.

During the course of the season, Ted and rookie Johnny Pesky both attended Naval classes in the evenings while in Boston. It's worth remembering that the Red Sox had never yet played in a night ball game.

92 (#1 of 1942) April 14 at Fenway Park. Pitcher: Phil Marchildon (Philadelphia Athletics). RH. Age 28.

Bottom of the first. Three-run homer.

A three-run homer in the first inning on Opening Day was a nice way to kick off the new season. He'd swung hard on a 2-1 pitch—and missed in entirely. On the next pitch, though, he "connected with a waist-high fast ball that rode down the wind into the second row of the open bleachers just back of the Boston bullpen." He hadn't known quite how he'd be accepted by the Boston fandom, but he'd been cheered early on and when he hit the home run, "the noise then loosened was sheer bedlam. And all afternoon the Splinter got ovations at every move" (*Herald*) Ted's homer wasn't the winning hit, but he had five RBIs on the day, an 8-3 Red Sox win.

The other Marchildon home runs are #120, 148, 180, and 196.

93 (#2) April 16 at Fenway Park. Pitcher: Les McCrabb (Philadelphia Athletics). RH. Age 27.

Bottom of the seventh inning. Two-run homer.

Williams drove in four more runs in this one, a lopsided 19-4 win, half of them on his homer in the seventh, by which time it was already 12-4. It was "a high loft which barely reached the covered grandstand sector just inside the right-field foul line. It couldn't have been better placed for a theatrical landing, however, since it dropped among a flock of soldiers and sailors who really went to town in fighting for possession of the souvenir sphere."

McCrabb had previously given up #54 to Ted.

94 (#3) April 30 at Fenway Park. Pitcher: Charlie Fuchs (Detroit Tigers). RH. Age 28.

Bottom of the third. One-run homer.

Ted led off the third inning and swung at the very first pitch. His third home run of the season "found a resting place in the Red Sox bullpen." (*Boston Traveler*) The homer gave Boston a 3-2 lead at the time. The Red Sox won the game, 5-3. The *Globe* said that the drive went deep into the pen.

This was the only homer Ted hit off Fuchs, but he did later hit one off the homo-phonic Johnny Kucks.

95 **(#4)** May 1 at Fenway Park. Pitcher: Johnny Niggeling (St. Louis Browns). RH. Age 38.

Bottom of the ninth inning. One-run homer.

The Red Sox assembled 11 hits, Ted getting a homer and two singles, and Jimmie Foxx hitting a big home run, too. As he had the day before, though this time with two outs, he swung at the first pitch and drove it about a dozen rows into the right-field grandstand seats. This homer was the first of an even dozen hit in May 1942. There was never a month in which he hit more.

In 1941, Niggeling had been nicked for homers #65, 71, 74, and 82.

96 **(#5)** May 2 at Fenway Park. Pitcher: Elden Auker (St. Louis Browns). RH. Age 31.

Bottom of the ninth. Two-run homer.

The Sox were down 10-8 heading into the bottom of the ninth, but Johnny Pesky beat out a bunt to set the table for Williams. For the third game in a row, Ted was first-pitch swinging. His blast tied the game, a ball hit so hard that everyone instantly knew it was gone, into the right-center-field bleachers. Not long afterwards, Foxx got on base, was replaced by a pinch runner, and Bobby Doerr doubled in the winning run.

#81 and #96 were the two homers the submariner Auker surrendered to The Kid.

97 **(#6)** May 5 at Fenway Park. Pitcher: Harry Eisenstat (Cleveland Indians). LH. Age 26.

Bottom of the fourth inning. Two-run homer.

A 13-3 win swept the three-game series against the visiting Indians. Ted's homer went into the bleachers, over the visitors' bullpen, a "mighty smash into the sunny center-field bleachers." (*Herald*) He also doubled in the third inning and even bunted for a single in leading off the sixth.

Ted had hit #21 off Eisenstat back in August 1939.

98 (#7) May 10 (second game) at Shibe Park, Philadelphia. Pitcher: Russ Christopher (Philadelphia Athletics). RH. Age 24.

Top of the ninth inning. Two-run homer.

The Red Sox lost two games to the Athletics, 4-2 and 6-5. Ted's homer sailed "far over the right-field wall of Shibe Park and onto the top of a two-story building on the other side of 20th street." (*Herald*) He'd hit it in the top of the ninth with Pesky on base tied the game but Philadelphia scored in the bottom of the ninth to re-take the lead and secure a win. It was Ted's first home run on the road in 1942.

Ted connected off Christopher for four home runs: #98, 104, 149, and 193.

99 (#8) May 16 at Sportsman's Park, St. Louis. Pitcher: Bob Muncrief (St. Louis Browns). RH. Age 26.

Top of the ninth inning. Two-run homer. GAME WINNER.

Tex Hughson threw a two-hitter, and the score was tied 2-2 after eight innings. Lou Finney doubled and then Ted Williams gave the Sox a 4-2 lead with a hard-hit ball that left the park "over the roof in right-center over the 354-foot mark."

Muncrief was mashed six times: homers #79, 80, 99, 177, 187, and 195.

100 (#9) May 21 at League Park, Cleveland. Pitcher: Joe Krakauskas (Cleveland Indians). LH. Age 27.

Top of the fourth inning. Two-run homer.

Ted played right field in the game, because he'd hit a ball off his foot in batting practice and there was less territory to defend. More significantly, he drove in four runs to beat the Tribe, 8-3. Half of the four came in the fourth, "over the right-field barrier wall at the 345-foot mark" (*Globe*) or "through the right-center-field barrier." (*Herald*) It wasn't the game winner, since the Sox already held a 6-0 lead at the time.

Ted hit #5 off Krakauskas. And now #100. It was the only homer "Krakky" gave up in 1942.

Speaking of batting practice, "Williams wanted the ball near the plate and he wanted tough pitches. To waste his time with bad balls in batting practice infuriated him, but to set them right down the middle was just as useless." And he was characteristically loud when he was in the cage, and calling out before the pitches, "creating situations, naming a late inning, a park, a quality pitcher, putting imaginary runners on base, demanding a pitch worthy of the circumstances."[28]

101 (#10) May 23 at Fenway Park. Pitcher: Roger Wolff (Philadelphia Athletics). RH. Age 31.

Bottom of the seventh inning. One-run homer.

Seaman Second Class Ted Williams had enlisted in the Naval Air Corps the day before, an offday. He celebrated with home run #10 on May 23. He might have had two more on deep fly balls, but for the heavy air. The one he hit landed in the Red Sox bullpen and tied the score 2-2 at the time. (The Red Sox lost, 4-2.) The proceeds from the day's game went to the Army and Navy Relief Societies.

Homers #106 and 128 came off Wolff pitches, too.

102 (#11) May 24 (first game) at Fenway Park. Pitcher: Jack Knott (Philadelphia Athletics). RH. Age 35.

Bottom of the fifth inning. Two-run homer.

The Red Sox lost the first game, 6-5, and won the second game by the same score. Ted's homer came in the first game, hit just barely over right-fielder Elmer Valo's head into the right-field stands. He drove in three of Boston's five runs.

Knott had given up #61 and 85 in '41.

1942 – Boston Red Sox Ted Williams shakes hands with Bobby Doerr (#1) as he crosses home plate in front of New York Yankee catcher Bill Dickey at Fenway Park.

103 **(#12)** May 26 at Yankee Stadium, New York. Pitcher: Atley Donald (New York Yankees). RH. Age 31.

Top of the third inning. Two-run homer.

The only two runs the Red Sox scored in the 9-2 Yankees win came in the third inning on Ted's home run. Pete Fox singled and was on first base when Ted hit a "prodigious poke, a towering drive that sailed into the third deck of the right-field stand with vociferous authority." Vociferous authority? That's what Arthur Sampson of the *Boston Herald* wrote. The *New York Times* described it as "a titanic smash."

Donald had also given up homer #46.

104 **(#13)** May 29 at Shibe Park, Philadelphia. Pitcher: Russ Christopher (Philadelphia Athletics). RH. Age 24.

Top of the first inning. Three-run homer. GAME WINNER.

The game started well for the Red Sox, and—with a 14-2 final score—it ended well, too. Christopher had walked Dom DiMaggio and Johnny Pesky on eight straight balls, then retired Pete Fox. Ted's homer was the only hit Christopher gave up through the first five innings, but it made all the difference in the game. "The ball landed on a roof behind the wall about 100 feet from the right-field foul line." (*Globe*)

His first homer (#98) off Christopher came in the ninth inning; this one came in the top of the first. He later hit #149 and 193.

105 (#14) May 29 at Shibe Park, Philadelphia. Pitcher: Dick Fowler (Philadelphia Athletics). RH. Age 21.

Top of the eighth inning. Four-run homer. Grand slam #5.

Ted's eighth-inning grand slam was icing on the cake in the 14-2 Red Sox win. Ted had already hit a three-run homer off Russ Christopher, "another prodigious homer onto a roof behind the right field." Bobby Doerr hit a home run off Fowler, too. Ted's seven RBIs were half the team's total.

106 (#15) May 30 (second game) at Shibe Park, Philadelphia. Pitcher: Roger Wolff (Philadelphia Athletics). RH. Age 31.

Top of the sixth. One-run homer.

The Sox split a doubleheader with the Athletics, despite Dom DiMaggio having a seven-hit day (five singles and two doubles, but with only one RBI and three runs scored.) He also made "two of the most sensational catches ever made at Shibe Park." As for Ted Williams, the *Herald* wrote, "[He] has found Wolff hard to hit all year and his homer to left was the only time he hit the ball with authority all afternoon."

It was Boston 10-6, then Philadelphia, 5-4.

The 12 homers Ted hit in May were the most he ever hit in any month. Only once did he match the 12—in June 1950.

#101, 106, 128—three homers off Roger Wolff.

107 (#16) June 23 at Briggs Stadium, Detroit. Pitcher: Dizzy Trout (Detroit Tigers). RH. Age 27.

Top of the seventh. Two-run homer.

Ted's two-run homer into the right-field stands was his first in more than three weeks. Williams and Jim Tabor both connected, and so did Red Sox pitcher Oscar Judd—and Judd's was the hardest-hit of the three. Ted was robbed of an earlier homer in the fourth inning when Barney McCosky made a great catch and prevented his ball from going out in left-center. When he did hit it out, his "long hoist…barely penetrated the lower right-field stand, about 375 feet from home." (*Herald*)

Six homers were hit off Detroit's Diz, perhaps the most meaningful of which was the last: #324. In between this one and that one were #144, 164, 221, and 283.

108 (#17) June 24 at Briggs Stadium, Detroit. Pitcher: Virgil Trucks (Detroit Tigers). RH. Age 25.

Top of the seventh. One-run homer. GAME WINNER.

Ted hit 12 homers off Trucks, more than any other pitcher. Needless to say, you have to be a good pitcher to even get into that many games. Trucks won 177 games in his career, but not this one. It was a "twilight" game, and there was only one run scored in the game—Ted Williams driving himself in with his home run into the Briggs Stadium right-field stands. He hit a 1-1 pitch and "met the ball so solidly that everybody in the park knew that it was ticketed for the circuit. It landed well up in the upper tier, out toward center." (*Herald*) Charlic Wagner threw a three-hitter for the victory, only facing 28 Tigers (none of whom got past first base.) In the fourth inning, Dom D. braced himself against the wall and grabbed what would have been a home run by Rudy York.

His 12 home runs spanned #108 to #444. The 12: 108, 115, 146, 174, 189, 226, 236, 243, 320, 342, 437, and 444.

109 (#18) July 4 (second game) at Fenway Park. Pitcher: Tiny Bonham (New York Yankees). RH. Age 28.

Bottom of the sixth inning. Two-run homer.

Ted hit Tony's first pitch for a "towering smash that dropped in the bullpen in front of the right-field bleachers." (*New York Times*). It gave the Red Sox a 2-1 lead at the time. The final score was Red Sox 6, Yankees 4. New York had won the first game, 6-3, with Yankees pitcher Red Ruffing driving in two of the runs.

Ted hit four homers off Tiny: #90, 109, 157, and 159.

110 (#19) July 15 (second game) at Fenway Park. Pitcher: Joe Haynes (Chicago White Sox). RH. Age 24.

Bottom of the seventh inning. Two-run homer.

It was quite an up-and-down day, with Tex Hughson and the Red Sox winning the first game, 11-1, but then losing the second, 11-6. Ted had five RBIs on the day, boosting his total to 86 on the season—and it was only mid-July. The home run he hit on a 0-1 count went "into the right-field corner bleachers" some 12 or 14 rows deep.

Haynes was also hit for homers #211 and 319.

111 (#20) July 26 (first game) at Sportsman's Park. Pitcher: Denny Galehouse (St. Louis Browns). RH. Age 30.

Top of the fourth inning. One-run homer.

It was a "drab matinee" according to the *Boston Globe*, but that may have reflected the team dropping two games (9-2 and 4-3) to the "bumptious Brownies." Facing a "screwy defense" the Browns mounted against him, Ted attempted a bunt but fouled it off. On the 0-1 count, he just drove one over the defense—way over it, and "lashed" one "well onto the right-center roof against the wind."

Galehouse also surrendered homers #77 and 124.

112 (#21) July 26 (second game) at Sportsman's Park. Pitcher: Al Hollingsworth (St. Louis Browns). LH. Age 34.

Top of the sixth inning. One-run homer.

Two homers this day catapulted Williams into the league lead in home runs. Hollingsworth fooled him on two slow curves, but it was hard to fool Ted Williams three times.

In the bottom of the ninth inning, with the score tied 3-3, St. Louis second baseman Don Gutteridge hit a ball which would have been a home run—but for Ted Williams, who made a "sensational one-handed catch" of the line drive with a "leaping catch" in front of the left-field bleachers. (*Herald* and *Globe)* But the Browns didn't wait long before drawing a base on balls and doubling to win the game.

Of all 521 home runs hit by Ted Williams, #111 is the only one for which we could not find a location. We checked the Boston papers—all of them—and both the *Globe-Democrat* and *Post-Dispatch* from St. Louis. No luck pinning down where Ted's homer was actually hit.

"Boots" Hollingsworth also helped Williams hit homer #142.

113 (#22) July 30 at League Park, Cleveland. Pitcher: Mel Harder (Cleveland Indians). RH. Age 32.

Top of the first inning. Two-run homer.

After Johnny Pesky singled, Ted Williams hit a high fly ball that went over League Park's right-center-field wall at the point where the distance was marked at 360 feet. The Sox got out to an early 2-0 lead. The Indians got one back in the third and three more in the bottom of the seventh. The final score was 4-3, Cleveland.

This was the fourth and final homer hit off Harder. The earlier three were: 20, 27, and 73.

114 (#23) July 31 at Briggs Stadium, Detroit. Pitcher: Al Benton (Detroit Tigers). RH. Age 31.

Top of the fifth inning. One-run homer.

The Sox won a 7-6 game to kick off a four-game series in Detroit. Ted "laced homer No. 23 on a line into the front of the upper right-field stands." (*Herald*) The ball struck something in the second row of the middle tier and caromed back onto the field. His hit gave the Sox a 5-3 lead, but the game wasn't over yet. Pitcher Tex Hughson left with a 7-4 lead and got the win, though things got close when Charlie Gehringer banged a two-run pinch-hit homer in the bottom of the ninth.

Benton's six homers: #43, 83, 114, 119, 161, and 277.

115 (#24) August 2 (second game) at Briggs Stadium, Detroit. Pitcher: Virgil Trucks (Detroit Tigers). RH. Age 25.

Top of the ninth inning. Two-run homer.

Combining elements of his last two homers, Johnny Pesky was again on first base. Again, Ted hit the ball into the middle deck in right field. It ruined Trucks's shutout. The final score was 6-2. The Tigers had won the first game, too, 8-4. All of the first game's Red Sox runs had scored on home runs, too, with Jim Tabor and Dom DiMaggio each smacking one.

Ted's 12 homers off Trucks: The 12: 108, 115, 146, 174, 189, 226, 236, 243, 320, 342, 437, and 444.

116 (#25) August 15 (first game) at Fenway Park. Pitcher: Sid Hudson (Washington Senators). RH. Age 27.

Bottom of the third inning. Two-run homer. GAME WINNER.

The Sox swept a doubleheader from the Senators, 2-1 and 7-6. The second game was a walkoff, when Lou Finney tripled with two men on and one out, lifting the Red Sox from a 6-5 deficit to a that 7-6 win. It was Ted who scored the tying run, and Tony Lupien who scored the winning run. In fact,

Ted Williams scored three of Boston's four runs in the nightcap, and *all* of the runs in the first game—both of them—with his two-run homer in the bottom of the third, driving in Johnny Pesky ahead of him. The homer was dropped into the right-field seats, inside the foul pole.

Hudson had allowed homer #40 in 1940, and later allowed #150 and 274.

117 (#26) August 19 (first game) at Fenway Park. Pitcher: Spud Chandler (New York Yankees). RH. Age 34.

Bottom of the first inning. Two-run homer.

Spurgeon Ferdinand Chandler was probably happy to have the nickname Spud. He certainly wasn't all that happy when he walked Dom DiMaggio in the bottom of the first and then saw Ted Williams jump on a pitch and bang it into the center-field bleachers, about ten feet to the right of the flagpole. Or for Jim Tabor to hit a two-run homer in the second, and then for Tabor to hit yet another in the sixth. Three homers, six runs, a 6-4 Red Sox win. The Yankees won game two, 2-1.

Later in 1942, Chandler also was hit for homer #125.

118 (#27) August 27 at Fenway Park. Pitcher: Jim Bagby (Cleveland Indians). RH. Age 27.

Bottom of the first inning. One-run homer.

The Red Sox had won nine games in a row and Tex Hughson had won 11 decisions in a row, but both streaks came to a halt when Jim Bagby threw a five-hitter and stifled the Red Sox, 4-2. One of the five hits was Ted's first-inning homer into the Red Sox bullpen, giving the Red Sox an early 1-0 lead, which lasted until the top of the third. The score was tied, 2-2, after eight—but the Indians scored two in the ninth and the Red Sox scored none.

Bagby had also given up homer #68.

119 (#28) September 2 (first game) at Fenway Park. Pitcher: Al Benton (Detroit Tigers). RH. Age 31.

Bottom of the eighth inning. One-run homer.

The Red Sox won two games, 3-2 and 4-2, and Ted Williams figured in all the scoring but one run—Johnny Pesky's two-out bases-loaded single that scored the tie-breaker in the first game. Williams was 5-for-8. It was Ted's homer which had created the tie in the bottom of the eighth. It was "a majestic first-pitch drive that landed in the bleachers beyond the Boston bullpen." The *Herald* wrote that Ted "had just finished look at some planes, far aloft."

Benton's six homers: #43, 83, 114, 119, 161, and 277.

120 (#29) September 5 at Fenway Park. Pitcher: Phil Marchildon (Philadelphia Athletics). RH. Age 28.

Bottom of the third inning. One-run homer.

It was an unusual Fenway doubleheader. The first game featured Ayer, Massachusetts-based Fort Devens beating Fort Terry of Montauk Point, L.I., 6-2, for the First Service Command's 1942 championship. In the second game, the Philadelphia Athletics beat the Boston Red Sox, 4-3. Williams hit a home run into the first row of the right-field grandstand seats. Ted's solo homer scored the third run of the third inning, but the last one the Red Sox scored.

This was Ted's second homer off the Canadian native in 1942 (see also #92); he later hit numbers 148, 180, and 196.

121 (#30) September 6 at Fenway Park. Pitcher: Lum Harris (Philadelphia Athletics). RH. Age 27.

Bottom of the eighth inning. One-run homer. GAME WINNER.

Sometimes a one-run homer is all you need. Connie Mack's men held a 6-2 lead over the Red Sox after 6 ½ innings, but then the Bostons scored five runs — three of them on Johnny Peacock's triple — in the bottom of the seventh. It was 7-7 an inning later, and Ted Williams hit one "into the right-field grandstand, around the bend, a circuit drive in any big-league ballpark and a game-winner." (*Herald*)

Chalmer Luman Harris had also been hit for homer #69.

122 (#31) September 10 at Briggs Stadium, Detroit. Pitcher: Hal Newhouser (Detroit Tigers). LH. Age 21.

Top of the third inning. One-run homer.

What could have been an inning-ending double play was mishandled by Bobby Doerr and the eighth-inning error let in the tying run while the umpire ruled Tony Lupien had been pulled off first base by a throw on the subsequent play, and the go-ahead run scored. Tex Hughson lost the game, 5-4, his record on the season now 18-6. Rookie shortstop Johnny Pesky had collected two more hits, giving him 190 on the season. Ted Williams had scored the first run of the game back in the third inning, "a terrific jolt into the upper right-center-field grandstand over the point on the ground marked as 370 feet from home." (*Boston Herald*)

"Prince Hal" granted three home runs — #122, 145, and 260.

123 (#32) September 13 (first game) at Comiskey Park, Chicago. Pitcher: Buck Ross (Chicago White Sox). RH. Age 27.

Top of the seventh inning. Two-run homer. GAME WINNER.

It was a close game, the White Sox winning 1-0 through six innings, when Johnny Pesky singled to lead off the top of the seventh. Next up — Ted Williams, on a 1-2 count, "spanked it wickedly to right, against an appreciable cross wind, into the fifth row of the lower grandstand." (*Herald*) The home run put Boston on the board and proved the game-winner; even though the Red Sox scored six runs in the top of the seventh, these first two runs were decisive in the 6-1 win. There had been a loud fan heckling Ted in the game, but the home run shut him up. The ball itself struck a fellow Navy man in the face, as Lt. Earl Newman had tried to catch it. The ball fell

521 — THE STORY OF TED WILLIAMS' HOME RUNS

into the lower right-field stands. Newman's cheek was cut and he had to go to Mercy Hospital for examination.

The Red Sox also won the second game, 5-0. Pesky added two more hits; he was now at 196.

Ross also served up homer #66.

124 (#33) September 17 at Sportsman's Park, St. Louis. Pitcher: Denny Galehouse (St. Louis Browns). RH. Age 30.

Top of the first inning. One-run homer.

Tex Hughson got his 20th win of the season and Ted Williams kicked things off with his 33rd home run of the year onto the roof of the right-field pavilion, hitting on a 2-1 count. Williams scored what proved the winning run after doubling to lead off the fourth — a ball he "intentionally slapped into wide open left field" against the shift — and scored on Bobby Doerr's two-out single. The Red Sox won, 5-1.

Galehouse had also given up homers #78 and 111.

125 (#34) September 19 at Yankee Stadium, New York. Pitcher: Spud Chandler (New York Yankees). RH. Age 34.

Top of the first inning. One-run homer.

Johnny Pesky's 201st base hit of the year led off the tenth inning of the 6-6 game. Ted Williams then drew his third walk. Going for the predictable sacrifice, Tony Lupien laid down a beauty and Yankees catcher Bill Dickey had no play but to first base. His throw was wild, umpire Bill McGowan ducked out of the way, and both Pesky and Williams scored as the ball went astray, Lupien reaching all the way to third base. He scored on Finney's single, and the Red Sox won, 9-6. Ted had scored the first run of the game back in the top of the first inning with a hard-hit ball that was "high off the face of the upper right-field tier" of Yankee Stadium.

Chandler also gave up #117.

126 (#35) September 20 (first game) at Yankee Stadium, New York. Pitcher: Red Ruffing (New York Yankees). RH. Age 37. Hall of Famer.

Top of the fourth inning. One-run homer.

After the September 20 double header, both the Red Sox and Yankees were 10-10 in head-to-head competition. The Yanks won this first game, 2-1, with the only Red Sox run coming on Ted's solo home run. Boston took the nightcap, 3-2. Ted led off the fourth, doing only one run's worth of damage on his drive "15 rows up into the very corner of the lower right-field stands." (*Herald*) The Yankees came from behind with single runs in the seventh and the bottom of the ninth.

Ruffing also gave up #7, #47, and #181.

127 (#36) September 21 at Yankee Stadium, New York. Pitcher: Marv Breuer (New York Yankees). RH. Age 28.

Top of the ninth inning. Two-run homer.

This was the last home run Ted hit before he went in the Navy. In a nation at war, no one could know if Ted Williams would ever play major-league ball again, much less survive the war. He homered three days in a row at Yankee Stadium to end his year. The Red Sox won the game, 3-2, in 11 innings. Johnny Pesky got three more base hits. Tex Hughson won his 21st game of the year.

The Yankees had a 2-0 lead until the top of the ninth inning, and Marv Breuer was working on a one-hitter, a Pesky single in the sixth. "Get on there and I'll knock you in," Williams said to Johnny before the Red Sox batted in the ninth. Pesky did his part and singled again, into left-center field. Ted took a ball on the first pitch he saw, a curve, but then correctly guessed fastball and got his first hit of the day, hitting it into the "right-field corner of the center-field bleachers, a four-bagger in any man's park." (*Herald*) In a flash, the score was tied. In the top of the 11th, Pesky singled again, took second base on Williams' grounder, and scored on Lupien's single to right.

It was the one and only homer Ted hit off Breuer, and the last of the 41 homers the Yankees pitcher surrendered.

Guessing that it would be a fastball paid off. It was an important part of success as a hitter. Guessing it was, though he something preferred to call it "anticipating." In *The Science of Hitting*, he wrote, "You've got to guess, you've got to have an idea. All they ever write about the good hitters is what great reflexes they have, what great style, what strength, what quickness, but never how smart the guy is at the plate, and that's 50 per cent of it. From the ideas come the 'proper thinking,' and the 'anticipation,' the 'guessing.'

"Obviously, you don't just 'guess' curve of 'guess' fast ball. You work from a frame of reference, you learn what you might expect in certain instances, and you guess from there. Certainly you won't guess a pitch the pitcher can't get over; he might have a terrific curve, but if he can't get it over, forget it. Certainly the pitch you anticipate when the count is 0 and 2 (a curve ball, probably, if the pitcher has one) is not the pitch you anticipate when the count is 2 and 0 (fast ball, almost without exception). Certainly if you are the kind of impatient hitter who will swing at anything at any time you will do yourself no good guessing at all because with that kind of latitude a pitcher will throw you nothing good to hit.

"But if you have developed discipline at the plate, and can wait for that good ball to hit, you have a right to think along with the pitcher, and you will surprise yourself how often you outguess him."[29]

Tommy Henrich said that Williams "did more than out-practice everyone… he out-thought the rest of us, too. He swung a lighter bat than most of us, 32 ounces compared with anything from 34 to 40 ounces for the rest of us, because he said bat speed was more important than a heavier bat that might give you distance. He said if you have enough bat speed, the home runs will come anyhow, and the lighter bat will give you more singles and doubles. He was also more disciplined at the plate than the rest of us…when you went for something that wasn't a good pitch, you'd hear it from him, usually at the top of his voice: 'Don't be so damn dumb.'"[30]

With 36 homers, 137 runs batted in, and a .356 average (down 50 points from the year before, but still spectacular), Ted Williams won the Triple Crown in the American League. He'd also led the league in runs scored (141), bases on balls (145), on-base percentage (.499), slugging (.648), and total bases (338). A shoo-in for league MVP? One would think so.

But the honor went to second baseman Joe Gordon of the Yankees. He had a good year, batting 322 with a .409 on-base percentage. But he drove in 34 fewer runs, scored 53 fewer runs, and hit only half as many homers (18 to Ted's 36). The only two categories in which Gordon led the league were in strikeouts (95) and grounding into double plays (22). And errors by second basemen. Ted struck out 51 times and grounded into 12 double plays, and had a .988 fielding percentage at his position. But the voting sportswriters, in their wisdom, determined Gordon as the more valuable player. Ted came in second, the vote 270-249. Gordon didn't even lead the Yankees in homers or RBIs (nor in hits, runs, doubles, triples, stolen bases, or total bases); he did in batting average but not in on-base percentage.

But Ted Williams was not always at his best diplomatically, and that undoubtedly cost him in his standing with the press. He had no problems with umpires, though. Ted was never ejected from even one of his 2,292 major-league games. On November 27, he officially began training in Naval aviation. For the next three years, he was in military service and had very little to do with the press.

1943 — Military service

Ted played some baseball during the war years, though not a lot. He did play on a couple of base teams, the Navy Pre-Flight Cloudbusters at Chapel Hill in 1943 and the Bronson Bombers at NAS Pensacola. He thought he might have played in 31 games for the Cloudbusters, and one of them was particularly notable — the only game in which he played on the same team as Babe Ruth. It was a benefit game at Fenway Park on July 12, pitting Ruth's Service All-Stars against the Boston Braves (Ruth's team was comprised of young men in the service and beat the Braves, 9-8). There was a home-run hitting contest before the game, Ruth vs Williams. Ted won that, three home runs to zero. He was fit, and Ruth was "fat and forty-eightish but still fabulous" in the words of the AP dispatch. During the game, Naval Aviation Cadet Ted Williams hit a three-run homer into the bleachers off Dave Odom to give Ruth's All-Stars the lead. Ruth pinch hit in the eighth but struck out. It was hit to "dead center, about the fourth row up." (*Boston Traveler*)

Williams said he really didn't focus much on baseball. "I rarely look at a box-score these days…But I figure I'm in a bigger game now, one that requires my full and complete attention." (*Traveler*)

There was another game, at Yankee Stadium on July 28, and this time Ruth and Williams were on opposing teams. Ruth drew a pinch-hit walk; Williams was 1-for-4, a single.

1944 — Military service

In 1944, Ted played some ball with the Bronson Bombers but one senses that he didn't go all out. The Bombers featured four former major leaguers — Bob Kennedy, Nick Tremark, and Ray Stoviak the other three. Ted's .300 batting average was the lowest of the four. And Pat McGlothin — later a big leaguer himself — held Ted hitless (0-for-7) in a 19-inning game at Corpus Christi.[31]

Michael Seidel says that Williams played in about 40 games in 1943, about half that number in 1944, and only seven in 1945.

1945—Military service

Lt. Williams began the year posted to NAS Jacksonville and later was stationed in Hawaii. Eager base commanders kept insisting he play baseball and he complied. The war was over by the time of the "1945 All-Star Game"—a scheduled best-of-seven series at Honolulu's Furlong Field beginning on September 26. He'd only played in four games before the series began. Around 26,000 turned out for the first game. Ted's teammates for the "American League" included Johnny Pesky, Dick Wakefield, and Bob Kennedy, with Freddie Hutchinson pitching. The National League team won four of the first six, but everyone agreed to play the seventh game anyhow, and the AL team won that one. Ted batted 3-for-11 (.272) in the games he played, with one home run.

The homer came in Game Three, a 6-3 win for the National League on September 30. Lou Tost pitched a complete game for the NL team, with the big hit being Ted's two-run homer completely over the right-field bleachers.[32]

1946

128 **(#1 of 1946)** April 16 at Griffith Stadium, Washington. Pitcher: Roger Wolff (Washington Senators). RH. Age 32.

Top of the third inning. One-run homer.

Away from baseball for more than three years, Williams picked right up where he left off with another home run on Opening Day—this time in Washington, in front of the President of the United States. "It's 'Play Ball' for the First Peacetime Season in Five Years" headlined the *Washington Post* above a story titled "Watching Williams Kept Fans and Players Entertained." The story's opening paragraph ended, "Williams smacked four home runs over the right-field wall in batting practice before yesterday's opening game, one up into the lights that tower over the wall, and another one over the scoreboard clock. A third disappeared into the tree that sticks up over the wall, while a fourth was just a bunt—probably didn't clear more than 374 feet."

President Harry S. Truman threw out the first ball and then watched the game. Truman and the rest of the crowd didn't have to wait long. On a 3-2 count his second time at bat, with two outs and no one aboard, Ted "sent the longest Griffith Stadium home run of a decade whistling into the dead-center-field bleachers, ten rows up…fully 440 feet from the plate." (Shirley Povich, *Washington Post*)

Truman's Opening Day pitch was the first ever delivered by a left-handed President. The Red Sox won the game, 6-3. Johnny Pesky resumed his hitting, too, with a two-run double in the seventh inning that provided the winning run. The *Boston Globe* cited "Washington historians" as saying that Lou Gehrig was the only hitter anyone could remember having hit one that deep in center field.

Wolff was with Philadelphia in 1942 and served up #101 and 106. He pitched through the war years, traded to Washington for Bobo Newsom in December 1943. This is the only other homer Ted hit off him.

129 (#2) May 2 at Fenway Park. Pitcher: Tommy Bridges (Detroit Tigers). RH. Age 39.

Bottom of the tenth inning. One-run homer. GAME WINNER.

Ted's first game-winner of the postwar years won the game for the Red Sox. He'd appeared "listless and lacking his usual verve as a result of a heavy cold," wrote the *Boston Globe*. He perhaps became energized in his self-directed anger at badly missing a pitch. Batting in the bottom of the tenth inning in a 4-4 game, he first fouled off a high, inside curve, then swung and missed by inches. "His head went up very soon after his swing," observed the *Boston Herald*. Bridges then threw a low one—perhaps a slider. "Where earlier swings had looked comparatively lazy and innocent, this one by Ted was his best cut. The ball went on a line, drilling right across the northwest wind and landed in the Tiger bullpen in far right-center." (*Herald*) Then Ted could return home and nurse his cold.

One couldn't blame Bridges were he politically confused, bearing the name Thomas Jefferson Davis Bridges.

Ted hit #138 off him, too.

130 (#3) May 3 at Fenway Park. Pitcher: Tom Ferrick (Cleveland Indians). RH. Age 31.

Bottom of the eighth inning. One-run homer.

Ted was back for more the very next day, but was walked his first three times up. When granted the opportunity to hit, he struck a double in the sixth inning (driving in the two runs that counted as game-winners), and wound up with a leadoff home run into the visitors bullpen in the eighth. Ferrick had come into the game in relief and Ted sauntered over a bit from the on-deck circle to watch him warm up. He swung at the first pitch and connected. For the Red Sox, it was their eighth win in a row, 9-4.

Ferrick furnished homers #77, 130, 247, and 304.

"He may have been the only hitter who a pitcher would never have to wait for. When the ball was hit while he was in the on-deck circle, by the time the ball got back to the pitcher, Ted was standing in the batter's box ready to hit. He had a chain of thought and it never got interrupted. He loved to swing that bat."— Fred Hatfield [33]

131 (#4) May 4 at Fenway Park. Pitcher: Bob Feller (Cleveland Indians.) RH. Age 27. Hall of Famer.

Bottom of the sixth inning. Two-run homer.

Homering for the third day in a row, Ted hit a 2-2 Bob Feller fastball and helped pad the 3-2 lead with a couple of insurance runs. It was a very cold day. "In spite or wind and weather, the ball had 'Destination: Home Run' written on it. It didn't quite make the bleacher, bouncing off the green concrete fence in back of the enemy bullpen." Feller said later, "It was a good fastball but Williams certainly hit the hell out of it, didn't he?" Feller grumped later that the Fenway mound wasn't high enough. The Red Sox their ninth in a row, 6-2. Johnny Pesky had walked and came in on Ted's homer. Johnny was 4-for-4 in official at-bats.

Only Virgil Trucks gave up more homers to Ted Williams than did Bob Feller. Trucks gave up 12; Feller (and Ned Garver) each gave up 10. Feller's were #131, 141, 203, 210, 227, 330, 351, 353, 374, and 416.

132 (#5) May 7 at Fenway Park. Pitcher: Jack Kramer (St. Louis Browns). RH. Age 28.

Bottom of the third inning. Two-run homer.

The Sox were in the midst of what became an early-season 15-game winning streak that separated them from the pack early on. To win this game, they had to overcome a 4-0 deficit. Ted hit a two-run homer over the Red Sox bullpen and quite a few rows up into the bleachers, which made it 4-2, but then the Browns scored two more. It was 6-6 after seven innings and stayed that way until the bottom of the 14th inning when Leon Culberson hit a first-pitch grand slam to win it. Ted had been 6-for-7 the day before, but—in the words of the *Herald*'s Bill Cunningham—"seemed to be disgusted." After playing that day, he said, "Tomorrow I'm going to rip one. I feel it." He was asked, "How do you feel when you feel it?" "I don't know. I just feel it." Cunningham wrote that the homer Ted ripped "was practically the longest one ever ripped...in that precise direction. It must have landed about 20 rows up in those benches."

Ted hit homers 16, 33, 132, 169, and 185 off Kramer—and then they became teammates for a couple of years, ending the possibility of adding to the list.

133 (#6) May 15 at Comiskey Park. Pitcher: Johnny Rigney (Chicago White Sox). RH. Age 31.

Top of the first inning. One-run homer.

After the war, Rigney and Williams had at it again. Ted had already hit six homers off Johnny. This would be his last. It came on the first pitch Rigney threw Ted in the game and was "a robust 400-foot belt up into the upper tier of the vacant right-field stands." The Red Sox only mustered three hits in the whole game, however, and lost, 3-2.

The earlier ones Ted hit off Rigney? #56, 57, 58, 64, 72, and 89.

134 (#7) May 18 at Sportsman's Park. Pitcher: Ellis Kinder (St. Louis Browns). RH. Age 31.

Top of the fifth inning. Four-run homer. Grand slam #6.

Kinder was in his rookie year, though age 31 (that's why he picked up the nickname "Old Folks".) The Browns weren't taking chances with Ted Williams and so, as the Red Sox racked up runs, they walked Ted four times. In the fifth, with the bases loaded, reliever Kinder's first pitch to The Kid was hit a ton. Ted hit it "well over the entire right-field pavilion and you could see the ball bound up from Grand Boulevard to the windows on the third floor on the far side of the street." (*Herald*) The grand slam "must have sailed almost 450 feet before colliding with some peaceful citizen's residence." (*Globe*) The Red Sox won with ease, 18-8.

Kinder also was tagged for another homer by The Kid, later in the year—#160.

135 (#8) May 22 at League Park, Cleveland. Pitcher: Pete Center (Cleveland Indians). RH. Age 34.

Top of the 12th inning. Two-run homer. GAME WINNER.

It was a 3-3 tie after nine innings. The Red Sox scored once in the 11th but so did the Indians. Throughout it all, Williams hadn't been able to get the ball out of the infield his first five times at bat. In the top of the 12th, Johnny Pesky singled and Center—just on in relief—"threw two pitches very close to The Kid's skull. Williams was raving mad. He stepped closer to the plate and took a tighter grip on his bat. Then Center tried to throw one by Williams. The Kid got a good cut at it and propelled it a good 400 feet off the roof of a house in back of the high fence in right-center." The *Herald* said it cleared the wall in right-center and the screen on top of the wall, but the *Herald* said it landed in a vacant lot on the other side of Lexington Avenue. Wherever it landed, it still served to win the game.

This was the only home run Ted ever hit off Center. He was no doubt happy to add it to his growing total, winning the ballgame for Boston as it did.

136 (#9) May 30 (second game) at Fenway Park. Pitcher: Ray Scarborough (Washington Senators). RH. Age 28.

Bottom of the fifth inning. Two-run homer.

Williams got equal coverage for a great catch he made in the game. His two-run homer on an 0-2 count was a "cloudbuster half a dozen rows up into the center-field seats, above the 420-foot sign." The Red Sox took two—6-5 and 7-2. The second game was a bit of a breeze. The first game was a thriller, the Sox coming back from being down 5-1, scoring three times in the eighth and twice in the ninth, coming from behind and winning when Bobby Doerr ran all the way from second base to home while Dom DiMaggio grounded to the shortstop, who kicked off a 6-4-3 attempt which didn't quite succeed in securing the doubleplay that would have sent the game into extra innings.

Ted's only homer off Ray Scarborough.

137 (#10) June 6 at Fenway Park. Pitcher: Ox Miller (St. Louis Browns). RH. Age 31.

Bottom of the seventh inning. Two-run homer. GAME WINNER.

With one out in the seventh, Pesky singled and Ted swung at the first pitch and slammed it into the Red Sox bullpen "where red-sleeved Mike Ryba made a nonchalant bare-handed catch as thousands cheered." The homer boosted Boston from a one-run deficit (4-3) to a one-run lead (5-4, the final score.)

Ted's only homer off Ox Miller.

138 (#11) June 9 (first game) at Fenway Park. Pitcher: Tommy Bridges (Detroit Tigers). RH. Age 39.

Bottom of the seventh inning. One-run homer.

Ted's "thump into the Tiger lair" was a "gargantuan smash" which just added another run to the seven Red Sox runs scored through the first seven innings. Mickey Harris got the fairly easy win over Dizzy Trout; Bridges had come on in relief.

Boston won, 7-1, and then the Red Sox won the second game 11-6. It was the fifth doubleheader they'd swept in 1946.

Ted hit #129 off him earlier in the year.

Talking about the spitball, Williams said, "Mike Garcia threw one at me one time, and the spit came up and hit me in the eye. The umpire threw the ball out. I didn't realize it, but Tommy Bridges said he threw one to me and I hit it out of the park."[34]

139 (#12) June 9 (second game) at Fenway Park. Pitcher: Fred Hutchinson (Detroit Tigers). RH. Age 26.

Bottom of the first inning. Two-run homer.

"How far away must one sit to be safe in this park?" That was Joseph A. Boucher's remark after Ted Williams' home run "bounced squarely off his head" putting a hole in his straw boater. He was sitting in the 33rd row of the right-field bleachers — the location is commemorated today by one red seat in the otherwise green bleachers. At the time, there were no individual seats in the bleachers, but instead fans sat on wooden planking. "I didn't even get the ball," Boucher said. "They say it bounced a dozen rows higher, but after it hit my head I was no longer interested." He was an engineer from Albany who had been working in Boston since the start of World War II. The red seat is 502 feet from home plate. Right now, it's Section 42, row 37, seat 21.

Ted's homer drove in Catfish Metkovich, who'd reached first on a drag bunt, and gave the Sox a 2-0 lead.

Hutchinson had been 19 years old when Ted first hit a homer off him, in 1939. Now he was 26. The eight homers he hit off Ted were #22, 139, 156, 163, 209, 225, 235, and 273.

NOTE: The 502-foot home run is said by the Red Sox to be the longest ever hit at Fenway Park, and the red seat is one of the features at Fenway always pointed out by the park tour guides. In 2001, Manny Ramirez hit a home run in the June 23 game which struck the top of one of the light towers in left field. A distance had to be assigned it, and it was declared to be 501 feet, which preserved Ted's mark.

But had young Ted once hit a homer that went 126 or more *miles*? According to a tale out of San Diego from Ted's time with the Padres in 1937, Teddy hit one out of Lane Field and into a freight car on the tracks beyond, only coming down once the train reached Los Angeles. Among those who told the tale was respected San Diego sportswriter Earl Keller, who wrote that he saw it with his own eyes.[35]

140 (#13) June 11 at Fenway Park. Pitcher: Red Embree (Cleveland Indians). RH. Age 28.

Bottom of the third inning. One-run homer.

Pinky Higgins was the star of this 10-5 Red Sox win, driving in six of the Sox's ten runs. Ted's homer was boomed into Fenway's center-field seats. "It looked like a high, but catchable, fly to deep center. The wind helped the flight of the ball, it is true, but the balls Williams hits always seem to have superior carry." (*Herald*)

Hit with one out, his homer "came at the right psychological moment," according to the *Herald*. The Indians had been up, 3-1, but Ted not only drew them within one run but then York doubled, Dom D drew a walk, and Higgins tripled them both in.

Ted hit Red for four homers — including a pennant-winner (see #165). His two later homers were #228 and 246.

141 (#14) June 12 at Fenway Park. Pitcher: Bob Feller (Cleveland Indians). RH. Age 27. Hall of Famer.

Bottom of the sixth inning. One-run homer.

Bob Feller brought out the fans — there were as many as 10,000 turned away once the park sold out — but he also brought another Red Sox winning streak to an end, this one a 12-game streak, with a 7-2 win over the Sox. It was a six-hitter and Ted Williams had three of the six — "one of them

Mr. Slug's 14th homer, into the Boston bullpen to spoil Rapid Roberts's bid for his fifth shutout....[Boston pitcher] Earl Johnson muffed the catch, but retrieved the souvenir." Feller had thrown a modified blooper pitch on the one beforehand, and both he and Ted smiled (it was called a ball), but Feller failed to fire the fastball by the Splendid Splinter.

The Feller homers: 131, 141, 203, 210, 227, 330, 351, 353, 274, and 416.

142 (#15) June 14 at Comiskey Park, Chicago. Pitcher: Al Hollingsworth (Chicago White Sox). LH. Age 38.

Top of the fifth inning. One-run homer.

Some 48,017 fans—the largest crowd to a night game in Chicago to that point—came out to see the two Sox teams face off against each other. The Red Sox scored four runs in the first inning, and Ted Williams tripled and homered. But rookie Mizell "Whitey" Platt of the White Sox had the game of his life, and drove in six runs, helping ensure a 9-5 Chicago win. Ted's homer was hit into the lower right-field stands "and he came only a few feet from getting No. 16 on the last out of the game when the contrarily-minded wind held up the ball just long enough for Wally Moon to catch it with his back against the concrete barrier." (*Boston Herald*)

Hollingsworth had given up homer #112 back in 1942.

143 (#16) June 23 (second game) at Cleveland Stadium, Cleveland. Pitcher: Don Black (Cleveland Indians). RH. Age 29.

Top of the third inning. Two-run homer.

Bill Zuber threw a three-hit shutout for Boston. Ted swung at Black's first pitch to him in the third and hit the ball 375 feet. "It was one of his characteristic Big Bertha whacks, a mile high and far. It landed a dozen deep in the lower right-field stands. The Red Sox won two games, 5-1 in the first and 6-0 in the second. The next time Ted was up, Catfish Metkovich stole home, with him leaping up while the sliding Catfish slid across the plate.

Black gave up one more homer, to Ted Williams: #152.

144 (#17) June 24 at Briggs Stadium, Detroit. Pitcher: Dizzy Trout (Detroit Tigers). RH. Age 31.

Top of the first inning. One-run homer.

Nobody won this game. It ended in a 5-5 tie. Ted "was quite lusty with the hickory" and gave the Red Sox an early lead, with his first-inning homer. (*Boston Traveler*) The ball shot into the right-center-field stands, about a 415-foot drive. The game ended because of "fast settling darkness that is hindered by the absence of daylight saving time." It was, though, almost the longest day of the year, and Detroit is on the western end of the Eastern time zone, and the game had only taken two hours and 25 minutes. It was a full nine innings, and the Red Sox had scored twice in the top of the ninth.

Other homers Ted hit off Trout: 107, 164, 221, 283, and 324.

145 (#18) June 26 (first game) at Briggs Stadium, Detroit. Pitcher: Hal Newhouser (Detroit Tigers). LH. Age 25.

Top of the sixth inning. One-run homer.

The Red Sox were slaughtered, 16-2, in the first game of two. One of their two runs came on Ted's solo homer, on a 2-1 pitch "lashed over the deep right-center-field lower stand barrier"—about a 420-foot home run. (*Herald*) By process of elimination this had to be the game Ted recalled when he wrote. "Newhouser knocked me down and struck me out that time, and I hit a home run the next time up."[36] After the brushback, Newhouser struck Williams out on three pitches. When Ted returned to the Boston bench, he made an offer: "I'll bet anyone here anything they want to bet that I hit one out of here next time up." Rip Russell put up $5.00—and lost it.[37]

Ted hit Hal for #122 and 260, too.

146 (#19) June 26 (second game) at Briggs Stadium, Detroit. Pitcher: Virgil Trucks (Detroit Tigers). RH. Age 29.

Top of the fourth inning. One-run homer.

The Tigers scored one run each in the first three innings of the second game and held a 3-0 lead. Ted started the scoring for the Red Sox with "a lulu, a wickedly crashed three-and-two liner into the left-center-field bleachers. It sailed well over the 365-foot mark, good for better than 400 feet on the level and as lusty a blow as he has made toward left-center all year, and that despite a slightly unfavorable wind." (*Herald*)

Ted's 12 homers off Trucks: 108, 115, 146, 174, 189, 226, 236, 243, 320, 342, 437, and 444.

147 (#20) June 28 at Fenway Park. Pitcher: Marino Pieretti (Washington Senators). RH. Age 25.

Bottom of the seventh inning. Two-run homer.

Two of the runs in a 12-1 whaling dished out to Washington came on Ted's 420-foot drive into the right-field bleachers on a 3-0 pitch that was sent six or seven rows deep "into the center-field bleachers, just beyond the grand-stand end of the Hose bullpen, a homer the moment it left the bat." (*Herald*)

The native of Italy allowed homers #147, 219, 230, and 253.

148 (#21) July 4 (first game) at Shibe Park, Philadelphia. Pitcher: Phil Marchildon (Philadelphia Athletics). RH. Age 32.

Top of the eighth inning. One-run homer.

Penetanguishene, Ontario's Marchildon was a war hero in the Allied cause during the Second World War. On the day the USA celebrates its inde-pendence, he gave up a third home run to Ted Williams. There were two one-run games this Fourth of July—the Athletics won the first game, 3-2, in which Ted homered with two out in the eighth. The ball left the park and landed on 20th Street outside Shibe.

Previous homers were #92 and 120. Later homers were #180 and 196.

149 (**#22**) July 4 (second game) at Shibe Park, Philadelphia. Pitcher: Russ Christopher (Philadelphia Athletics). RH. Age 28.

Top of the fourth inning. One-run homer.

The Red Sox had a come-from-behind 9-8 win in the second game, with Williams contributing another solo home run. It also left Shibe Park and "landed on top of a series of two-story homes on the far side of the street." (*Herald*)

#98, #104, this one, and #193 — the four HRs Ted had off Christopher.

150 (**#23**) July 7 (first game) at Griffith Stadium, Washington. Pitcher: Sid Hudson (Washington Senators). RH. Age 31.

Top of the third inning. Two-run homer. GAME WINNER.

The Red Sox had a field day, with wins of 11-1 and 9-4. Ted built up a better on-base percentage, reaching base in nine out of 11 plate appearances. He was 4-for-6 and walked five times. His homer went over Griffith Stadium's right-field wall. With Dom DiMaggio on first after singling, the two runs were the first two scored and enough to win the game for Tex Hughson.

Ted had gone deep off Hudson twice before — for homers #40 and 116. He later allowed HR #274.

July 9, 1946 — All-Star Game at Fenway Park

The 1946 All-Star Game was played at Boston's Fenway Park, and Ted Williams was 4-for-4 with two home runs. Facing Claude Passeau, he walked. Passeau probably pitched around Ted, remembering the game-winning homer Ted hit off him in the 1941 game. In the fourth inning, "I homered off Kirby Higbe into Fenway's center-field bleachers." He singled off Higbe in the fifth, and off Ewell Blackwell in the seventh. Ted came up again in the eighth, facing Rip Sewell, known for his high arcing "eephus" pitch. "Sewell developed it after he got hurt. Damn near got his foot blown off in a hunting accident. He would put a lot of backspin on the ball, almost like a damn shot put. It would fly up in the air — up, high up — a 25-foot arc. Looked like a pop fly. A lot of batters were just too surprised to swing.

And it you did hit it, well it wouldn't go anywhere. Wouldn't go anywhere because you had to supply your own power. Sewell never put a damn thing on it, that's for sure. Before the game, I asked Sewell, 'you're not going to throw that pitch to me, are you?' Sewell said he was.

"Bill Dickey gave me some advice on how to hit it. He said the only way to generate enough power to hit it out was to get a little running jump on. Take a couple of steps in toward Sewell. I fouled Sewell's first pitch back. I watched his second pitch go outside. His third pitch was a fastball—called strike two. Then came another eephus. I did just like Bill Dickey said—I slammed that piece of junk right into the right-field bullpen—380 damned feet—for a three-run homer."[38] Williams was almost certainly out of the batter's box at the time he hit the ball, but no one worried much about that.

Boston pitcher Mickey Harris caught the ball. The American League won the game, 12-0. Williams had five RBIs.

"I've been tossing that ball up there for five years," Sewell said right after the game. "Nobody has ever hit a homer off that pitch of mine before. I didn't think it was possible until Williams did it this afternoon." (*Boston Herald*)

151 (#24) July 14 (first game) at Fenway Park. Pitcher: Steve Gromek (Cleveland Indians). RH. Age 26.

Bottom of the third inning. Four-run homer. Grand slam #7.

Ted hit three home runs in this one game, kicking things off with a third-inning grand slam. It banged off the back wall of the visiting team's bullpen, and then bounced back onto the field of play. He was the first Red Sox batter to hit three homers in a game at Fenway. Not even Babe Ruth had done that. Each home run was off a different pitcher.

The grand slam helped tie the game, 5-5. The Red Sox went on to win it, 11-10, but the winning run didn't score until the bottom of the eighth, part of a three-run rally.

Gromek also surrendered homers #155, 205, 263, 437, and 354.

152 (#25) July 14 (first game) at Fenway Park. Pitcher: Don Black (Cleveland Indians). RH. Age 29.

Bottom of the fifth inning. One-run homer.

The Indians had pulled ahead, 8-6, but Ted's solo home run off Don Black brought them back to within a run, 8-7. This one was pulled more than the first one, and went into the gap between the bleachers and the right-field grandstand, and then took a notable bounce: "This one bounded high and majestically into the upper regions" of the covered grandstand.

Black's other homer was #143.

153 (#26) July 14 (first game) at Fenway Park. Pitcher: Joe Berry (Cleveland Indians). RH. Age 41.

Bottom of the eighth inning. Three-run homer. GAME WINNER.

This was the only home run that "Jittery Joe" Berry allowed Ted Williams, but it won the game With Culberson and Pesky on base, he pulled it progressively further to right, just inside the foul pole—down the right-field line and just a few rows into "homer heaven." The three-run homer propelled the Sox from being down, 10-8, to being up, 11-10—the final score. Ted had driven in eight runs—and that was just in the first game.

There was another game to come, a 6-4 Red Sox win. He was 1-for-2 with a double in the second game (without an RBI), a game in which Cleveland player-manager Lou Boudreau put on a bizarre (at the time) defense which stacked up all the defenders on the right side of the field, leaving only left-fielder George Case playing shallow, behind shortstop, on that side of the field. It was known as the "Boudreau Shift" or—later—the "Williams Shift" and was effective. Many teams use the extreme shift today against certain left-handed pull hitters.

An apocryphal story: The story was written by *Sport* magazine's Ed Fitzgerald. "Between innings during the first game—in which, as mentioned before, he hit three homers—Ted stepped to the scoreboard instead of heading for the Boston bench. Slipping out a trapdoor leading to the street, he ran across to a small restaurant and asked the waiter for a dish of ice cream. Everybody in the place had been listening to the radio and discussing Ted's home runs. They sat openmouthed at the spectacle of the uniformed ball player sitting next to them while the radio blared an account of the game in which he was supposed to be playing. Ted paid no attention to their astonishment. Parking his spikes on the foot rail, he gobbled up his ice cream, handed the waiter a coin, and dashed back across the street. He ducked through the trapdoor and into the ballpark just in time to resume his position in left field."[39]

It was a wonderful story and fit nicely with The Kid's earlier image of a "screwball." But it was simply made up. There was no door through which Ted could have ducked out of the scoreboard. There had been the Pennant Grille across the street at the corner of Lansdowne Street and Brookline Avenue. But there never could have been (because the playing surface of the field is below street level) any form of door in the back of the left-field scoreboard. We should take the story as reflecting the sort of fantastical personality that Ted Williams was, someone about whom almost any story was believable.

154 (#27) July 21 (second game) at Fenway Park. Pitcher: Cliff Fannin (St. Louis Browns). RH. Age 22.

Bottom of the first inning. One-run homer.

Boston residents picking up the morning *Globe* on July 22 read the headlines: PRESIDENT OF BOLIVIA SLAIN; Sox Win 2 As Ted Hits Cycle. Indeed, Ted Williams had hit for the cycle, hitting seven hits in a row. He flied out his first time up, but then singled and singled and doubled in the first game, a 5-0 win for Boo Ferriss. First time up in the second game, he homered on a 1-1 pitch some "eight or nine rows into the right-field stands, around the bend a trifle, and more notable than usual because the wind was a bit hostile." (*Herald*) It kicked off the scoring in the 7-4 second game. Ted came up again in the second inning and tripled off the visiting bullpen wall. He singled to center in the fourth and then doubled down the first-base line leading off the seventh. Oddly, when he batted a final time in the eighth, he never swung the bat—he struck out on three pitches, all looking. Going 7-for-9 bumped up his average by 12 points, no mean feat in the latter part of July. His .365 average gave him the league lead over Mickey Vernon who only had a 4-for-8 day.

Fannin gave up five homers to Ted: this one, a cluster of three in 1947, and a final one in 1950: #182, 183, 186, and 280.

155 (#28) July 30 at Cleveland Stadium, Cleveland. Pitcher: Steve Gromek (Cleveland Indians). RH. Age 26.

Top of the fourth inning. One-run homer. GAME WINNER.

The grand slam on July 14 wasn't enough to win the game, but this solo home run was. More than 56,000 Clevelanders were disappointed at the 4-0 defeat. The first run scored in the game was Ted's home run into the first row of the lower deck of the right-field seats in the fourth. Boo Ferriss shut out the Indians, allowing just three hits, all singles.

In addition to #151 and this one, Gromek later surrendered homers #205, 263, 437, and 354.

156 (#29) August 3 at Briggs Stadium, Detroit. Pitcher: Fred Hutchinson (Detroit Tigers). RH. Age 26.

Top of the first inning. Three-run homer.

Wally Moses singled, Johnny Pesky doubled, and up came Ted Williams in the top of the first inning. Nobody out, and first base open—but the Tigers pitched to him, and the result couldn't have been worse. Gerry Moore of the *Boston Globe* said it was the first time he could recall all year when the opposition hadn't intentionally walked him. There were over 50,000 fans somehow crammed into the ballpark in Detroit. On a 1-2 count, Ted "unloaded on a high fastball and lined it into the lower right-field seats, a dozen feet to the left of the 325-foot sign at the foul pole." The final score was 5-3, so while Ted's runs were crucial, the homer wasn't truly the game-winning hit.

This was the second of three homers Ted hit off Hutchinson in 1946. He hit eight in all: #22, 139, 156, 163, 209, 225, 235, and 273.

157 (#30) August 10 at Yankee Stadium, New York. Pitcher: Tiny Bonham (New York Yankees). RH. Age 32.

Top of the seventh inning. Three-run homer.

The score had been 1-1 when Ted stepped into the batter's box in the top of the seventh. Pesky had singled and Dom had walked. Bonham threw one pitch, a slow ball or changeup to Ted, who crushed it into the top deck in right field. After the game, Ted said the only one he'd hit better at Yankee Stadium was the one he'd hit on May 26, 1942 off Atley Donald. The Yankees matched the three runs in the bottom of the seventh and the game progressed until the 12th inning...(see homer #158 below).

Ted hit four homers off Tiny: #90, 109, 157, and 159.

158 (#31) August 10 at Yankee Stadium, New York. Pitcher: Johnny Murphy (New York Yankees). RH. Age 37.

Top of the 12th inning. One-run homer.

Ted's second home run of the day looked like it might be the game-winner. Ted was facing Johnny Murphy now and he fouled off three pitches in a row. Then he took a low and outside pitch, refusing to bite. "The next pitch was a curve and Williams gave it a high ride, almost up as high as the roof of this lofty grandstand, but it landed 20 rows back in the first deck, or lower grandstand." (*Boston Herald*) Unfortunately for Ted, there was another player who hit two home runs in the game—and Aaron Robinson's second homer, for the Yankees in the bottom of the 12th, was a three-run homer that erased the fresh Red Sox lead and won the game—much to the delight of Robinson's father, watching his son for the first time in a major-league game.

Murphy had been hit for Ted's homer #35 back in 1940.

159 (#32) August 17 at Fenway Park. Pitcher: Tiny Bonham (New York Yankees). RH. Age 32.

Bottom of the third. Two-run homer.

Doerr and Williams both hit two-run homers, and pitcher Boo Ferriss even drove in two runs on his way to winning #21 (against only four defeats). The Red Sox won, 7-4, though only after the Yankees rallied in the top of the ninth for three more runs. Bobby Doerr's homer came in the bottom of the first after "Timber Ted" took a base on balls, a liner which just reached into the screen above the wall in left-center. The drive boosted Doerr's RBI total to 97. The *Herald*, which seemed to favor the "Timber Ted" nickname for Mr. Williams during 1946 described his blast as "a lordly smash over the Yankee bullpen in right-center field, six rows into the center-field stands, with Johnny Pesky on base and one out." Bonham's first three pitches were all low and outside. The fourth one was right over the plate. Cronin had given Ted the green light on 3-0, and Ted "gave it the merriest of sleigh rides into the sun lovers, a tremendous wallop on such a warm and humid afternoon when the ball usually is more than a little bit on the dead side."

After the game, Ted talked to Hy Hurwitz. "I only wish that before the season ends some Yankee pitcher will give me a pitch to hit like the one Mickey Harris gave Joe DiMaggio this afternoon. Yankee pitchers have been feeding me a lot of swill all season. I hardly remember one good ball that I've seen one of their pitchers throw at me. But some day one of them is going to make a mistake and, Brother, I'll knock it a mile. I'm waiting for that one pitch." Bonham walked Ted on four pitches in the first inning and none of this first three of the third were near the plate. "It had the earmarks of a semi-intentional pass. But The Kid was ready. He had been waiting for the dream pitch through 15 straight games."

One week after Ted had hit #157 off Bonham at Yankee Stadium, he hit another, this time at Fenway. In earlier years, he'd hit #90 and 109. By 1947, Bonham was pitching in the National League.

160 (#33) August 20 (second game) at Fenway Park. Pitcher: Ellis Kinder (St. Louis Browns). RH. Age 31.

Bottom of the eighth inning. Two-run homer.

The Red Sox had taken the first game, 5-1, but it was the Browns who held a 5-1 lead in the second game until Johnny Pesky set the table for Ted with a sharp single to left in the bottom of the eighth and, on a 1-0 count, Ted hit a homer into the runway between the right-field grandstand and the bleachers. That made it 5-3, and the Red Sox scored one more in the ninth, but fell one run short.

Kinder had served up a grand slam in May (#134) and then this one in August. They were the only two Ted hit off him. From 1948 through 1955, the two were teammates. Any homers there would have to be if Kinder felt like throwing batting practice.

161 (#34) August 29 at Fenway Park. Pitcher: Al Benton (Detroit Tigers). RH. Age 35.

Bottom of the third inning. Two-run homer.

Former Red Sox player Doc Cramer did in the Red Sox, driving in the first run of the game and—in the 14th inning—the final run, as the Tigers beat the Red Sox, 9-8. Leon Culberson had walked when Ted came up in the third. On Benton's first pitch, Ted swung and the ball "sailed right across the southeast wind and penetrated the right-field wing of the far grandstand to the depth of five or six rows." (*Herald*) The Tigers walked Ted four times in the game.

Benton's six homers: #43, 83, 114, 119, 161, and 277.

There were times Ted was robbed of home runs. He might have wound up with 524, had it not been for Elmer Valo and one weekend in Boston. Valo robbed Ted Williams of more homers, in a very short period of time, than any other defender. On August 30, 1946, at Fenway Park, "Williams was victim of as spectacular a catch as has been witnessed in any ballpark this year or any other year. Elmer Valo was the villain." In the bottom of the sixth inning, Ted hit a hard shot off the pitching of Philadelphia pitcher Everett Fagan. It was headed for the right-field seats when Valo "went into the seats to grab the ball with a leaping, glove-handed catch. He crashed into the wall and for a moment as Elmer hit the turf with the ball still in his possession, it seemed that he might have cracked his spine." Ed Linn wrote, "If he had fallen into the bleachers, Williams still would have had a home run. Instead, he slid very slowly down the low wall and crumpled into a heap on the grass. Valo had to be carried off the field. Williams had been robbed."[40] It was, Ted wrote in his column for the *Globe*, "one of the best catches I've ever seen."

It wasn't as spectacular, but the very next day, he "propelled a terrific drive into the teeth of a hostile wind in the third inning which Elmer Valo grabbed in front of the Red Sox bullpen just before the separation in right-center field."

And on September 1, in the ninth inning, Williams "laced into a Savage offering and backed Valo up against the right-field stands to haul down another terrifically-stroked drive." It was the third time in the one home-stand that he had grabbed a ball that Ted would otherwise have hit into the seats.

162 (#35) September 7 at Shibe Park, Philadelphia. Pitcher: Jesse Flores (Philadelphia Athletics). RH. Age 31.

Top of the ninth inning. One-run homer.

"Don't Be Crude When You're Booed"—that was Bobo Newsom's advice to Ted Williams, according to a story in the September 8 *Washington Post*. He was offering free advice to Williams as to how to disarm the fair-weather fans at Fenway who sometimes booed him and sometimes cheered. A long feature in the September 8 *Boston Globe* by San Diego newspaperman Forrest Warren told of how Ted's mother May Williams told Teddy that she hope he'd become a captain in her beloved Salvation Army when he grew up (Teddy was purportedly 9 at the time), but he answered, "I'm gonna be a Babe Ruth." The story provided readers a lot of details of Ted's childhood. There was a great appetite for stories on Ted Williams.

The game accounts of the September 7 game at Shibe told the story of the first loss Boo Ferriss had suffered since July 4. He'd won 12 consecutive games as was 24-4. But after the 4-2 loss to the Athletics, he was 24-5. Ted drove in the second of the two Red Sox runs, after there were two outs in the top of the ninth, homering off Guadalajara's Jesse Flores. First-pitch hitting, Ted struck "a majestic clout that easily cleared the right-field fence and possibly landed on the front porch of a house across the street from the ballpark."

In 1950, Ted hit homer #278 off Flores.

163 (#36) September 10 at Briggs Stadium, Detroit. Pitcher: Fred Hutchinson (Detroit Tigers). RH. Age 26.

Top of the sixth inning. One-run homer.

The Red Sox were trying to clinch the pennant, but this 9-1 loss was their fourth in a row. The only run the Red Sox scored came on Ted's solo home run in the sixth. On an 0-2 pitch, he hit one "up into the stratosphere. Its better than 400-foot journey was interrupted by the press-box extension in right-center field. It was the first time that any major-league player had dumped in this area in a league game." At the point the ball struck the press box extension was about 15 feet below the roofline—and Williams remained the only batter to ever hit one onto the roof. The third-deck press gallery seats were, the *Herald* said, 125 feet above ground level. Burt Whitman guessed the ball would have traveled "500 or 575 feet on the fly on level ground."

This was the third homer (see also #129 and 156) Ted hit off Hutchinson in the Red Sox drive for the pennant. He'd earlier hit #22, and later hit #209, 225, 235, and 273.

164 (#37) September 11 at Briggs Stadium, Detroit. Pitcher: Dizzy Trout (Detroit Tigers). RH. Age 31.

Top of the fourth. One-run homer.

Again, the Sox were frustrated in their attempt to clinch, with Dizzy Trout beating them, 7-3, despite Ted Williams having himself a 4-for-4 day with a home run. The homer was almost a carbon copy of the monstrous drive of the day before, a "fierce fly" (*Herald*) also into the press-box seats up by the roof but about five feet from the foul line; the September 10 one had been more to right-center. Harry Heilmann sat on the bench with Williams before the game and told him he ought to be able to hit .400 again (as Heilmann had done himself in 1923) if he'd consistently bunt toward third base whenever they pulled the shift on him. "You can bunt yourself into leading the league in hitting…What Ty Cobb would do with that sort of defense would be to get 4-for-4 every game." (*Boston Herald*) Ted did indeed bunt to third base for a base hit in this very game, and helped achieve that 4-for-4. The Red Sox still failed to win, and did the next day, too.

Six homers off Trout also included #107, 144, 221, 283, and 324.

165 (#38) September 13 at League Park, Cleveland. Pitcher: Red Embree (Cleveland Indians). RH. Age 28.

Top of the first inning. One-run homer. GAME WINNER.

This one was not only a game-winner; it was also a pennant-clincher. And the only inside-the-park homer Ted ever hit. The champagne that had traveled with the Sox from Washington to Philadelphia and then to Detroit was again placed on a train and traveled on to Cleveland. One never would have guessed how the Red Sox would clinch the 1946 pennant, though that Ted Williams might be key wouldn't have been a bad guess. Tex Hughson won the game, a 1-0 victory.

It was Cleveland's Lou Boudreau who'd developed the extreme shift to defend against Williams. The *Boston Globe*'s headline the next day: "Weird Indian Defense Finally Boomerangs to Give Sox Pennant." On a 1-1 count, with two outs and no one on, Ted—perhaps still remembering Harry Heilmann's advice—deliberately slashed a ball to left-center and he hit it hard. It would have been, the *Globe* wrote, "a routine out against an orthodox defense." But League Park had a very deep left-center field and the Tribe's defense had opened up huge holes on the left side of the field. The centerfielder himself, Felix Mackiewicz, was to the right of center field, while leftfielder Pat Seerey was "about 20 feet back of the grass behind third base, 15 or so feet from the foul line"—guarding against one down the line. Everyone else was shifted to the right side of the field. Ted's drive traveled about 375 feet before it hit the ground and then skittered up to 400 or 430 feet before it settled into a gutter at the base of the wall. By the time Mackiewicz got to it, Williams was almost to third base. He slid across home plate as Boudreau's relay home was a bit off the mark.

Ted wanted to give Tex Hughson all the credit for the win. "He pitched a helluva game. My home run didn't mean a thing when I hit it."[41]

Williams, years later: "Someone said, 'Is that the easiest homer you ever got?' And I said, 'Hell no, it was the hardest. I had to run!'"[42]

It was Ted's 38th home run of the year, a new season high. It was also his last of the year—and didn't hit one in the World Series, either.

Red allowed Ted four home runs: #140, 165, 228, 246.

Ted Williams was voted Most Valuable Player in the American League in 1946. He led the league in walks with 156 and in runs scored with 142. He hit 38 homers, as we have seen, and drove in 123 runs. For the fourth year in a row, he led the league in getting on base, with a .497 on-base percentage. He beat out Detroit's Hal Newhouser for MVP. Second place was Bobby Doerr and third place was Johnny Pesky. With Boo Ferriss #7 and Dom DiMaggio #9, the Red Sox had five of the top nine positions in the MVP voting. Given that they won the A.L. pennant with such ease, finishing 12 games ahead of the second-place Tigers, it wasn't surprising that Ted got the nod.

The World Series was another matter. Widely favored to beat the Cardinals, the Sox in fact lost in seven games. Ted Williams—in the only World Series appearance of his long career—hit zero home runs and batted only .200. He didn't even have a double, not a single extra-base hit. Ted hit five singles, and drove in only one run in the entire Series.

It wasn't as though Ted was unfamiliar with the park—Sportsman's Park, home of the Cardinals, was also home to the Browns. The problem was his elbow. The Red Sox finished so far in front of the pack that they some time off (literally so for the first-stringers), and then had to wait for the Cardinals to win in a playoff. To keep fresh, Joe Cronin brought in a makeshift team of American Leaguers (including Dom's brother Joe) to play in some mock games against the Red Sox. Unfortunately, one of Mickey Haefner's pitches struck Williams on the elbow, and it swelled up to twice its normal size. Though x-rays were negative, it was at first thought there was no chance for Ted to play. He did, but with poor results.

There was a near home run Ted hit—his first time up. "Pollet and the rest of the Cardinal pitchers crowded me the whole Series, trying to force me to pull. The first time up I hit a shot to right field and as soon as I hit it I thought, Boy, that's out. It hit the screen a foot foul. Then I grounded out."[43] It was as close as he ever came to hitting a homer in the World Series.

In fact, the last time he hit a home run had been weeks earlier—the clincher on September 13, and that was an inside-the-park home run. The last time Ted had hit one out of the park was on September 11.

1947

During spring training, the Sox played a game against the Dallas Rebels on April 2 and the Texas League team put on "the shift of all shifts"—as the *Dallas Morning News* explained: "When Ted stepped to the plate for the first time, the Rebels drew an approving cheer from the crowd when all the men except the battery raced out into the right-field bleachers and climbed to the top row." After the fun subsided, the fielders did indeed shift on Williams and held him to one single on the day.

Williams did admit that he could have beaten the shift, but was too stubborn to. "I can hit to left field. But when they try to make me do it, I just don't want to do it."[44] Of course, he was have had to compromise on power, to some extent, and he'd worked so hard to hone the craft of hitting that there was something about having to adjust to pitchers that rubbed him the wrong way.

166 (#1 of 1947) April 18 at Shibe Park, Philadelphia. Pitcher: Bob Savage (Philadelphia Athletics). RH. Age 25.

Top of the fifth inning. Three-run homer.

In the third game of the year, Ted got his first home run of the new season. The Sox only held a 2-1 lead after the first four, so a three-run homer offered some much-welcome insurance. It was a "high wind-blown fly, which sailed over the right-field fence." (*Herald*) The *Globe* figured it would have been caught in front of the bullpen at Fenway Park—but this was Shibe Park and it was a home run.

Ted's first home run of 1947. He also hit #178 off Savage in late June.

167 (#2) April 19 at Shibe Park, Philadelphia. Pitcher: Joe Coleman (Philadelphia Athletics). RH. Age 24.

Top of the ninth inning. Two-run homer.

The Red Sox hadn't scored a run all day, while Philadelphia had scored once in the first and once in the eighth. Twice earlier in the game, Ted had pushed balls to left field against the shift and earned himself a single and then a double. Pesky was on second and Williams at bat in the top of the ninth. The Athletics again put on a shift. This time, Ted put one *over* the shift. "The Kid was in no kidding mood. He scorned the open spaces in left. He set his sights on the right-field fence and with a full swing at the first pitch he met the ball squarely. There never was any doubt where that ball was destined to land. The flight of the ball was high enough to scale a fence twice the size of this one." (*Herald*) It was a knee-high fastball and the Athletics had failed to position an outfielder on 20th Street, where the ball game down. Ted had tied the game. Dom DiMaggio hit a two-run single in the top of the tenth, which won the game.

Later this year, Boston area native Coleman gave up #194. In 1951, Coleman got hit for #318.

168 (#3) April 22 at Yankee Stadium, New York. Pitcher: Bill Bevens (New York Yankees). RH. Age 30.

Top of the third inning. One-run homer.

The visiting Red Sox hit three home runs in the game. The Yankees only managed three base hits. But the Yankees won, 5-4. One of the Yankees' hits was a three-run first-inning homer by King Kong Keller. Ted's came in the third and the *Herald*'s Arthur Sampson said it "bounced into the vacant chairs in the third deck and made Keller's…look like a drag bunt."

The *Globe*'s Hurwitz came up with the same analogy; Keller's "was a bunt compared to the Williams wallop."

#176 was the other homer Ted hit off Bill Bevens.

169 (#4) May 6 at Sportsman's Park, St. Louis. Pitcher: Jack Kramer (St. Louis Browns). RH. Age 29.

Top of the ninth inning. One-run homer.

"Williams' Homers Tie Game in Ninth, Win It in 11th, 6-5"—so read the *Boston Globe* headline the next morning. Before the game, Jack Kramer was holding court and "casually remarked that the only way to pitch to Ted if a run meant the ball game is to walk him." The top of the ninth rolled around and Kramer had a 3-2 lead. There was one out. Ted Williams left the on-deck circle and came to bat. "This was when Kramer forgot his pre-game sermon. He pitched to Williams. The Kid drove a 400-footer into right center that caromed off a steel girder" and tied the game.

Kramer was also responsible for #16, 33, 132, and 185.

170 (#5) May 6 at Sportsman's Park, St. Louis. Pitcher: Fred Sanford (St. Louis Browns). RH. Age 27.

Top of the 11th inning. Three-run homer. GAME WINNER.

Next time up, Williams faced Fred Sanford, on in relief of Kramer. Pellagrini had doubled and Pesky had walked. After laying off one that went for a ball, Ted saw a pitch to his liking and "unloaded. He gave it a terrific ride. It cleared the ten-foot high screen at the back of the right-field pavilion. It crossed Grand st. in back of the pavilion...a three-run smash." The *Herald* writer said, "We could see it bound up to the third story of a house on the other side of the boulevard." Every one of those three runs was needed, as the Browns scored twice in the bottom of the 11th.

Sanford also served up #188 and #202.

171 (#6) May 13 at Fenway Park. Pitcher: Earl Harrist (Chicago White Sox). RH. Age 28.

Bottom of the seventh inning. One-run homer.

It was his sixth year playing for the Red Sox but not until this day had Ted hit a home run to left field at Fenway. The day before, Ted had visited 11-year-old Glenny Brann at the hospital in Malden. The young boy had lost both legs to amputation after being "burned at the stake" in a game of cowboys and Indians. It was just that day that Glenny learned his legs were gone. Ted—who'd been in a bit of a slump—promised Glenny he'd try to hit a home run for him. In the bottom of the seventh, on a 0-1 pitch, he hit one out toward the center-field flagpole, "yards above the wall" to the left of the flagpole.

It wasn't the first time Williams had promised to try and hit a homer for a boy who was ill. During the springtime, the Red Sox had played a game in Chattanooga on April 7 against the Cincinnati Reds. Tommy Seessel's father spotted The Kid on the street before the game and told Ted his son Tommy was home ill and sad because he unable to go to the game—so Ted went to visit him. This author interviewed Seessel in 1997, and he recalled, "I forget how it came up, whether he offered or whether I asked for him to hit a home run for me that day. But he did."[45]

Harrist got off light; this was the only homer Ted ever hit off him and it was a solo home run at that.

172 (#7) May 13 at Fenway Park. Pitcher: Eddie Smith (Chicago White Sox). LH. Age 33.

Bottom of the eighth inning. One-run homer.

The inning after he hit #171, he hit #172—also to left field, this one into the screen in more or less straightaway left. He'd been talking with Joe Cronin before the game, and Cronin had told him he could hit homers to left field—just to use his wrists to propel the ball that way. He did it, and it worked—twice in one day. The solo home run in the eighth hadn't made that much of a difference in the game, either—the Red Sox won, 19-6.

Glenny Brann hadn't heard the first home run but was listening to the radio with other patients on the sunporch of Malden Hospital when Ted hit this one.

Like Harrist on the same day, Smith also skated through. He'd been pitching since six years before Williams joined the league, and worked in 282 games but this is the only homer Ted collected off him. Later this season, he joined the Red Sox and closed out his career with Boston.

173 (#8) May 16 at Fenway Park. Pitcher: Walter Brown (St. Louis Browns). RH. Age 32.

Bottom of the fifth inning. Four-run homer. Grand slam #8. GAME WINNER.

Ted resumed hitting to right field. Every base hit in his six previous home games had each been hit to either center or left. Whether or not this was simply to prove he could do it is something we cannot know for sure. The only year the Browns' Walter Brown worked in the big leagues was 1947. He relieved in 19 games and gave up three home runs. This was the first. The other two were both hit by Roy Cullenbine, more than a month apart from each other. Though Ted's homer won the game, providing runs 8 through 11 in a 12-7 game, the loss was given to starting pitcher Jack Kramer, who'd gotten the Browns in a 7-0 hole. The homer followed a walk, a single, and another walk, and was "a 400 ft. wallop over the Sox bullpen and ten rows high in the right-field bleacher area." Vic Johnson's sports page cartoon in the *Herald* showed it landing in what is today Section 1. Doerr drove in three runs without a hit, on three sacrifice flies.

174 (#9) May 19 (second game) at Fenway Park. Pitcher: Virgil Trucks (Detroit Tigers). RH. Age 30.

Bottom of the ninth inning. Two-run homer. GAME WINNER.

The Red Sox lost a 3-2 heartbreaker in the 12th inning in game one and were down by a 4-3 score when they got to the bottom of the ninth in game two. (The Tigers had just taken the lead with a run in the top of the ninth.) Then

Wally Moses singled to center field. Virgil Trucks was trying to avoid giving Williams a fastball to hit, but his first three pitches were off the plate. It was 3-0 and he either had to risk putting the winning run on base or throw one over. He fired a fastball, high and up by the letters, and Ted hit it and it went out—a walkoff, we'd call it today—about five or six rows in the same are depicted by Johnson's cartoon showing #173—maybe 10 feet further toward the front of Section 2.

Ted's 12 homers off Trucks: 108, 115, 146, 174, 189, 226, 236, 243, 320, 342, 437, and 444.

175 (#10) May 20 at Fenway Park. Pitcher: Johnny Gorsica (Detroit Tigers). RH. Age 32.

Bottom of the fourth inning. One-run homer.

The Sox had been chasing the Tigers in the A.L. standings, and this 8-3 helped them get with a game. The two teams also traded catchers—Boston getting Birdie Tebbetts for Hal Wagner. The Tigers got two early runs off Joe Dobson, and Dizzy Trout struck out Williams in the first. Boston scored seven runs and had a solid lead by the fourth, when sinkerballer Johnny Gorsica came on in relief. Swinging at Gorsica's second serve, Ted "sent it about a mile in the air. The wind took it for a ride and just made the center-field bleacher."

Gorsica had previously given up homers #55 and 59.

176 (#11) May 25 at Yankee Stadium, New York. Pitcher: Bill Bevens (New York Yankees). RH. Age 30.

Top of the ninth inning. Two-run homer.

The Yankees almost obliterated the Red Sox, with a 17-2 win. It was New York's fourth win in a row and the first three had been shutouts: 5-0 over the Tigers and then 9-0 and 5-0 over the Red Sox. And it was 17-0 through eight innings on May 25. Only Ted Williams' two-run homer in the top of the ninth prevented the Yankees from setting a new American League record for consecutive shutouts. Bevens even had a no-hitter for six innings, until Pesky doubled in the seventh. Pesky was on base again in the ninth when Ted hit one in Yankee Stadium's right-field upper deck. On a 1-0 count, he "gave the next pitch the old glory ride high up against the adverse wind, 10 rows or more deep into the third tier in right field." (*Herald*)

#168. That was the other homer Ted hit off Bevens.

177 (#12) June 4 at Sportsman's Park. St. Louis. Pitcher: Bob Muncrief (St. Louis Browns). RH. Age 31.

Top of the sixth inning. One-run homer. GAME WINNER.

The Red Sox were in danger of falling into fifth place, but a 5-2 win in St. Louis staved off that concern for another day. Sam Mele and Ted Williams each homered for the Red Sox, while Joe Dobson threw a four-hitter. Ted's broke a 2-2 tie, a "liner which landed on the right-field roof."

Jeff Heath played with the Browns in 1947 and he talked about how some of the St. Louis pitchers lost the guessing game against Ted Williams. "He wore us out, and the reason was that our pitchers wanted to throw to him. They wouldn't walk him, like other sensible pitchers. They kept thinking they'd found his weakness. If he took a swing and missed, the pitcher would say, 'Ah, now I got it. I know how to pitch to him.' The next time Ted batted the pitcher would throw the same pitch, but this time Ted would hit it out of the park."[46] Ted hit 11 home runs against Browns pitchers in 1947.

#79, 80, 99, 177, 187, and 195 — Ted's homers off Bob Muncrief.

178 (#13) June 29 (second game) at Shibe Park, Philadelphia. Pitcher: Bob Savage (Philadelphia Athletics). RH. Age 25.

Top of the fifth inning. Two-run homer.

Connie Mack's Athletics won both halves of a doubleheader, 3-2 and then 6-5. Ted was 0-for-3 in the first game and only managed one hit in three at-bats in the second. That hit was a two-run homer in the top of the fifth inning and it temporarily gave the Red Sox a 4-0 lead but then the A's scored five times in the bottom of the fifth and the game tilted their way. It was Ted's first home run in 25 days, reckoned to be the longest stretch he'd had without homering since he joined the big leagues (winters and wartime excepted!) Johnny Pesky had singled and Ted "unleashed…a mighty blast over the right-center-field wall." (*Herald*)

Savage's second home-run pitch. Ted hit #166 on April.

179 (#14) July 2 at Fenway Park. Pitcher: Carl Scheib (Philadelphia Athletics). RH. Age 20.

Bottom of the first inning. Two-run homer.

Williams and Doerr and Tebbetts all homered, the Red Sox had six runs. But it was 6-6 after eight innings and Philadelphia scored once more in the top of the ninth, while Boston failed to do so. The game stands out in the chronology of Ted Williams home runs in that it was the first he ever hit in a night game at Fenway Park. Lights had been installed in 1947 and occasional games played after dark. This was the fifth in which he had played, but the first in which TSW homered. It came after Pesky walked and was "a blistering smash into the third row of the bleachers over the Sox bullpen." (*Herald*) Ted had just returned from doing some fishing in the Bangor area, apparently a quick trip as the team had only had one day off, but the schedule afforded him a little extra time with the game set at night. A bit of a novelty at the time (it occasioned comment in a few newspapers) were three signs some boys had in center field, one reading "TED" in big letters and the other two readying "Teddy's Our Boy" and "Teddy the Kid."

And when they held this night game at Fenway, it was a *night* game — the scheduled start was 8:45 PM. June 13 had been the first night game, and Ted had been 2-for-4 with two RBIs, but no home run.

Carl Scheib later contributed home runs #192 and 234 to the cause.

180 (#15) July 3 at Fenway Park. Pitcher: Phil Marchildon (Philadelphia Athletics). RH. Age 33.

Bottom of the eighth inning. One-run homer.

The Red Sox scored three runs in the first inning, but saw their lead disappear when the Athletics scored five times in the top of the fifth, bringing them to a 6-3 lead. It was 7-3 when Ted added just one more run with an eighth-inning homer into the Red Sox bullpen.

When it was learned that the Indians had signed "Negro Larry Doby" (as the *Globe* put it) as the first black player in the American League, only pitcher Bob Klinger knew who he was. Or maybe. "I can't recall Doby but he must have been with the Negro team we faced" in a couple of games at the Great Lakes Naval Training Center. In southern California, Ted had once played in the Pomona tournament at the same time as Jackie Robinson, but the Red Sox had not availed themselves of Robinson's services despite a 1945 tryout at Fenway Park, and Robinson ended up in the National League. It would be 12 more years before the Red Sox had an African American ballplayer in Boston.

Ted hit five homers off Phil: 92, 120, 148, 180, and 196.

181 (#16) July 16 at Comiskey Park, Chicago. Pitcher: Red Ruffing (Chicago White Sox). RH. Age 42. Hall of Famer.

Top of the third inning. Two-run homer. GAME WINNER.

Boston's Denny Galehouse pitched shutout ball for eight innings, then allowed two Chisox runs in the bottom of the ninth. In the third, "Ted thumped a 370-foot home run into the right-field stands" and doubled the lead from 2-0 to 4-0, thus ultimately providing the winning runs in the 7-2 game. Pesky was on board; Ted's homer went into the lower part of the stands.

This was the last year of Ruffing's 22-year major-league career, now working for the White Sox. This was the first home run off him in 1947, but the last three all came in the same game, hit by Sam Mele, Bobby Doerr, and Dom DiMaggio (and none of them back-to-back.)

182 (#17) July 18 at Sportsman's Park, St. Louis. Pitcher: Cliff Fannin (St. Louis Browns). RH. Age 23.

Top of the first inning. Two-run homer.

Ted Williams had a 5-for-5 day, with 11 total bases — two homers and three singles. He drove in five runs, all on the homers. The rest of the Red Sox drove in three more runs. Sam Mele was on first base (he singled four times) when Ted gave the Sox a 2-0 lead in the top of the first. Homer #17 of the year was "a gentle little liner which barely landed on top of the right-field pavilion roof." (*Herald*) For readers accustomed to accounts of Ted's "gargantuan blasts" and the like, to have a writer like Burt Whitman describing a "gentle little liner" may have been a surprise.

This was the first homer Fannin gave Ted on this day.

183 (#18) July 18 at Sportsman's Park, St. Louis. Pitcher: Cliff Fannin (St. Louis Browns). RH. Age 23.

Top of the seventh inning. Three-run homer.

His two homers on the day drove in five runs, but the Browns scored nine runs in the game, thanks in part to three homers of their own. Number 18 was "a most lordly one…which cleared everything in deep right-center, a ball which must have landed over on the far side of Grand Boulevard, and one to rank right up with his most ferocious jolts."

Former Negro Leaguers Willard Brown and Henry Thompson both played in this game, the first time the Red Sox had played in an "integrated" ballgame.

Ted's five homers off Fannin: #154, 182, 183, 186, 280.

184 (#19) July 24 at Fenway Park. Pitcher: Gordon Maltzberger (Chicago White Sox). RH. Age 34.

Bottom of the seventh inning. Two-run homer.

Over the back of the Red Sox bullpen, and 10 to 12 rows up in the right-field bleachers. Ted had gone nine at-bats without so much as a base hit, so a hard-hit homer like this was very welcome. It was an 8-2 win for boys from Boston, already 5-2 heading into the seventh. Ted's homer produced runs 6 and 7. The Sox added one more later in the inning.

Ted's only homer off Maltzy.

185 (#20) July 25 at Fenway Park. Pitcher: Jack Kramer (St. Louis Browns). RH. Age 29.

Bottom of the first inning. Two-run homer.

Ted started the scoring for the Red Sox with a two-run homer in the first inning, but it was a squeeze play by Sox pitcher Harry Dorish which scored Dom DiMaggio in the fifth inning with the seventh run of a 7-6 night-game victory. Ted had scored the tying run earlier in the inning. He was 3-for-3 with a base on balls. Pesky had singled in the first and Williams was given new life when Browns catcher Les Moss dropped a high-hit foul ball off Ted's bat. The Kid then banged a home run into the third row of the right-field grandstand seats, and then Bobby Doerr homered on the very next pitch.

Five homers off Kramer: 16, 33, 132, 169, and 185.

186 (#21) July 26 at Fenway Park. Pitcher: Cliff Fannin (St. Louis Browns). RH. Age 23.

Bottom of the first inning. Two-run homer. GAME WINNER.

Ted hit a homer for the third day in a row. It was also his third home run off Fannin in an eight-day stretch. Once again, he kicked off the first inning with a two-run homer—always a good way to start a game. This time, Pesky had walked and Ted swung on a 3-1 count and drove it over the Red Sox bullpen and eight rows up in the bleachers. It gave the Red Sox a 2-1 lead.

His first homer off Cliff was #154—then 182 and 183 and this one—and then 280.

187 (#22) July 26 at Fenway Park. Pitcher: Bob Muncrief (St. Louis Browns). RH. Age 31.

Bottom of the third. Two-run homer.

The score after two innings was 4-1 Red Sox, and in the third inning, the Thumper hit another one out, this time off reliever Bob Muncrief. It went to the same location, but a few rows higher. He almost hit a third home run later in the game. Willard Brown backed up against the gate to the Red Sox bullpen, reached up high, and snagged the ball. The final score of the game was a "picnic" at 12-1.

Ted caused Muncrief grief with this one. It was the second of the six homers the Browns pitcher surrendered which were true game-winning hits. His other HRs were #79, 80, 99, 177, and 195.

188 (#23) July 27 (first game) at Fenway Park. Pitcher: Fred Sanford (St. Louis Browns). RH. Age 27.

Bottom of the sixth inning. Two-run homer.

Ted had now hit homers four games in a row, and five home runs over the four games. The Red Sox won seven games in a row, by sweeping two games from St. Louis, 4-3 and 11-2. The first game, clearly, was the close one. Boston scored once in the second and once in the eighth, with Ted's two-run homer in the middle. The game might have been 4-2, but Ted dropped an easy fly ball with two outs in the ninth inning, letting in the third run of the game for the Browns (and the second in the ninth.) Sam Mele made a great one-handed running catch, crashing into the grandstand wall to end the game. Ted's homer was the "grandpappy of all center-field high blasts…six rows into the center-field bleachers, a little to the right of the little yellow pole which is labeled at 420 feet from home plate, over the center-field tip of the visitors' bullpen and also over the little lower leg of the bleachers which goes into center field like a slice of pie." (*Herald*)

Ted also hit #170 and 202 off Sanford.

189 (#24) August 2 at Fenway Park. Pitcher: Virgil Trucks (Detroit Tigers). RH. Age 30.

Bottom of the first inning. Two-run homer. GAME WINNER.

It was Bobby Doerr Day at Fenway and he received a Cadillac, Monica got a milk stole, and there was good feeling all the way around. The Tigers, though, got a run off Tex Hughson in the top of the first. Sam Mele hit the first pitch to a Boston batter and drove it to center field for a triple. Two outs followed, and Mele had to hold at third on both of them. Ted Williams then clouted one to left-center field, not that far from the flagpole, for a two-run homer, a "smack of genuine authority." (*Herald*) Neither team scored for the rest of the game.

Ted's 12 homers off Trucks: 108, 115, 146, 174, 189, 226, 236, 243, 320, 342, 437, and 444.

190 (#25) August 7 at Griffith Stadium, Washington. Pitcher: Early Wynn (Washington Senators). RH. Age 27. Hall of Famer.

Top of the second inning. One-run homer.

It was really the six runs the Red Sox scored in the fourth inning which broke the back of the Senators. Ted's solo homer in the second was the only run of the game to that point. Ted beat out a bunt down the third-base line later in the game, in the fifth, leading to another run. It was a 2-1 pitch and Ted hit it over the right-field wall, which was 320 feet from the plate and stood 30 feet high.

Ted hit eight homers off Early Wynn. Though they'd broken in the same year—1939—six of Ted's homers hadn't come until Wynn turned 36 years of age. The eight home runs: #190, 334, 405, 433, 434, 447, 489, and 497.

191 (#26) August 26 (second game) at Briggs Stadium, Detroit. Pitcher: Hal White (Detroit Tigers). RH. Age 28.

Top of the first inning. Two-run homer. GAME WINNER.

First there were the Yankees. Then, ranging from 12 to 14 games behind the Yankees, there were four teams battling for second place—the Red Sox, Tigers, Athletics, and Indians. On August 26, Boston and Detroit split a doubleheader, each team having its way with the other in one of the games: the Tigers took the first, 12-1, and the Red Sox the second, 9-1. Williams was 3-for-7 on the day, driving in the only run in the first game and five of the nine in the second. His two-run homer led the way and was the game-winner in game two. Compared to other homers he hit at Briggs Stadium, this was a more modest one—"into the lower deck in right field"—but it was a home run all the same, and gave Tex Hughson all he needed for a four-hit victory.

Hal's other homer was #276.

192 (#27) August 31 at Fenway Park. Pitcher: Carl Scheib (Philadelphia Athletics). RH. Age 20.

Bottom of the sixth inning. Two-run homer.

The Red Sox won their fifth game in a row with a 5-1 win (Joe Dobson's 15th of the year). Ted Williams threw out a runner at home plate—one of a league-leading 11 assists in 1947—and drove in three runs. The first came on a sacrifice fly in the first inning; the other two were on the homer providing insurance runs in the sixth. Dom had walked and, on an 0-2 count, Williams hit one into the Red Sox bullpen.

Ted also hit #179 and 234 off Scheib.

193 (#28) September 5 at Shibe Park, Philadelphia. Pitcher: Russ Christopher (Philadelphia Athletics). RH. Age 29.

Top of the ninth inning. One-run homer.

The A's tied the game, 6-6, in a wild seventh inning that saw Eddie Pellagrini and Ferris Fain get into a fight and Joe Cronin thrown out for heckling the umpires from the bench. Then the A's scored three more in the eighth. Ted Williams got one back with his homer in the ninth, though Ted had almost given up before getting something like a second life. Ted swung and missed, thought he'd been struck out by Christopher, and started trudging toward the dugout, and had to be called back and told it was only strike two. Given one more chance, he swung and hit the ball over the right-field wall.

The final of the four Ted hit off Russ Christopher. See also #98, 104, and 149.

194 **(#29)** September 7 (first game) at Shibe Park, Philadelphia. Pitcher: Joe Coleman (Philadelphia Athletics). RH. Age 24.

Top of the seventh inning. Two-run homer.

The Red Sox hold on second place was jeopardized by 7-4 and 4-3 losses in the day's Philadelphia twinbill. Pesky had four hits and Williams had three, including his 29th homer which accounted for half of the first game's runs. With Dom DiMaggio about, the four-base hit "cleared the works in right field." Ted was leading the league in hitting.

Earlier in the season, Coleman served up #167. And, in 1951, #318.

195 **(#30)** September 17 (first game) at Fenway Park. Pitcher: Bob Muncrief (St. Louis Browns). RH. Age 31.

Bottom of the fourth inning. Three-run homer.

The Sox split with the Browns, losing 9-4 but then winning 4-0 on Joe Dobson's one-hitter (the only hit coming in the seventh on Wally Judnich's broken-bat single that plopped into right field.) Ted's 30th homer on a 2-0 pitch put him at 100 RBIs on the year. He drove in another run later in the game. This was his 11th home run of the year off Browns pitching; he rubbed it in by hitting it off the back wall of the Browns' bullpen.

It was Ted's third homer of the year off Muncrief (the others were #177 and 187). Previously, he'd hit 79 and 80, and #99.

196 **(#31)** September 23 (first game) at Fenway Park. Pitcher: Phil Marchildon (Philadelphia Athletics). RH. Age 33.

Bottom of the fifth. One-run homer.

Harry Hooper of the World Champion Red Sox teams of 1915, 1916, and 1918 was at Fenway Park but he and Duffy Lewis went out on the roof for a few minutes to talk with a couple of newspapermen and missed seeing Ted's home run land in the Red Sox bullpen. "I missed seeing my fellow Californian knock one out of the ballpark. Is my face red!" said a disappointed Hooper. It was the last home game for the Red Sox in 1947, and the team dropped to third place with a 9-3 loss in the first game and a 6-5 win in the second. Williams held the league lead in the three Triple Crown categories and worked his 159th base on balls. Only Babe Ruth had ever had more (170 in 1923) in a season. Ted ultimately walked 162 times—and then matched that total in 1949. His 20.75 walks percentage remains the highest even achieved by any major-league ballplayer.

This was the fifth of five hit off Marchildon. See also #92, 120, 148, and 180.

"I was walked more frequently than Ruth and struck out less—once every 11 times up to Ruth's one in six. I had to be doing something right, and for my money the principal something was being selective."[47]

197 (#32) September 27 at Griffith Stadium, Washington. Pitcher: Walt Masterson (Washington Senators). RH. Age 27.

Top of the first inning. Three-run homer. GAME WINNER.

Williams gave Dobson all the runs he needed with a three-run homer in the top of the first inning. Joe won the game, 8-1. An on 0-2 count, Ted hit a ball that "hit the top of the right-field fence and dropped over on the far side." (*Washington Post*)

It was 155 homers after Ted hit #42 that he struck again. In all, he hit five homers off Masterson: #6, 42, 197, 218, and 402.

Ted Williams won the Triple Crown in 1947. His 32 home runs were three more than Joe Gordon, now with the Indians. His 114 runs batted in were well above second-place Tommy Henrich of the Yankees, who had 98. His .343 batting average was 15 points above Barney McCosky of the Athletics. Williams boasted a .499 on-base percentage and led the league in slugging with .634, well above Joe DiMaggio's second-ranked .522. He scored 125 runs, topping Henrich at 109. His 162 walks, including 24 intentional walks, led all of baseball.

Did he win the Most Valuable Player award? Nope. That went to Joe DiMaggio—by one vote, thanks to the spite shown by at least one BBWAA writer who refused to rank Ted even in the top ten. Despite the obvious animus that reflected, Joe D accepted the award rather than decline it under the circumstances. *The Sporting News* named Williams the Major League Player of the Year.

1948

198 (#1 of 1948) April 23 at Yankee Stadium, New York. Pitcher: Spec Shea (New York Yankees). RH. Age 27.

Top of the fifth inning. One-run homer.

It was manager Joe McCarthy's first game managing the Red Sox as the visiting team at Yankee Stadium. The former New York manager saw his new team beat his former team, 4-0, behind the five-hit pitching of Mickey Harris. Joe DiMaggio was presented the 1947 MVP award in pregame ceremonies. In the game itself, he was "clearly outshadowed" by Ted Williams. (*New York Times*)

The Red Sox only got seven hits, but three of them were Ted's. The Sox scored once in the third and once in the fourth and twice in the fifth, one of the fifth-inning ones coming on Ted Williams' first home run of the year. The first run came in when Ted singled in the third, though he didn't earn an RBI because the run scored on Joe DiMaggio's fielding error. As for his home run, Ted "hit the ball over the head of the leaping Henrich into the right-field stands at the 340-foot mark. And we mean leaping—Henrich all but dismembered himself jumping and half-falling into the stands trying to reach the drive."

Speaking of leaping, back in the second inning, Ted backed up to the left-field wall, leapt, and stole a home run away from Gus Niarhos.

Several hundred fans watched the game at the Parker House in downtown Boston, among them Tom and Jean Yawkey. It was, according to the April 24 *Boston Globe*, "the first television presentation of a ball game in Boston." The *Herald* noted that for the first time, viewers in Boston had now seen a televised Ted Williams home run. "A great roar went up from the Parker House select group when Ted Williams connected for his first home run of the season."

The Yankees and then Senators pitcher saw Ted hit five home runs: #198, 224, 309, 326, and 328.

199 (#2) April 24 at Yankee Stadium, New York. Pitcher: Allie Reynolds (New York Yankees). RH. Age 31.

Top of the fourth inning. One-run homer.

In the fourth, Williams "opened the inning with a terrific smash into the upper right-field tier" (*New York Times*) but it was one of only two runs the Red Sox scored, as the Yankees prevailed, 7-2. The *Globe* wrote that the ball went high into the upper deck.

The *Globe* also reported another story involving a Red Sox/Yankees broadcast. Mel Allen's game account was being transmitted by telephone wires when somehow the lines got crossed. Radio station WINS issued a statement saying that the studio apparently "had been hooked into a public circuit and some irate person trying to put through a call heard the broadcast and broke into it." The station's statement didn't mention that the irate patron had uttered an obscene word, which was sent out over the airwaves before the station hastily cut off its broadcast and replaced it with recorded music. The Associated Press said the epithet was "one not used in public society."

Reynolds' name stands next to six Ted Williams home runs: #199, 216, 251, 265, 290, and 344.

200 (#3) April 29 at Shibe Park, Philadelphia. Pitcher: Bill McCahan (Philadelphia Athletics). RH. Age 27.

Top of the first inning. Two-run homer.

The Red Sox hit four home runs while beating the Athletics, 7-4. Ted led the parade, later joined by Sam Mele, Jake Jones, and even pitcher Joe Dobson. He'd hit one back in 1941; the two were the only two he ever hit. Johnny Pesky had walked and on a 1-0 pitch Williams "deposited McCahan's next serve well over the 311-foot right-field wall." It wasn't fair by much, but it was fair. Mele was next, in the second inning, with Dobson and Jones getting into the act only in the top of the ninth.

This was the only homer McCahan gave up to Ted Williams.

201 (#4) May 2 at Fenway Park. Pitcher: Joe Page (New York Yankees). LH. Age 30.

Bottom of the eighth inning. Three-run homer.

The Yankees had put on a shift against Ted in the May 1 game and he faked a bunt at one point, but he said, "the Yankees didn't move a step...They want me to bunt. Well, I'm not going to. I'm going to keep swinging." (*Boston Herald*) He tripled and homered, driving in five runs. His first-inning triple had been the game-winning hit in the 7-1 Red Sox win. It was Ted's third homer of the year off Yankees pitching, one more than he hit in all of 1947.

He'd received a telegram during the game from 19-year-old Charles Walsh, sent from Springfield, Massachusetts. It read, "Will you hit a home run for me today, Ted? I am sick in Mercy Hospital." The telegram arrived late in the game, more or less around the time of his home run. The *Herald* wrote, "He whistled the ball high, wide, and handsome, down the wind, over the Yankee bullpen, and a couple rows into the bleachers."

This was the only homer Page gave up to Ted Williams.

202 (#5) May 8 at Fenway Park. Pitcher: Fred Sanford (St. Louis Browns). RH. Age 28.

Bottom of the eighth inning. One-run homer.

In the early going of the 1948 season, the Red Sox were barely keeping above .500 and their 9-4 loss to St. Louis this day actually dropped them below the mark. Ted sent Sanford's offering "into the right-field seats, yards inside the foul pole." And Stan Spence hit a homer on the very next pitch, but there was too big a deficit to make up.

Sanford of St. Louis also was the pitcher who gave up #166 and 178.

203 (#6) May 9 (first game) at Fenway Park. Pitcher: Bob Feller (Cleveland Indians). RH. Age 29. Hall of Famer.

Bottom of the fourth inning. One-run homer.

One in the first game, one in the second game. But it wasn't a good day for the team. The Red Sox lost both games, 4-1 and 9-5. Simple math tells you that Ted's home run off Feller was the only run the Red Sox scored in

1948-9 against the Indians. #5 is Vern Stephens.

the first game. Ted hit a 1-1 pitch into the Red Sox bullpen. It actually gave Boston the lead until Ken Keltner matched it with a homer of his own in the top of the fifth. Ted's was a very important home run at the time, since it kept the Sox in the game through nine. It was the top of the tenth when the Indians scored three times—on another Keltner home run—and the Red Sox were unable to match it.

Ten homers Ted hit off Rapid Robert: 131, 141, 203, 210, 227, 330, 351, 353, 374, 416.

204 (#7) May 9 (second game) at Fenway Park. Pitcher: Lyman Linde (Cleveland Indians). RH. Age 27.

Bottom of the fifth inning. One-run homer.

Ted hit another one into the bullpen, this time "a high, fast ball directly on a line off the back of the visitors' bullpen." It was again a solo homer. It provided the fifth and final run for the Red Sox, and the lead at the time, but the lead evaporated over time and the Tribe prevailed.

This was the only homer Linde gave up to Ted Williams.

Ted said that the home-run hitter swings harder because he swings faster. And he swings faster because he waits longer. "The average hitter," he said, "tries to hit the ball too hard. The secret of hitting is to get your power one hundred percent from your forearms, wrists, and hands."[48]

205 (#8) May 21 at Cleveland Stadium, Cleveland. Pitcher: Steve Gromek (Cleveland Indians). RH. Age 28.

Top of the sixth inning. One-run homer.

Some words carried different meanings in 1948. *Boston Herald* readers were likely not startled to read, "Williams had a gay afternoon." He hit a homer, three singles, and walked twice for a perfect offensive afternoon." The four-base hit was a "jumbo homer…a magnificent better-than-400 drive into the upper right-field grandstand." The solo home run was Ted's only RBI in an 11-5 beating put on the Indians.

Gromek surrendered homers #115, 155, 205, 263, 437, and 354.

206 (#9) May 23 (second game) at Comiskey Park, Chicago. Pitcher: Glen Moulder (Chicago White Sox). RH. Age 30.

Bottom of the fifth inning. One-run homer.

Their two losses this day (4-3 and 4-3) saw the Red Sox drop to seventh place in the standings. Ted Williams' home run into the upper right-field deck at Comiskey Park gave the Red Sox a 3-2 lead in the second game, but it didn't last long. The White Sox got another run and sent the game into the tenth inning, but Joe Dobson's wild pitch with the bases loaded in the bottom of the tenth was fatal. Ted's homer came on a 3-0 count and was a "man-sized homer" according to a *Boston Herald* subhead. The game story said, "The Splinter lashed it on a line against the very strong north wind into the upper tier of the right-field grandstand, a smack which would have been good for 450 feet on the level, any time, any where."

This was the only homer Moulder gave up to Ted Williams.

207 (#10) May 29 (second game) at Griffith Stadium, Washington. Pitcher: Dick Welteroth (Washington Senators). RH. Age 20.

Top of the third inning. One-run homer.

The number of games lost continued to climb—10 of their last 12 games—as they dropped another pair (this made four doubleheader sweeps in a row, all on the losing side), 5-4 and 7-6. Burt Whitman started his *Herald* column, "It's a good thing that the A.L. rules do not allow the hapless and maladroit Red Sox to play more than two times a day." Williams was doing his part; he was hitting .391 after he hit two singles, one double, one triple, and one home run over the course of the two games. He drew two walks, too, and had three RBIs. His homer was hit on the first pitch he saw in the third inning and went over the 40-foot wall in right field that was 330 feet from the plate. On May 30, the *Globe* ran a Harold Kaese column with a headline that was repeated for a generation or two that followed: "What's the Matter With the Red Sox?"

Welteroth also surrendered #232.

208 (#11) May 31 (first game) at Shibe Park, Philadelphia. Pitcher: Lou Brissie (Philadelphia Athletics). LH. Age 24.

Top of the first inning. Two-run homer.

The Sox earned a split in this doubleheader. Dobson beat war hero Lou Brissie, 7-0, in the first game, with two of the runs coming on Ted's homer. Philadelphia won the second game, 2-1, a run scoring on a sixth-inning balk by Mickey Harris. Ted's home run followed a base on balls granted Dom DiMaggio. It went over the high right-field wall that was 331 feet distant.

Brissie gave up #208 and #288.

209 (#12) June 6 (second game) at Fenway Park. Pitcher: Fred Hutchinson (Detroit Tigers). RH. Age 26.

Bottom of the sixth inning. Two-run homer.

There was a reversal of fortune as the Red Sox won back-to-back double-headers on June 4 and June 6. The scores on the 6th were 5-4 and 12-4 and there was a stretch in this game when the Sox hit three home runs in the course of nine pitches. Williams, Spence, and Stephens were the homer-hitters. Ted had only had one hit in the first game — he "homered into the curving seats at the foul line on the 3-1 serve." He had a double and two singles to go with his homer in the nightcap. The wins had helped the Sox to climb into fourth place.

Hutchinson homers: #22, 139, 156, 163, 209, 225, 235, and 273.

210 (#13) June 16 at Cleveland Stadium, Cleveland. Pitcher: Bob Feller (Cleveland Indians). RH. Age 29. Hall of Famer.

Top of the seventh inning. Two-run homer.

The Kid had another four-hit day — and hit three of the hits to left field, frustrating Lou Boudreau's shift. The three were two doubles and a home run over the left-field wall at the 365-foot mark. Ted was hitting .408. Boudreau, credited as the author of the shift, watched Williams "hit to left with astounding ease and nonchalance" and that Boudreau may have inadvertently handed "a deadly new weapon to The Kid's offensive arsenal"—an ability to hit as well to left as to right.

Also hit off Feller: 131, 141, 203, 210, 227, 330, 351, 353, 374, 416.

211 (#14) June 24 (second game) at Comiskey Park, Chicago. Pitcher: Joe Haynes (Chicago White Sox). RH. Age 30.

Top of the fifth inning. Two-run homer.

After the Red Sox lost the first game of the doubleheader, 3-1, Ted stepped in and hit two homers—both of them two-run jobs—to help Boston to an 8-5 win in the second game. The White Sox had been winning 5-1 when Ted hit the first home run as part of a three-run fifth, "a beautiful line homer… into the deep left-center-field lower stands." (*Herald*) Roger Birtwell of the *Globe* asked him why he seemed to be hitting more to left field. His answer: "Because they're pitching me outside."

#110 and #319 were both hit off Haynes, too.

212 (#15) June 24 (second game) at Comiskey Park, Chicago. Pitcher: Earl Caldwell (Chicago White Sox). RH. Age 43.

Top of the eighth inning. Two-run homer.

Though he drove in half the runs in the second game, neither of them was the game-winning hit. Boston held a 6-5 edge; his second homer added two insurance runs. This one "was a sure homer the moment it left the bat. It landed half a dozen rows up in the upper right-field stands, a sure homer in anybody's ballpark." (*Herald*)

This was the only homer Caldwell gave up to Ted Williams. He'd pitched off and on in the majors since 1928. A month after this home run (on July 26) the White Sox placed him on waivers and he was picked up by Boston.

213 (#16) June 27 (second game) at Sportsman's Park, St. Louis. Pitcher: Ned Garver (St. Louis Browns). RH. Age 22.

Top of the first inning. Three-run homer.

2-0 and 6-3—the Red Sox took a doubleheader. They were still in fourth place, but the teams were bunched up a bit and they were only 5 ½ games out of first. The first game was a two-hitter thrown by Joe Dobson. Ted's homer came on a 2-1 pitch and went into the right-center-field pavilion.

Tied with Bob Feller for second place in the number of home runs allowed to Ted Williams was Ned Garver, with 10: #213, 245, 272, 282, 337, 375, 385, 422, 436, and 459.

"The first time that you faced him as a pitcher—the first time you faced him—he had never seen you. That was the best chance you had of striking him out. So the first time I pitched against him, it so happens, he did strike out and went back to the dugout and hit his bat on something and cracked the bat." So recalled Ned Garver, who talked the Browns trainer into getting the bat for him. Years later, Garver got Ted to sign it for him, and some years after that, Garver sold the cracked, game-used bat for $28,000.[49]

214 (#17) August 1 (second game) at Cleveland Stadium, Cleveland. Pitcher: Sam Zoldak (Cleveland Indians). LH. Age 29.

Top of the ninth inning. One-run homer.

What happened to July? No home runs for a full month? Williams played in 17 games during July. He'd also missed a lot of games. He hit seven doubles and 15 singles. His average dipped from .407 at the end of June to .388 at the end of July. He'd driven in 12 runs. But didn't hit a home run.

He hit one this day, though it came in the last inning of the second game and was the only run of the game. The Red Sox lost two games, 12-2 and 6-1. Ted "blistered his home run drive off the far right-field wall," wrote Henry McKenna in the *Boston Herald*.

Zoldak also allowed homer #317.

Ted launches another one, in this photograph thought to be from 1948.

215 (#18) August 3 at Sportsman's Park, St. Louis. Pitcher: Bryan Stephens (St. Louis Browns). RH. Age 27.

Top of the third inning. One-run homer.

During July, the Red Sox had managed to get into first place for seven days. They'd dropped back to second place but when the Red Sox won this game, 15-8, the win put them back on top. The home run hit by Ted Williams was "a mighty wallop onto the street beyond the park." (*Herald*)

This was the only homer Stephens gave up to Ted Williams.

216 (#19) August 11 at Yankee Stadium, New York. Pitcher: Allie Reynolds (New York Yankees). RH. Age 31.

Top of the seventh inning. One-run homer.

The homer Ted hit on August 11 was the first one he'd ever hit into the left-field stands at Yankee Stadium. But out it went. The Sox held a slim 3-2 lead after six innings, Denny Galehouse on his way to an effective 5-2 victory. Williams was the leadoff batter for Boston in the seventh and on a 2-0 count, he drove Reynolds' pitch right down the line in left. Keller couldn't get to it in time and it "dropped into the first section of boxes, just inside the foul pole, as the crowd howled. It's only 301 feet to the left-field line, so the ball probably went 310 or 315 feet, no more." (*Boston Herald*)

But it provided an important insurance run for the Red Sox. *The New York Times*, calling Williams "the siege gun of the Red Sox" said the home run was, by Ted's standards, "anything but a distinguished blow — merely a high slice that drifted into the left-field stand just inside the foul pole…[but] it greased the skids under Reynolds."

Every one of Williams' six home runs off Reynolds (#199, 216, 251, 265, 290, and 344) came after the pitcher joined the New York Yankees.

217 (#20) August 15 (first game) at Griffith Stadium, Washington. Pitcher: Forrest Thompson (Washington Senators). LH. Age 30.

Top of the ninth inning. Two-run homer.

The two games played in Washington were both filled with late-inning drama. The Senators won the first game, though the Red Sox crept closer when Ted's two-run homer in the top of the night scored Pesky ahead of him and brought Boston to within one run. Ted "screamed it far over the right-field wall." (*Herald*) That made the score 5-4 in Washington's favor and the Sox put two more men on the bases before Jake Jones took a 3-2 called strike that ended the game. In the second game, it was the Red Sox who staved off a ninth-inning rally and squeaked in to salvage a 7-6 win.

This was the only homer Thompson gave up to Ted Williams.

218 (#21) August 20 (second game) at Fenway Park. Pitcher: Walt Masterson (Washington Senators). RH. Age 28.

Bottom of the fifth inning. One-run homer.

Five home runs helped the Red Sox take two from the visiting Senators, 5-4 (in 10 innings) and 10-4. Stan Spence's walkoff homer in the first game won that one. It was a game Vern Stephens had tied with a three-run homer in the ninth, Pesky and Williams on base at the time. Dom DiMaggio homered in the second game, as did Bobby Doerr, and Ted Williams hit one into the runway again — the gap between the bleachers and the right-field grandstand seats.

Five home runs were how many Ted bagged off Walt Masterson pitches: #6, 42, 197, 218, and 402.

219 (#22) August 27 at Fenway Park. Pitcher: Marino Pieretti (Chicago White Sox). RH. Age 27.

Bottom of the sixth inning. Three-run homer. GAME WINNER.

Family and friends back home in San Diego no doubt enjoyed seeing the *San Diego Union* headline: WILLIAMS CLOUTS HOMER TO HELP RED SOX WIN, 10-5. The sixth-inning smash broke a 5-5 tie as it "dropped into the right-field bleachers 400 feet from the plate," the accompanying story explained. Ted had come close to hitting a grand slam in the second inning but White Sox centerfielder Dave Philliey backed up to the Boston bullpen and caught the ball. His homer reached the third row of the bleachers, comfortably coming down on the other side of the Chicago bullpen. Frank Bell of Needham was one of many who scrambled for the souvenir; he came out with some scrapes that had to be treated by team doctor Ralph McCarthy, and he didn't even get the ball to show for his effort.

Homers #147, 219, 230, and 253 were all charged to Pieretti.

220 (#23) August 29 (first game) at Fenway Park. Pitcher: Karl Drews (St. Louis Browns). RH. Age 28.

Bottom of the first inning. Three-run homer. GAME WINNER.

Another game-winner for Ted Williams, and this one came early — in the bottom of the first. The final score was uneven, a 10-2 Red Sox win, but it had been a three-run first-inning homer and that sufficed to win the game. Drews had walked Dom DiMaggio on four pitches, then promptly walked Johnny Pesky on four pitches. This left him facing The Thumper. He threw two balls to Ted, but then got one over the plate, and Ted "hit it sky-high. The heavy wind caught the ball and sent it sailing into the concrete bleacher" wiping out the early 1-0 Brownie lead. The second game was a lopsided 12-4 loss for the Red Sox.

This was the only homer Drews gave up to Ted Williams.

221 (#24) September 19 (first game) at Briggs Stadium, Detroit. Pitcher: Dizzy Trout (Detroit Tigers). RH. Age 33.

Top of the ninth inning. One-run homer.

Ted hadn't had a home run in three weeks, and the Sox were jostling for first place. Ironically or otherwise, the day he came through again, they lost two games to the Tigers. They still held a half-game lead, but a precarious one. His homer tied the score in the top of the ninth in the first game, but the game went into extra innings and the Tigers won it in the 12th. Ted was 0-for-3 in the second game (but still batting .376.) The homer had been a deep one, "belted 425 feet into the lower deck in the deepest part of the park, right-center field." The *Herald* account was a little more precise: he hit a 2-0 pitch "high to the wilderness in center field, the ball hitting the top of the 12-foot railing in front of the lower stands a few feet to the center-field spot labeled as 415 feet from home plate and bounding far into the crowd."

Dizzy Trout's six homers: 107, 144, 164, 221, 283, and 324.

222 (#25) October 2 at Fenway Park. Pitcher: Tommy Byrne (New York Yankees). LH. Age 28.

Bottom of the first inning. Two-run homer. GAME WINNER.

It was Saturday, October 2, the 153rd game of the 154-game season. The Red Sox and Yankees were tied at 94-58, both just one game behind the league-leading Cleveland Indians. Whoever lost this day's game would be eliminated, should the Indians win their game — and the Indians did, downing Detroit, 8-0. The Red Sox beat the Yankees, 5-1, behind Jack Kramer's pitching, to remain in contention. Like Kramer, New York's Byrne, and three relievers, only gave up five hits but they walked 11. Ted Williams was walked three times, singled, but first—on a 1-1 pitch with Johnny Pesky on board, having reached on four straight pitches—hit one into the "center-field end of the Yankees bullpen. It was one of those old-time lordly and high affairs." (*Boston Herald*)

This was the only homer Byrne gave up to Ted Williams.

Then there was the homer that Ted *didn't* hit. He didn't hit one in the single-game playoff necessitated after the Indians and Red Sox finished the season in a dead heat. Williams was 1-for-4 in the playoff game and scored once, but the final was 8-3. Even if Ted had homered every time up, and hit four home runs, the Sox would have fallen short, since there was only once he came up with anyone on base—and that was with Pesky on second in the first (and Pesky scored anyway, thanks to Vern Stephens.)

Ted ended 1948, having—as in 1946—seen the Red Sox lose an elimination game. He'd hit 25 homers, the lowest since the 23 he hit in 1940. His 44 doubles led the league and he led in walks, with 126. Both helped him to his sixth season in a row leading in on-base percentage, this time .497. His .369 batting average led the league as did his .615 slugging percentage. He came in third in the MVP voting, with DiMaggio second, and Cleveland's player/manager Lou Boudreau deservedly coming in first. Boudreau had hit two homers in the playoff game and went on to lead his team to win the World Series.

1949

223 **(#1 of 1949)** April 28 at Fenway Park. Pitcher: Jim Wilson (Philadelphia Athletics). RH. Age 27.

Bottom of the fifth inning. Three-run homer.

Just before the Red Sox went on a long 18-game trip, Ted hit a three-run homer for his first of the season to help the team build a 12-5 triumph over the A's. He drove in a run in the first inning with a single. He got another with a bases-loaded walk (one of three walks on the day). And three after he got a reprieve in the fifth—a foul fly ball fell down untouched in between first baseman Ferris Fain and catcher Joe Astroth. Granted new life, he hit a "vivid line drive, across the lusty wind…into the center-field bleachers" and over the bullpen. Thus, five RBIs for Mr. Williams.

Ted smacked three home runs off Jim Wilson. The other two were #448 and 477.

Back in November 1948, Ted had sent a signed baseball to 14-year-old Bob Peterson of Omaha, a polio victim from Stanton, Nebraska. On it he had written, "To Bob Peterson, the first home run of next season will be for you. Lots of luck, Ted Williams." Tom Yawkey had helped arrange it; he was friends with Boston radio personality Johnny Kowalski, whose parents lived in Omaha and had reached Kowalski with the request.[50]

224 (#2) May 1 at Yankee Stadium, New York. Pitcher: Spec Shea (New York Yankees). RH. Age 28.

Top of the sixth inning. Four-run homer. Grand slam #9.

It was Ted's first grand slam at Yankee Stadium. Even Johnny Pesky got into the act with a homer, and the Red Sox beat New York, 11-2. It was another five-RBI day for Williams. In the third inning, he swung at the first pitch and singled. After Parnell singled, and Dom singled, and Pesky beat out a bunt for another single. Williams came up again in the sixth and "again Ted slashed at the first pitch and there never was a doubt as to its four-ply quality. The only question was whether it would get into the upper or lower stands. It landed in the lower deck." (*Boston Post*)

Spec Shea saw Ted hit five home runs: #198, 224, 309, 326, and 328.

225 (#3) May 3 at Briggs Stadium, Detroit. Pitcher: Fred Hutchinson (Detroit Tigers). RH. Age 29.

Top of the fourth inning. Three-run homer.

This game was an extraordinary 13-inning tie game that ended with the score 14-14. It was the second tie game in which Ted Williams homered. And it was a real see-saw battle, with the Red Sox overcoming a 10-4 deficit they faced after three innings. Boston built a 14-11 lead after seven innings, but Detroit's Pat Mullin tripled with the bases loaded in the bottom of the ninth to tie the game. There were no outs at the time, but the Red Sox held the line. Neither team scored in the next four innings, by which time the game had to be called due to darkness. Ted's homer halved the distance from the 10-4 deficit, making it Detroit 10, Boston 7.

Of the eight homers hit off Hutch (#22, 139, 156, 163, 209, 225, 235, and 273), this was the sixth.

226 (#4) May 4 at Briggs Stadium, Detroit. Pitcher: Virgil Trucks (Detroit Tigers). RH. Age 32.

Top of the seventh inning. One-run homer.

The Red Sox lost this game, 5-1—Williams' home run was the only run they scored. It was one of only three hits the Red Sox got off Virgil Trucks. Ted singled for one of the other two hits. The home run was "slapped...far and high into the upper right-center deck." Jack Malaney told *Boston Post* readers where the ball came down: "At the front of the upper deck in right field here, it is only 315 feet from home. Where Ted's home run went in today, it is about 325 feet and the ball landed about 20 feet back in the stand, so it was not much of a wallop for Ted."

Ted's 12 homers off Trucks: 108, 115, 146, 174, 189, 226, 236, 243, 320, 342, 437, and 444.

227 (#5) May 5 at Cleveland Stadium, Cleveland. Pitcher: Bob Feller (Cleveland Indians). RH. Age 30. Hall of Famer.

Top of the eighth inning. One-run homer.

Bob Feller beat the Boston Red Sox, 7-3, throwing a six-hitter. Ted hit a solo home run as leadoff batter in the top of the eighth, knocking it over the right-center field fence which stood at 365 feet from the plate. Cleveland Stadium had a temporary fence that had been installed some years earlier. "Ted led off with a 390-foot blast to deep right center, well over the little wire fence which shortens home run territory greatly in this expansive ball yard." (*Herald*) This was Williams' fourth homer in four consecutive games, but the Red Sox hadn't won even one of the last three.

131, 141, 203, 210, 227, 330, 351, 353, 374, 416—the numbers of Ted's homers off Bob Feller.

228 (#6) May 10 at Sportsman's Park, St. Louis. Pitcher: Red Embree (St. Louis Browns). RH. Age 31.

Top of the first inning. One-run homer.

Ted's homer came with two outs in the top of the first. "Ted Williams' swishing bat and a favoring tail wind put the ball in the right-center-field stand." (*St. Louis Post-Dispatch*) From that point on, Embree pitched shutout ball. The Browns got one run in the third inning and then won it on Gerry Priddy's home run off Chuck Stobbs in the bottom of the ninth.

Ted's four homers = #140, 165, 228, and 246.

229 (#7) May 11 at Comiskey Park, Chicago. Pitcher: Howie Judson (Chicago White Sox). RH. Age 23.

Top of the eighth inning. Two-run homers.

This was the fifth game in which Ted homered but the Red Sox lacked a win. The first was the 14-14 tie, and then followed four losses including this one. The White Sox scored one or more runs in every inning, winning 12-8. Bobby Doerr quite uncharacteristically committed three of Boston's four errors. Johnny Pesky singled and Ted hit one about 370 feet. It was, the *Herald* wrote, "a long poke into a stiff gale" which the *Chicago Tribune* said was "looped into the lower right-field seats."

Judson gave up a remarkable five home runs to Ted in one year—1949: #229, 248, 255, 256, and 262. He later also gave up #300.

230 (#8) May 18 at Fenway Park. Pitcher: Marino Pieretti (Chicago White Sox). RH. Age 28.

Bottom of the third inning. Two-run homer. GAME WINNER.

Finally came a game in which Ted Williams homered and the Red Sox won. It was his homer that was the game-winning hit. The score was 7-4, Boston. Ted's was the game-winner, with Dom on board, "a tremendous belt about 10 rows up in the right field stands—a lordly poke with plenty of carry." (*Herald*)

Marino Pieretti gave up four homers to Ted Williams: #147, 219, 230, and 253.

Why did bat speed matter? Ted referred to the Bernoulli effect, developed by 18th-century Swiss mathematician Daniel Bernoulli, which told him why a curve ball curved, and also was the fundamental principle on which aviation is based. "Here's where it helped me with hitting. You can take a 20-ounce bat and move it at 50 miles an hour, say, and you've got a 1,000 factor there, and you can take a 35-ounce bat and move it at 20 miles an hour, and you've only got 700 at the end result of the swing. So there's more power in a light bat going faster than a heavy bat going slower....So what's the advantage of the lighter bat. You can wait longer. Understand that? The lighter bat goes faster. Even if you don't hit the ball any father, you're going to be able to wait longer and be fooled less." [51]

231 (#9) May 24 at Fenway Park. Pitcher: Art Houtteman (Detroit Tigers). RH. Age 21.

Bottom of the first inning. One-run homer.

Ted struck out in the eighth inning and showed his displeasure with himself by flinging his bat high in the air; fortunately plate umpire Joe Paparella claimed not to have seen it — and did say after the game that Williams hadn't said a negative word to him. It put a sour ending on a good day for Ted. He'd "homered into the chummy left-field netting, doubled high off the left-field wall, and doubled to his favorite right sector." The Tigers scored twice in the ninth to tie the score, and one in the top of the tenth to take a 7-6 lead, but Dominic and Johnny got on board, Williams advanced them both with a high-bounding grounder, and Doerr's bloop hit scored both for a walkoff win. It was "the teammates" in action.

Houtteman was hit hard — six home runs: #231 (this one) and 239, 249, 275, 285, and 350.

232 (#10) May 28 at Fenway Park. Pitcher: Dick Welteroth (Washington Senators). RH. Age 21.

Bottom of the fifth inning. One-run homer. GAME WINNER.

The Red Sox scored four runs in the third inning and the Senators matched that with four in the bottom of the fourth. The score tied, Williams strode to the plate in the bottom of the fifth. He swung at relief pitcher Dick Welteroth's first pitch of the frame, and hit "a high drive which dropped into the bullpen reserved for visiting firemen." Tex Hughson, working out of the Red Sox pen, threw four innings of shutout ball and so Ted's blow held up as the hit that won the game.

Welteroth also surrendered #207.

233 (#11) May 29 at Fenway Park. Pitcher: Paul Calvert (Washington Senators). RH. Age 31.

Bottom of the eighth inning. One-run homer.

This was the only homer ever Calvert gave up to Ted Williams. Calvert was born in Montreal. His 6-17 record put him first in the league in losses in 1949, though this game was one of his wins (Washington won the game, 10-4) and the solo home run was easily one he could spot the Red Sox. The Red Sox had actually spotted the Senators a 10-0 lead and even the hardiest of Red Sox fans, who often stayed to see Ted Williams get "one more time up," had left the park. In the bottom of the eight, Ted "detoured a Paul Calvert 'highball' into the visitors' bullpen…for the first Boston run." It may have sparked a rally of sorts; the Red Sox scored three more times in the ninth but were in way too deep a hole to climb out from.

234 (#12) May 30 (second game) at Fenway Park. Pitcher: Carl Scheib (Philadelphia Athletics). RH. Age 22.

Bottom of the eighth inning. Two-run homer. GAME WINNER.

Ted hit his 11th homer of the month. The Red Sox won both games of the Memorial Day doubleheader, 10-2 and 4-3, but Ted hadn't helped much until the eighth inning of the second game. In fact, he grounded out three times in a row. "I pitched him curveballs low and inside and got him out three times at bat. A story later was that he told the guys on the bench, if I started him again on curveballs, he would hit a home run…and he did. It beat me in the ball game."[52] The Athletics had just scored twice in the top of the eight of game two to take a 3-2 lead. Johnny Pesky walked on five pitches in the bottom of the eighth. The *Boston Herald* set the stage for Ted Williams: "He was due. He hadn't hit the ball out of the infield all day. He had walked twice in the first game but had slapped harsh drives into double plays twice in the opener and been thrown out by the over-shifted Philadelphia infield three times in the nightcap." Ted swung at Scheib's first pitch and connected. "The towering drive stayed up long enough to give the fans a thrill. When it came down it was well over the screen in front of the Sox bullpen."

In 1947, Williams hit #179 and 192 off Scheib. All three were hit at Fenway Park. Sadly, he never hit a homer off Scheib at Shibe Park.

235 (#13) June 4 at Briggs Stadium, Detroit. Pitcher: Fred Hutchinson (Detroit Tigers). RH. Age 29.

Top of the first inning. Three-run homer.

The day before in Cleveland, Ted had three times swung at a first pitch and each time grounded out weakly in the infield. The June 4 game had its ups and downs. A three-run homer in the first caromed off the right-field façade in front of the second deck, the skyview seats. The Red Sox got off to a 7-1 lead but the Tigers kept coming back. Boston still held a 9-6 lead after 7 ½ innings. But Red Sox pitchers, throughout the game, kept walking Detroit batters—including walking Connie Berry (who was batting .085) with the bases load for a 10th run, which won them the game.

Homers allowed by Fred Hutchinson: #22, 139, 156, 163, 209, 225, 235, and 273.

236 (#14) June 5 (first game) at Briggs Stadium, Detroit. Pitcher: Virgil Trucks (Detroit Tigers). RH. Age 32.

Top of the first inning. Two-run homer.

The Red Sox won the first game, 5-3, and lost the second, 11-5. Ted's homer "landed well into the upper tier of stands in right field." (*Boston Herald*) It gave the Sox a 2-0 lead right from the start of the game through the midway point. The Tigers then scored three times in the bottom of the fifth to take the lead, but then Boston came back with another pair in the top of the sixth—and added another run in the eighth.

Ted hit an even dozen 12 homers off Trucks: 108, 115, 146, 174, 189, 226, 236, 243, 320, 342, 437, and 444.

Ted Williams: [Birdie Tebbetts] came as close as anybody to get me to tip my hat. We were on the train to Boston after a series in Chicago and he and

Bobby Doerr and Joe Reichler of the Associated Press—one of the most accurate journalists I have known—were giving me the business, telling me how I could be Mayor of Boston if I would just once acknowledge the cheers. I said, 'No, I can't. It wouldn't be me.' Birdie said, 'OK, I've got a better idea. How you can really put one over on 'em. The next time you hit a home run, tip your hat and smile and look up at them, and while they're cheering and you're smiling, you yell, 'Go to hell, you S.O.B.'s.' They won't know what you're saying. That kind of appealed to me a little bit, and I said I might just do it. But there was a rainout the next day, and by the time I hit my next home run, the day after, the mood had passed."[53]

237 (#15) June 17 (second game) at Fenway Park. Pitcher: Bill Wight (Chicago White Sox). LH. Age 27.

Bottom of the third inning. Three–run homer.

The Red Sox took two from the White Sox by scores of 4-3 and 10-8. Chicago's Bill Wight was pounced on in the third inning for two homers, seven hits, and six runs. Hitchcock doubled and Pesky singled, Hitchcock unable to score. Ted Williams "whacked a high inside curve well into the bleachers in right center." Matt Batts hit a two-run homer later in the inning.

This was one of two homers Wight gave up to Ted Williams. The other was #392.

238 (#16) June 19 at Fenway Park. Pitcher: Randy Gumpert (Chicago White Sox). RH. Age 30.

Bottom of the seventh inning. Three-run homer.

Chuck Stobbs won a 9-2, his first major-league win. Both Dom DiMaggio and Ted hit three-run homers. Rookie outfielder Herb Adams crashed hard into the fence in front of the Fenway Park bullpen "in a vain attempt to reach Williams' high hoist...Adams bounced back across the cinder path and went down and out, his badly-cut head streaming blood." (*Boston Herald*)

This was Ted's first homer off Gumpert in 1949. In 1951, he hit another pair. The four home runs: 238, 261, 313, and 323.

239 (#17) June 21 at Fenway Park. Pitcher: Art Houtteman (Detroit Tigers). RH. Age 21.

Bottom of the sixth inning. Three-run homer.

The Tigers scored once in the top of the first, but Mel Parnell held them at bay from that point on and the next seven runs all came off the bats of the Red Sox. Ted's supplied the last three of the seven runs. It was a "high wind-blown poke which looked like a long fly when it left the bat but which ultimately landed in the third row of the center-field bleachers about 430 feet from the plate." (*Herald*)

Houtteman homers: #231, 239, 249, 275, 285, 350.

240 (#18) June 24 at Fenway Park. Pitcher: Joe Ostrowski (St. Louis Browns). LH. Age 32.

Bottom of the first inning. Three-run homer. GAME WINNER.

It was really a slaughter: Boston Red Sox 21, St. Louis Browns 2. Given the final score, the three runs Ted drove in were enough to win the game, though the Sox added 18 more before it was all over. The first of Ted's two homers was "a terrific wallop which landed about eight rows up in the center-field stands." (*Boston Post*) The *Globe* thought it landed about 15 rows up. Ellis Kinder held the Browns to two runs and five hits.

This was the only homer Ted hit off Ostrowski in his career, but not the only one he hit in the June 24 game. See #241.

241 (#19) June 24 at Fenway Park. Pitcher: Ray Shore (St. Louis Browns). RH. Age 28.

Bottom of the seventh inning. One-run homer.

Ted's second home run of the game was just additional icing on the cake. It was "a line drive which went into the right-field end of the grandstand." (*Post*) A third of the runs—seven of the 21—were batted in by Williams. Home run #240 had given the Red Sox enough runs to win the game.

This was the only homer Ted hit off Shore.

242 (#20) July 10 (second game) at Fenway Park. Pitcher: Dick Fowler (Philadelphia Athletics). RH. Age 28.

Bottom of the fourth inning. One-run homer.

The Red Sox won two games, 8-5 and 11-10, running a winning streak to seven games in a row. The homer went deep into the tenth row of the right-field grandstand. Matt Batts and Bobby Doerr each drove in three runs, in the second game. Given the one-run margin, each run made a difference in the end. The game-winner came when Batts drove in Billy Goodman in the fourth. The one run Ted drove in came on a "a high belt into the curving right-field pavilion sector." The Red Sox had already scored eight runs before the fourth inning had begun.

The following day it became known that Ted had fractured a rib on July 4 at Yankee Stadium. He'd been scheduled to take part in a home-run hitting contest before a charity benefit game against the Boston Braves on July 11, but was unable to.

Ted hadn't hit a homer off Fowler since 1942, but he hit his third one on this day. He later hit #252, 267, and 295. The first two had been #91 and 105.

243 (#21) July 16 at Briggs Stadium, Detroit. Pitcher: Virgil Trucks (Detroit Tigers). RH. Age 32.

Top of the first inning. Two-run homer. GAME WINNER.

Ted bunted safely toward third base against the shift. But before that, his two-run homer got the Sox enough runs to win the 11-1 game. Pesky had reached on an error and Williams hit a Trucks fastball "about 12 rows back in the upper right-center tier." Tebbetts, Zarilla, and Doerr all homered for the Red Sox, too. It was Ted's third homer of the year off Virgil Trucks and his seventh of the year against Tiger pitching. In the fourth inning, with a shift on, he "bunted the first pitch down toward the third base and didn't even have to hurry to get himself a base hit." (*Boston Post*) He later hit another towering smash, but it came down in from of the stands in right-center and became an out.

244 (#22) July 20 at Comiskey Park, Chicago. Pitcher: Bob Kuzava (Chicago White Sox). LH. Age 26.

Top of the ninth inning. Three-run homer.

There was a lot of late scoring in this game. Ted's three-run homer into the lower left-field tier at Comiskey tied the game, 7-7, but Chicago scored a run in the bottom of the ninth on a triple, two intentional walks, and a sacrifice fly to right field.

Ted later hit his 296th home run off Kuzava.

245 (#23) July 22 at Sportsman's Park, St. Louis. Pitcher: Ned Garver (St. Louis Browns). RH. Age 23.

Top of the eighth inning. One-run homer.

Vern Stephens hit a homer to left in the second. Ted Williams hit one "high atop the right-center roof" to lead off the eighth, and the Red Sox beat the Browns behind Mel Parnell, 4-2. Stephens was leading the league in homers with 24, one more than Williams. Ted was batting an even .333.

#213, 245, 272, 282, 337, 375, 385, 422, 436, and 459 — the 10 homers Ted hit off Ned.

246 (#24) July 23 at Sportsman's Park, St. Louis. Pitcher: Red Embree (St. Louis Browns). RH. Age 31.

Top of the third inning. Two-run homer.

Doerr hit two homers and Williams hit one. The Red Sox handily beat the Browns, 16-5. Pesky had bunted to get on base in the third and Williams "belted his round-tripper onto the roof of the right-field seats, on a two-nothing serve." St. Louis catcher Sherm Lollar said that Williams had been "barbering" as he stepped into the batter's box, saying, "This guy really bothers me, throws slow stuff…then faster, mixes 'em up. It isn't that he's tough, but he's bothersome…." Then, BAM!

The four Embree home runs: #140, 165, 228, and 246.

247 (#25) July 24 (first game) at Sportsman's Park, St. Louis. Pitcher: Tom Ferrick (St. Louis Browns). RH. Age 34.

Top of the seventh inning. Two-run homer.

The Red Sox battled back from being down 7-1, even taking the lead in the seventh with a five-run inning. Ted's two-run homer "into the left-field stands" (*Post*) was part of the rally. The three runs he drove in during the first game put him at 100 RBIs, leading the league. His 25th homer also put him first, and he was first in base hits and runs scored, and tied for tops in batting average. His 25th homer matched his total for all of 1947. But the Browns scored twice in the eighth and won, 9-8. Boston won the day's second game, 8-4.

Ferrick furnished homers #77, 130, 247, and 304.

248 (#26) July 28 at Fenway Park. Pitcher: Howie Judson (Chicago White Sox.) RH. Age 23.

Bottom of the fifth inning. One-run homer.

Ted's 26th home run was hit "on a dead line 420 feet into the lower corner center field bleachers." The *Boston Post* agreed: "a tremendous wallop which went into the corner of the center-field bleachers just a few feet from the 420-foot marker."

This was the second of the five homers Howie gave up to Ted Williams in 1949: #229, 248, 255, 256, and 262. He later also gave up #300.

249 (#27) August 7 at Fenway Park. Pitcher: Art Houtteman (Detroit Tigers). RH. Age 21.

Bottom of the seventh inning. One-run homer.

Houtteman beat Mickey McDermott and the Red Sox, 6-4. Ted Williams had a single and a double, and he "pulled one into the right-field stands over Mr. Wertz's head" in the seventh for the second of the Sox runs. They added two in the bottom of the ninth, but two was not enough.

Hit off Houtteman: #231, 239, 249, 275, 285, 350.

Unhappy about hitting a home run? It's hard to know if this is the home run that visiting team batboy George Sullivan had in mind when he re-told the story. He had thought the pitcher might have been Fred Hutchison, but he put it against the Tigers at Fenway in August 1949 and thought it had been after the sixth inning. He'd had to duck into the Red Sox clubhouse to get some fresh towels (the visiting clubhouse was next to the Sox clubhouse in those days), and he saw Ted hit the homer. "I was dying to see his reaction as he came back and down the stairs. Among the first things they were saying to him was, 'What kind of pitch was it?' He was ticked off. He had hit a ball that was not a strike. 'I never should have swung at the ball. Lousy pitch.' That hit me as a 15-year-old. I loved the guy. But here was a titanic home run that probably was going to win the game. And he was mad about it. At the very least, unhappy about it."[54] The artistry had been lacking and he'd swung at a bad pitch.

250 (#28) August 9 at Fenway Park. Pitcher: Vic Raschi (New York Yankees). RH. Age 30.

Bottom of the third inning. Two-run homer. GAME-WINNER.

The Sox won, 6-3, Ellis Kinder improving his record to 13-5, Williams driving in the fourth and fifth runs of the game after Pesky doubled in the bottom of the third. Ted "parked his 28th homer of the year into the Red Sox bullpen in right-center." (*Herald*) It was hit, the *Globe* wrote, on a direct line.

The Yankees' Raschi donated five homers to the cause: HRs #250, 266, 292, 293, and 321.

251 (#29) August 11 at Fenway Park. Pitcher: Allie Reynolds (New York Yankees). RH. Age 32.

Bottom of the first inning. One-run homer.

Ted had two singles and reached on an error, but his biggest hit was, of course, the homer he hit into the Red Sox bullpen in the first inning. That accounted for the first run of the game. Twice the Yankees overcame three-run deficits, but Ted scored the winning run on his single in the sixth after he advanced to second on Vern Stephens' walk and Bobby Doerr drove him in. The final score was 7-6, Sox. Mel Parnell was now 17-6.

Six home runs Ted hit off Reynolds: #199, 216, 251, 265, 290, and 344.

252 (#30) August 17 at Shibe Park, Philadelphia. Pitcher: Dick Fowler (Philadelphia Athletics). RH. Age 28.

Top of the first inning. One-run homer.

It was another first-inning homer, this one on the road and off Dick Fowler, who'd allowed the hit and the homer that had boosted him over .400 on the final day of the 1941 season. It was an important run in the game, hit "into 20th Street, far over the right-field wall" since it was the only one the Red Sox scored through the first nine innings. Had Ted not hit it, Fowler would have shut out the Sox. Chuck Stobbs allowed one run, too, and the game went into the 10th.

The fourth of six homers: Ted also touched Fowler for #91, 105, 242, 267, and 295.

253 (#31) August 26 (first game) at Comiskey Park, Chicago. Pitcher: Marino Pieretti (Chicago White Sox). RH. Age 28.

Top of the seventh. One-run homer.

The Red Sox beat the White Sox twice, 11-4 and 10-7. The first game gave Mel Parnell his 20th win (he became 20-6). Boston only had five runs when Ted led off the seventh with a solo home run, serving at the time as a significant insurance run. The *Chicago Tribune*'s Edward Burns wrote, "Ted tagged one of Chico Pieretti's specials for a smash against the upper-deck balustrade." The balustrade separated Comiskey's upper and lower tiers in right field.

The second homer Marino granted Ted in 1949. His earlier three were #147, 219, and 230.

254 (#32) August 26 (first game) at Comiskey Park, Chicago. Pitcher: Max Surkont (Chicago White Sox). RH. Age 27.

Top of the ninth inning. One-run homer.

This home run landed in the lower seats in right field. The score being 8-4 at the time, it wasn't essential—but every run counts, even the two scored later in the top of the ninth. Ted had three hits in both games of the double-header, with a pair of RBIs in each game.

This was the only homer Ted hit off Surkont.

255 (#33) August 27 at Comiskey Park, Chicago. Pitcher: Howie Judson (Chicago White Sox). RH. Age 23.

Top of the fifth inning. Two-run homer.

For the second day in a row, Ted hit two home runs. He drove in five of the seven runs in the 7-2 win. With one out in the top of the fifth, and Dom DiMaggio on second, the White Sox elected to pitch to Williams even with first base open. That was a mistake. "The Kid promptly parked his 33rd homer well into the lower right-center tier for a 2-1 lead." It was a 400-foot drive, newspapers agreed, and landed about 15 rows deep in the stands.

On August 27, Judson gave up two more of the five 1949 homers he allowed Ted Williams. The full list: #229, 248, 255, 256, and 262. He later also gave up #300.

256 (#34) August 27 at Comiskey Park, Chicago. Pitcher: Howie Judson (Chicago White Sox). RH. Age 23.

Top of the eighth inning. Three-run homer.

It was 4-2 Red Sox heading into the eighth. Stobbs and Pesky were on the bases; Ted hit Judson's fast ball "on a bee line" into the same lower right-center tier. This gave Boston their final three runs.

This was the second August 27 homer, which added to five RBIs during a 7-2 Red Sox win.

257 (#35) August 29 (second game) at Cleveland Stadium, Cleveland. Pitcher: Mike Garcia (Cleveland Indians). RH. Age 25.

Top of the seventh inning. Two-run homer.

The Sox had lost the first game, 5-2, but had some hope in the second game when Dom DiMaggio singled to lead off the seventh and Ted Williams homered over the right-field fence to break a 2-2 tie and give Boston the lead. But the Indians tied it with two in the bottom of the ninth, then won it with another run in the tenth.

This was the first of six homers Ted hit off Mike: see also 284, 314, 325, 331, and 380.

258 (#36) August 31 at Briggs Stadium, Detroit. Pitcher: Lou Kretlow (Detroit Tigers). RH. Age 28.

Top of the ninth inning. Two-run homer.

Bobby Doerr's two-run homer was the game-winner, giving the Red Sox a 5-4 lead. Ted's two-run homer "off a girder high in the upper deck of the right-field stands" (*Herald*) provided welcome insurance for reliever Tex Hughson to close out the game and get a win for Sox starter Chuck Stobbs. The win put the Red Sox just two games behind the Indians in the American League standings.

This was the only homer Ted hit off Kretlow.

259 (#37) September 3 at Fenway Park. Pitcher: Bubba Harris (Philadelphia Athletics). RH. Age 23.

Bottom of the eighth inning. One-run homer.

With this 10-3 win, despite walking six, Ellis Kinder had won 14 consecutive decisions in a row dating back to June 9. Everyone in the Red Sox lineup got at least one hit. Ted's home run into the screen over the left-field wall—it even went to the left of the light tower—was the *coup de grace*, providing the tenth and final run of the game.

This was the only homer Ted hit off this Harris.

260 (#38) September 14 at Fenway Park. Pitcher: Hal Newhouser (Detroit Tigers). LH. Age 28.

Bottom of the sixth inning. One-run homer. GAME WINNER.

The Red Sox won the game, and Kinder collected his 20th win. It would seem that all was good—but they lost ground because the Yankees played two and won them both. Ted's home run was pretty significant; in fact, it was the only run of the whole game. Kinder threw a six-hit shutout. Newhouser threw a four-hitter but one of the hits was the home run. Like #37, this one also went to left field. With homer #38, Williams had tied his career high in the homer department. It was also Ted's 145th run batted in of the year, tying his personal best (1939). It was "a high fly to the right of the scoreboard in left."

Ted hit two earlier homers off Newhouser: 122 and 145.

261 (#39) September 18 at Fenway Park. Pitcher: Randy Gumpert (Chicago White Sox). RH. Age 30.

Bottom of the first inning. Two-run homer.

The Red Sox won the game, 11-5, and Ted Williams drove in six runs. Dom DiMaggio doubled in the bottom of the first inning, and Ted hit a 2-0 slow pitch "ten rows up into the section that starts the grandstand in right field." Today we would call that Section 1. It was his 39th home run of the year and tied him with teammate Vern Stephens at 150 RBIs apiece, putting him one homer up on Stephens, who—waiting in the on-deck circle—had 38. So Stephens homered to left field, re-tying Ted at 39, but taking the RBI lead with 151. And the Red Sox had a 3-0 lead. Ted's two-RBI single in the second inning gave him 152 RBIs.

This was Ted's second homer off Gumpert in 1949. In 1951, he hit another pair. The four home runs: 238, 261, 313, and 323.

262 (#40) September 18 at Fenway Park. Pitcher: Howie Judson (Chicago White Sox). RH. Age 23.

Bottom of the fourth inning. Two-run homer.

This homer evened up Ted's home and away totals; he'd now hit 20 on the road and 20 at home. His 40th home run inched him one ahead of Stephens again, and he'd added two more RBIs. The homer was hit on a 2-1 count "low and fast down the right-field line. The ball crashed against the screen extending out into fair territory off the foul line pole up about 12 feet and caromed into the stands." (*Boston Herald*) The Red Sox were 2½ games behind New York with only ten games left on their schedule.

1949-50 – Boston Red Sox Ted Williams crossing home plate in front of Chicago White Sox catcher Eddie Malone (#28) as Boston Red Sox Vern Stephens (#5) and unknown umpire look on at Fenway Park. (probably July 28 or September 18, 1949)

Judson gave up a remarkable five home runs in one year—1949, for a total of ten RBIs. This was the fifth. They were #229, 248, 255, 256, and 262. He later also gave up #300.

263 (#41) September 21 at Fenway Park. Pitcher: Steve Gromek (Cleveland Indians). RH. Age 29.

Bottom of the seventh inning. One-run homer. GAME WINNER.

Initially down, 4-1, the Sox caught up and went ahead, but were tied, 6-6, at the time of the seventh-inning stretch. Williams homered a 2-1 pitch into the Red Sox bullpen, inches over Luke Easter's glove. There was one on board. The final score was 9-6, and it was the seventh win in a row (as well as the 19th consecutive at Fenway Park.)

Gromek surrendered homers #115, 155, 205, 263, 437, and 354.

264 (#42) September 24 at Fenway Park. Pitcher: Eddie Lopat (New York Yankees). LH. Age 31.

Bottom of the third inning. One-run homer.

The Red Sox continued to fight for the flag, pulling to within one game of the Yankees in the battle for first place. Ellis Kinder threw a 3-0 six-hit shutout. The Red Sox scored two runs in the second. Ted's first-pitch home run into the 15th row (*Globe*) or the 23rd row (*Herald*) of the right-field grandstand seats.

Ted hit homer #393 off Lopat, after Eddie went to the Orioles on July 30, 1955.

265 (#43) September 25 at Fenway Park. Pitcher: Allie Reynolds (New York Yankees). RH. Age 32.

Bottom of the seventh inning. Two-run homer.

Mel Parnell threw a four-hit, 4-1 win over the Yankees and pulled into a first-place tie with New York. The Sox had a 2-1 lead through six innings. The score was "tight as a miser's fist" until Ted's two-run homer provided welcome insurance. He swung at Reynolds' first pitch and sent it 15 rows deep into Section 2, a "soaring drive deep into the curved wing of the right-field grandstand." (*Herald*) "That was the first fast ball I threw that fellow all afternoon," Reynolds said. "I mean the first fast ball that was over the plate. It was on the inside and about four inches above his knees. It looked good starting out, but you never know what's going to happen when he swings."

The most homers Ted hit in a single season were the 43 he hit in 1949. This was #43 of the year. Two of them came off Reynolds, this one and #251. There were two 1948 homers off Reynolds (#199 and 216), and two later ones (#290 and 344).

This was the last year that Ted led the league in homers. He still had many home runs to come, but—for a variety of reasons—only in 1957 did he exceed 30 homers in a season. In 1949, he came as close as one could to winning a third Triple Crown—something no batter has ever done. His 43 homers did lead the league and so did his 159 RBIs, which also stands as his personal best. He drew 162 walks, matching his total from 1947. And he was named the American League MVP for the season time. But he fell just short in batting average.

He hit .343 and so did George Kell—but if one extends to more decimal places, Kell takes the lead and was indeed honored as the leader. Kell's average was .3429 to Ted's .34275. If Ted had made one less out or had made one more hit, things would have come out otherwise. Kell had three homers to Ted's 43, and 100 fewer runs batted in—59 to Ted's 159. But for batting average, he came out on top. In terms of on-base percentage, Williams was .490 and Kell was .424, because Williams drew those 162 bases on balls and Kell walked 71 times. It was the seventh year in a row that Williams had led the league in OBP.

It's remarkable to note that from 1941 through 1949, Williams' on-base percentage was .5026—more than half the time he came to the plate, he reached base safely.

1950

266 (**#1 of 1950**) April 19 (first game) at Fenway Park. Pitcher: Vic Raschi (New York Yankees). RH. Age 31.

Bottom of the third inning. Two-run homer. GAME WINNER.

It was a chilly Patriots' Day morning game against the visiting team from New York and the Red Sox won it, 6-3. Building on a 2-0 lead, the Sox scored two more in the third after Pesky walked and Williams hit his first homer of the year, "well stroked because it had to soar through a stiff east wind before it dropped into the Yankees bullpen." (*Herald*) Williams was 1-for-3 with three walks. The Yankees won the 3:00 PM afternoon game, 16-7. Ted was 1-for-2 with two walks.

Ted kicked off Patriots Day with a homer run off Vic Raschi. He hit five in all off the New York right-hander: #250, 266, 292, 293, and 321.

267 (**#2**) April 30 (first game) at Fenway Park. Pitcher: Dick Fowler (Philadelphia Athletics). RH. Age 29.

Bottom of the second inning. Three-run homer.

The Red Sox swept a doubleheader from the Athletics by two very different scores, 19-0 and 6-5. They'd held a 5-0 lead at one point in the second game, but only barely won it. The first game was clearly another story. With Joe Dobson throwing a five-hit shutout, the four runs the Red Sox scored in the first inning were enough to win the game, with Johnny Pesky's triple after Dom's leadoff walk being the game-winner. Ted singled in Johnny. Both Dom and Johnny walked in the second inning, and Ted homered for three more runs. It landed in one of his favorite spots, the runway between the bleachers and the right-field grandstand.

This was #5 off Dick Fowler, the others being 91, 105, 242, 252, and 295.

268 (#3) April 30 (first game) at Fenway Park. Pitcher: Harry Byrd (Philadelphia Athletics). RH. Age 25.

Bottom of the fourth inning. Three-run homer.

A third consecutive walk to DiMaggio and then a single by Pesky put two men on the bases when Ted came up in the fourth, and he homered them both in again, hitting it 10 rows into the bleachers over the bullpen (there was some difference of opinion as to which team's bullpen but there's no doubt it was hit deep into the stands.) This accounted for three runs in the 11-run fourth. He walked his second time up in the inning. Ted had seven RBIs in the first game.

Ted neither homered nor drove in a run in the second game, though he scored two runs and advanced baserunners a couple of other times.

Byrd was another pitcher who gave up five home runs to The Thumper. They were #268, 340, 360, 367, and 381.

Catcher Neil Watlington told a story he'd heard after he got to the majors. "We, the Philadelphia A's, had a pitcher named Harry Byrd, who proclaimed that he was going to see how Ted hit laying flat on his back. He found out—the first time Byrd faced him, he knocked him down—Ted got up, brushed himself off, and proceeded to hit the next pitch nine miles out of the park." [55]

269 (#4) May 2 at Fenway Park. Pitcher: Gene Bearden (Cleveland Indians). LH. Age 29.

Bottom of the seventh inning. One-run homer.

It was a 6-1 win on a Ladies Day at the park. Ted's solo home run produced the sixth and final run. It was a liner into the Indians bullpen. His game was marred by his first strikeout of the season. As he had in 1941, Williams finished the season with more home runs than strikeouts. McDermott pitched a four-hitter.

The pitcher who won the 1948 playoff game for the Indians gave up the first of two home runs to Ted Williams. The other was #301. He was with the Tigers by then.

Ted Williams, on guesswork: "A pitcher at work, he believed, tended to fall into observable patterns. A certain succession of movements was a tipoff that a certain pitch was coming. Given a particular situation and a particular count, he would go to a particular pitch. Most pitchers, he discovered, would go to their 'out' pitch, the pitch they wanted the batter to swing at, one a 2-2 count. He discovered that if a run-of-the-mill pitcher struck him out, he would never come back with the same pitch, in a key situation, during the same game. A good pitcher, on the other hand, would almost always come back with it on Ted's very next time at bat—possibly because the pitcher had more confidence in throwing his best pitch against Ted and possibly because he figured Ted would not be looking for it again. As a result, time after time, Ted was able to go back to the bench after striking out and predict a home run on his next time at bat." [56]

270 (#5) May 5 at Fenway Park. Pitcher: Billy Pierce (Chicago White Sox). LH. Age 23.

Bottom of the seventh inning. Two-run homer. GAME WINNER.

"You see, it's like this. You get the guy out a couple of times and the law of averages is bound to catch up with you. That Williams is quite a hitter and you just can't keep getting him out forever."—White Sox starter Billy Pierce. He'd already struck Ted out once and got him to pop up to third base with the bases loaded in the fourth. The teams were tied, 2-2, in the seventh when Pesky drew a walk and Williams hit a curve that didn't curve into the lower seats in Section 1 out in right field.

The other homer Pierce provided Ted was #356.

Third time around was sometimes magic for Williams. He'd had more than enough opportunities to suss out the pitcher. And he was ready for revenge. He even allowed, "Nothing pleases me more than to get a second chance to a pitcher who got me out on something he thought had fooled me. I couldn't *wait* to get up again, because I knew he would throw it again."[57]

271 (#6) May 6 at Fenway Park. Pitcher: Ken Holcombe (Chicago White Sox). RH. Age 31

Bottom of the first inning. Three-run homer. GAME WINNER.

Ted's homer over the left-center-field wall was the first of six home runs hit by Red Sox batters as they battered the White Sox, 11-1. Birdie Tebbetts hit two homers, and Vern Stephens, Dom DiMaggio, and Bobby Doerr each hit one. Chuck Stobbs more or less cruised to victory, only allowing four hits.

Holcombe was later hit for homers #279 and 310.

272 (#7) May 7 (first game) at Fenway Park. Pitcher: Ned Garver (St. Louis Browns). RH. Age 24.

Bottom of the third inning. One-run homer.

It was a "clean sweep of a sloppy double header" as the Sox took two from the St. Louis Browns, 8-6 and 6-2. The Browns committed four errors in the first game, and were described by the *Globe* as "a bush league outfit posing as major leaguers." Dom DiMaggio tripled to lead off the third; he scored on Pesky's sac fly. And then Ted homered, making it 4-3 in favor of the Red Sox. It was "a well-tagged drive which landed 20 rows deep into the right-field grandstand." (*Herald*)

#213, 245, 272, 282, 337, 375, 385, 422, 436, and 459. Those were the 10 homers Garver gave up to Williams.

273 (#8) May 11 (first game) at Fenway Park. Pitcher: Fred Hutchinson (Detroit Tigers). RH. Age 30.

Bottom of the eighth inning. Four-run homer. Grand slam #10.

One might think a grand slam in the bottom of the eighth would just about sew up a game for the Red Sox. Well it might, but not this day. The Tigers already had a 13-0 lead at that point. The ball just made it out, hopping out of Vic Wertz's glove and over the Tigers' bullpen fence. Hutchinson said, "I'm not sore about the home run. Wertz had the ball in his glove, but it fell out when he hit the railing. But I am sore about the two walks I gave before the home run. I just couldn't get the ball over."

The Red Sox also lost the second game, 5-3, the first time in 19 doubleheaders that the Red Sox had been swept. The four RBIs gave Ted 26, in 15 games. But he wasn't happy. He committed a fielding error in the first game and another in the second game, and responded to the boos and catcalls with rude gestures in three directions, and he spat once toward the crowd. He was quote in the next morning's *Globe*, saying, "I don't mind the errors, but those ---- ---- fans, they can -------- ----- and you can quote me in all the papers. They're ------, ------."

Hutch's homers: #22, 139, 156, 163, 209, 225, 235, and 273.

Years later, Ted wrote of the incident and the way the fans got on him, "I'd have been better off striking out."[58] Bob Feller understood why Williams found it hard to countenance the fickle fans. "The fans would let him have it one day, and then cheer the next day when he pumps one out of the park."[59]

274 (#9) May 13 at Fenway Park. Pitcher: Sid Hudson (Washington Senators). RH. Age 35.

Bottom of the sixth inning. One-run homer.

It was Birdie Tebbetts' 1,000th game in the American League and a 5-4 Red Sox victory, which he'd provided with a single to drive in Doerr with the tiebreaker in the bottom of the eighth. Boston had built a 4-0 lead, with Ted's leadoff homer in the sixth accounting for the third run and first baseman Walt Dropo's homer later that inning accounting for the fourth. Four

Senators runs in the top of the seventh brought them even. Dropo's had been hit into the screen in left-center. Ted's hit the top of the screen behind the Red Sox bullpen and hit with such force that "it bounced 75 feet back on the field of play." (*Herald*)

The Senators righty had previously allowed homers #40, 116, and 274.

275 (#10) May 16 at Briggs Stadium, Detroit. Pitcher: Art Houtteman (Detroit Tigers). RH. Age 22.

Top of the third inning. Two-run homer. GAME WINNER.

Ted's first nine homers of the year had all come at home. This one came in his favorite homer haven, Briggs Stadium in Detroit. And so did #11. Ted hit two homers in the same, and so did Vern "Junior" Stephens. Both of Ted's were two-run homers. Both of Junior's were solo home runs. Between them, they accounted for all the Red Sox runs in the 6-1 win.

Ted hit Art Houtteman for homers numbered 231, 239, 249, 275, 285, and 350.

276 (#11) May 16 at Briggs Stadium, Detroit. Pitcher: Hal White (Detroit Tigers). RH. Age 31.

Top of the ninth inning. Two-run homer.

Both of Ted's home runs went into the upper right-field deck, against a stiff wind, and both times Al Zarilla was on board at the time, first with a single and then with a walk. For Joe Dobson, it was his 100th career win.

Hal's other homer was #191.

277 (#12) June 2 at Fenway Park. Pitcher: Al Benton (Cleveland Indians). RH. Age 39.

Bottom of the second inning. One-run homer.

Ted Williams was "cheered tumultuously every time he so much as lifted a finger" as he hit the first of the game's four home runs—two for each team—into the right-field stands. When the "stringy outfielder" hit #12, it lifted him above Walt Dropo and Al Rosen, each of whom hit #11 in the same game.

Benton's six homers: #43, 83, 114, 119, 161, and 277.

278 (#13) June 3 at Fenway Park. Pitcher: Jesse Flores (Cleveland Indians). RH. Age 35.

Bottom of the fifth inning. Two-run homer. GAME WINNER.

The Red Sox had a 9-7 lead just after the halfway point of the game, after Tebbetts hit a leadoff home run. With Pesky on base, Ted popped one "deep in the right-field bleachers beyond the visiting bullpen." (*Herald*) Larry Doby hit a two-run homer in the top of the ninth, so Williams' drive was the one which made the difference in the 11-9 ballgame.

Home run #162 was another one hit off Jesse Flores.

279 (#14) June 6 at Fenway Park. Pitcher: Ken Holcombe (Chicago White Sox). RH. Age 31.

Bottom of the seventh inning. One-run homer.

The White Sox won this game, 8-4, with four homers of their own. Ted Williams' home went into the Red Sox bullpen for the fourth Red Sox run. It went in on a line "like a tennis expert's forehand drive skims over the net." (*Herald*)

Holcombe's other homers were #271 and 310.

280 (#15) June 8 at Fenway Park. Pitcher: Cliff Fannin (St. Louis Browns). RH. Age 26.

Bottom of the second inning. Three-run homer.

This was the day the Red Sox slaughtered St. Louis, 29-4. Bobby Doerr hit three homers and Ted only hit two. Ted's five RBIs only placed him third on his team—Doerr drove in eight and Dropo drove in seven. It was the most runs ever scored by one team in a major-league ballgame; the record lasted 57 years until the Texas Rangers beat Baltimore, 30-3. On June 7, the day before this day's game, the Sox had beaten the Browns, 20-4. Ted had three RBIs in that game, but no home runs.

Ted's first home run came in the eight-run second inning. It went 10-12 rows up in the right-field bleachers over the Red Sox bullpen. It gave the Red Sox a modest 4-0 lead at the time.

The fifth and final Fannin gopher ball. The first four: #154, 182, 183, and 186.

281 (#16) June 8 at Fenway Park. Pitcher: Sid Schacht (St. Louis Browns). RH. Age 33.

Bottom of the eighth inning. Two-run homer.

The Red Sox batted around in the second inning, the third inning, and the fourth inning. In the fourth inning, he got up twice — but made two of the inning's three outs. By the time Ted got up in the eighth, it was 24-3. He homered, hitting the other way, over the left-field fence, improving the Red Sox score to 26.

This was the only homer Ted hit off Schacht.

282 (#17) June 9 at Fenway Park. Pitcher: Ned Garver (St. Louis Browns). RH. Age 24.

Bottom of the first inning. Two-run homer.

The Red Sox scored seven more runs, for a total of 56 over three games which outstripped the prior record of 52. Ted's first inning homer with Billy Goodman on base gave Boston a quick 2-0 lead, but this time the Browns turned the tables in the scoring department and won, 12-7. Ted's homer went over Fenway's left-field wall.

Ted hit Ned for homers #213, 245, 272, 282, 337, 375, 385, 422, 436, and 459.

283 (#18) June 10 at Fenway Park. Pitcher: Dizzy Trout (Detroit Tigers). RH. Age 35.

Bottom of the first inning. One-run homer.

It was Ted's fifth homer in five days, and for the third day in a row he hit a homer to left. The Tigers upped the run total over the dozen runs the Browns had scored the day before, beating the Bosox, 18-8. The home run went into the left-center-field screen. Was this the game Trout knocked him down? We've not been able to definitively locate the game, but — talking about the relatively few times he'd ever been knocked down by a pitcher — he remembered one time when "Trout knocked me down, and I hit a home run on the next pitch. Same thing happened with Wynn."[60]

Before this, Ted hit #107, 144, 164, and 221. After this, he hit one more: #324.

284 (#19) June 14 at Cleveland Stadium, Cleveland. Pitcher: Mike Garcia (Cleveland Indians). RH. Age 26.

Top of the third inning. Two-run homer.

A home run thought to be from the early 1950s.

The home run Ted hit went 10-12 rows up into the lower right-field seats at Cleveland Stadium. He was always known for his willingness to talk hitting—even with the opposition. Before the game, Ted spent five minutes or so speaking with Al Rosen, second only to Williams in the league's home run totals. Rosen hit #16 in the game, one of three hits he had.

Ted's six homers off Garcia: #257, 284, 314, 325, 331, and 380.

285 (#20) June 18 at Briggs Stadium, Detroit. Pitcher: Art Houtteman (Detroit Tigers). RH. Age 22.

Top of the fourth inning. One-run homer.

The Red Sox lost their fifth game in a row, and they lost it by a lot—12-2. Stephens and Williams each hit solo home runs for the two Red Sox runs. Ted's was "a solid sock into the right-center-field seats."

Ted Williams hit homers #231, 239, 249, 275, 285, and 350, off young Art Houtteman.

286 (#21) June 24 at Sportsman's Park, St. Louis. Pitcher: Tommy Fine (St. Louis Browns). RH. Age 35.

Top of the sixth inning. One-run homer.

Billy Goodman hit a grand slam and Bobby Doerr drove in four runs with a homer, a double, and a single. First-pitch swinging, Ted hit his homer onto the top of the roof in right-center. Stephens hit a homer, too. This was the fifth game under new manager Steve O'Neill, who'd taken over on the 20th and the second game of a seven-game winning streak, a 12-3 win for Ellis Kinder.

This was the only homer Ted hit off Fine. When he'd pitched for the Red Sox in 1947, Fine worked 36 innings and didn't allow a home run. In 1950, he worked for the Browns and gave up three.

June 26—The Red Sox played an exhibition game at Forbes Field against the Pittsburgh Pirates (losing, 4-3). Before the game there was a home-run hitting contest. Ralph Kiner won, with eight home runs. Walt Dropo came in second with six. Ted Williams hit four.

During the game itself, Ted hit a 375-foot drive into the lower deck in right field.

287 (#22) June 27 at Shibe Park, Philadelphia. Pitcher: Bobby Shantz (Philadelphia Athletics). LH. Age 24.

Top of the third inning. Two-run homer.

The Red Sox won the game in the 11th inning, scoring twice and holding on to the 7-5 lead. Ted's home run had put his team ahead, 4-1, back in the third. "Williams socked a long drive onto the roof tops across the street from the ballpark." The *Boston Herald* was a little more precise, saying the ball had "landed squarely on the roof of an apartment house on 20th Street beyond the right-field fence." A few years later, Shantz said, "There's no sure-fire way to get him out, but I find that prayer helps a little." (*Cleveland Plain Dealer*, April 7, 1956)

The other homer Ted hit off Shantz was #403.

288 (#23) June 28 at Shibe Park, Philadelphia. Pitcher: Lou Brissie (Philadelphia Athletics). LH. Age 30.

Top of the eighth inning. Two-run homer. GAME WINNER.

"Ted Williams belted one of the longest home runs of his life…a twisting smash just inside the foul line," wrote the *Globe*. It, like his homer the day before, landed on the roof of a 20th Street structure. It was fair by about five feet. The home run gave the 6-2 game to the Red Sox.

Readers will remember that the 43 homers Ted hit in 1949 were his all-time high. He had hit his 23rd homer on July 22 that year. In 1950, he'd hit #23 about 3 ½ weeks earlier.

Brissie gave up homers #208 and 288.

289 (#24) June 29 at Shibe Park, Philadelphia. Pitcher: Moe Burtschy (Philadelphia Athletics). RH. Age 28.

Burtschy had 12 1/3 innings of major-league experience under his belt.

Top of the seventh inning. Two-run homer.

There were 34 games in 1950 in which the Red Sox scored ten or more runs. This was the third in which they scored more than 20. It was a 22-14 victory. Williams' homer was "blasted over the right-field wall." He drove in six runs to lead the parade. The 36 runs scored set an American League record.

With 12 home runs in June, Ted matched his best month ever. He'd also hit 12 in May 1942.

This was the only homer Ted hit off Burtschy.

290 (#25) July 7 at Yankee Stadium, New York. Pitcher: Allie Reynolds (New York Yankees). RH. Age 33.

Top of the eighth inning. Two-run homer.

"Reynolds lost his shutout when he walked Dom DiMaggio and Ted Williams sent a fast ball soaring into the top deck of the right-field stands for his 25th homer." That said, the Yankees still won the game, 5-2, despite Ted's third-deck drive. With 25 homers before the All-Star break, Williams was on the way to what was looking like his best year ever.

This was the fifth of the six Ted hit off Allie Reynolds. The list: #199, 216, 251, 265, 290, and 344.

The 1950 All-Star Game was played at Comiskey Park and it was one which proved fateful for Ted Williams. He broke his left elbow fielding, crashing into the wall as he caught a long drive from Ralph Kiner in the very first inning. He knew it hurt, but he tried to play through it and didn't leave the game until the eighth inning. He'd been on his way to a career year, perhaps not in average but in power—home runs and runs batted in. And now he lost more than six weeks.

291 (#26) September 15 at Sportsman's Park, St. Louis. Pitcher: Don Johnson (St. Louis Browns). RH. Age 23.

Top of the sixth inning. Three-run homer.

Ted Williams' return to playing with the Red Sox finally came on September 7, in a pinch-hitting role. He pinch-hit on the 7th, 10, and 14th. This day, September 15, was his first full day back. He had a 4-for-6 day with a three-run home run. "It felt strange at first. I had trouble with inside pitches. All of the hits I made were on pitches away from me. But don't tell the New York and Detroit writers about it." It wasn't any cheap homer; Ted "powered a fast ball over the roof in right center." The homer went "completely over the roof…and bounced in the street beyond." (*Herald*) Clearly, his elbow was sufficiently healed that he could hit a home run onto Grand Avenue. The homer also concluded a six-run rally that broke a tie and gave the Red Sox an 8-2 lead. The final score was Boston 12, St. Louis 9.

This was the only homer Ted hit off this Johnson.

292 (#27) September 24 at Yankee Stadium, New York. Pitcher: Vic Raschi (New York Yankees). RH. Age 31.

Top of the first inning. One-run homer.

The Yankees beat Boston, 9-5, almost mathematically eliminating the Sox from the race, but Ted did his part with two home runs. Both home runs were hit with two outs and both were solo home runs. He swung at the first pitch he saw in the game and sent it "deep into the lower right-field stands." (*Herald*) That homer briefly gave the team a 1-0 lead.

Williams closed out the year that might have been his best, save for the injury that cost him more than two months, with two homers off Raschi — #292 and 293. He'd kicked off the year with a home run off Raschi — #266.

293 (#28) September 24 at Yankee Stadium, New York. Pitcher: Vic Raschi (New York Yankees). RH. Age 31.

Top of the fifth inning. One-run homer.

The Yankees held a 6-1 lead when Ted drove in Boston's second run of the game in the top of the fifth. This one was "a man-sized homer a good ways up in the top deck of the right-field stands."

His second homer of the game. The five homers he hit off Vic: #250, 266, 292, 293, and 321.

Ned Garver told a story he'd heard, how Williams had hit two homers but then Yogi Berra complained on a later pitch to Ted that the umpire called ball four. "Well, at least I held him to first base," the umpire said. Garver said, "If you walked him, he only got to first. If you pitched to him, you didn't know what the hell was going to happen."[61]

It could well have been Ted's best year. At the time of the All-Star Break, which came at the precise midpoint of the season (the 77th game of 154), he had 25 homers and 83 RBIs. Double those figures and he would have had 50 home runs and 166 runs batted in. He still finished with a remarkable 97 RBIs—three short of 100—despite only appearing in 89 games.

1951

294 **(#1 of 1951)** April 21 at Fenway Park. Pitcher: Bob Hooper (Philadelphia Athletics). RH. Age 29.

Bottom of the first inning. Two-run homer.

Just the day before, the Athletics had won their first game at Fenway since 1948. After three losses, the Red Sox secured their first win of the 1951 season by the same 6-3 score. Ted Williams started the scoring for the Sox with a home run into the bleachers a couple of rows over the Red Sox bullpen in the bottom of the first.

Hooper was Ted's first victim of 1951. In July, he gave up #308 and in 1953, #335.

295 **(#2)** April 22 (first game) at Fenway Park. Pitcher: Dick Fowler (Philadelphia Athletics). RH. Age 30.

Bottom of the first inning. Two-run homer.

The Red Sox took both halves of a doubleheader, 6-5 and 7-4, at half-frozen Fenway. In the first game, Williams again homered in the first inning, again with one man on, again over the bullpen and into the seats. This time, it was over the visitors' bullpen. It was his only hit of the day; he didn't get the ball out of the infield after that, though he did walk three times and score two more runs.

The last of six homers struck off Dick Fowler pitches. See also homers #91, 105, 242, 252, and 267.

296 (#3) April 24 at Fenway Park. Pitcher: Bob Kuzava (Washington Senators). LH. Age 28.

Bottom of the eighth. One-run homer.

Three Red Sox errors were dispiriting, but all seven of the Senators runs were earned. The Red Sox scored five, the last one coming on Ted's solo home run in the bottom of the eighth. This one dropped into the Red Sox pen where it was caught on the fly by one of the players.

#244 had been hit off Kuzava, too. Both had come in losses; the Sox lost this one, 7-5.

297 (#4) April 29 at Shibe Park, Philadelphia. Pitcher: Johnny Kucab (Philadelphia Athletics). RH. Age 31.

Top of the 13th inning. Two-run homer.

In the top of the 13th inning, Ted Williams punctuated a Red Sox win with a "sky-rocket home run…that soared 30 feet above the high right-field wall at Shibe Park and bounced on the flat top roof of an apartment house across the street." (*Boston Herald*) He'd drawn four walks earlier in the game. Pesky and Goodman had each driven in a run already, so it was a four-run burst that gave Boston a 12-8 win. There was a second game, which started with the Red Sox ahead, 6-0, but it had to be called after just two innings. No Williams homer was noted.

This was the only homer Ted hit off Kucab.

298 (#5) May 6 (first game) at Sportsman's Park, St. Louis. Pitcher: Lou Sleater (St. Louis Browns). LH. Age 24.

Top of the tenth inning. One-run homer. GAME WINNER.

The Red Sox left 16 men on base (two shy of the league record at the time) but had worked a 4-4 tie against the Browns through nine innings. Actually, they'd held a 4-3 lead after eight innings and with two outs and two strikes on the batter in the bottom of the ninth. The Browns tied it and set the stage for extra innings. Ted Williams was the first man up in the tenth, and it was no small homer he hit (his only hit of the day). It was "a towering drive that sailed far over the roof of the right-field pavilion at Sportsman's Park." (*Herald*)

Ted also hit #441 off Sleater.

299 (#6) May 13 at Griffith Stadium, Washington. Pitcher: Alton Brown (Washington Senators). RH. Age 26.

Top of the ninth inning. Two-run homer.

The Red Sox won the game, 10-1, with Vern Stephens and Ted Williams each collecting three RBIs. Ted's home run came in the final inning; as it happens, this was the third Sunday in a row he'd homered (without any intervening weekday home runs) and all three homers were hit in the final inning. This was hit over the right-field wall. He was a little down on himself, saying he was undercutting the ball too much and that he probably ought to start trying to hit to left field a little more as a corrective measure.

This was the only homer Ted hit off Alton Brown, and the only homer Brown ever gave up during his brief time in the big leagues. Brown threw 11 2/3 innings in seven innings of relief, but managed to walk 12 batters in those innings and was tagged for 14 hits and 12 earned runs.

300 (#7) May 15 at Fenway Park. Pitcher: Howie Judson (Chicago White Sox). RH. Age 25.

Bottom of the fourth inning. One-run homer.

The White Sox were leading, 7-6, in the ninth inning when Williams came up for the last time. Ted already had a double and a homer in the game. Manager Paul Richards moved his pitcher, Harry Dorish, to third base and brought in the left-handed Billy Pierce to pitch to Williams. Ted popped up to the shortstop, at which point Richards moved Dorish back to the mound and brought in Floyd Baker to play at third. The Red Sox scored anyway, though it was the White Sox who won it in the 11th on career home run #1 by Nellie Fox.

Ted's 300th home run came with two outs in the fourth, on a 3-2 count, hit into the right-field seats. He became just the tenth player to reach 300 home runs. Ruth, Foxx, Ott, Gehrig, DiMaggio, Mize, Greenberg, Hornsby, and Chuck Klein (who had exactly 300) were the names that preceded him.

In 1949, Ted hit five homers off Howie Judson. In 1951, he hit the only other one he hit — this one, #300.

301 (#8) May 21 at Fenway Park. Pitcher: Gene Bearden (Detroit Tigers). LH. Age 30.

Bottom of the seventh inning. Two-run homer. GAME WINNER.

Had Ted once more worked himself up in a way to boost his productivity? He'd been hitting .226 and Ty Cobb was in town, again critical of Ted for not hitting to left field. Trying to break out of his slump, Williams banged three hits — every one of them to left field — a single, a double off the wall, and a home run into the screen in left. He added 21 points to his average. The two runs were the margin of difference in the game.

Williams had previously hit #269 off Bearden.

302 (#9) May 25 at Fenway Park. Pitcher: Connie Marrero (Washington Senators). RH. Age 40.

Bottom of the second inning. One-run homer.

The Red Sox beat the Senators, 14-2, with 19 base hits. Ted's second-inning shot was a "well-stroked homer into the Red Sox bullpen." He also hit two doubles and drove in four of the 14 Red Sox runs.

Marrero made the majors for the first time the year before at age 39 — and then pitched in 118 major-league games. In 1954, he gave up two homers to Ted in the same game — #358 and 359.

303 (#10) May 27 (second game) at Fenway Park. Pitcher: Julio Moreno (Washington Senators). RH. Age 30.

Bottom of the third inning. Four-run homer. Grand slam # 11. GAME WINNER.

Williams finally pushed his batting average over .300, thanks to going 4-for-7 in the doubleheader. The Red Sox won 9-3 and then 7-1, with Ted's four-run homer driving in the winning run. His first grand slam of 1951 also gave him the league lead in runs batted in; he'd driven in six on the day. Moreno's first two pitches were in tight on him, but Ted unloaded on the third pitch. "Williams pulled and sent the pitch high and far to the Red Sox bullpen, where Mickey Harris made a back-hand stab of the four-run clout." (*Herald*)

This was the only homer Williams hit off Moreno, but a game-winning grand slam is one of the most satisfying of home runs.

304 (#11) May 30 (first game) at Fenway Park. Pitcher: Tom Ferrick (New York Yankees). RH. Age 35.

Bottom of the eighth inning. Two-run homer.

"Ted Williams had his greatest day against the Yankees in yesterday's Memorial Day doubleheader…the story was Williams and his seven hits in 13 at-bats, his game-tying homer in the opener and his game-tying double in the nightcap."—Harold Kaese, *Boston Globe*. The Red Sox won the first game, 11-10, though it took them 15 innings. It was Ted's homer that tied the game, 10-10, for Boston. After Billy Goodman singled, Williams hit it into the bleachers, over the visitors bullpen. They beat the Yankees, 9-4, in the second game. And Ted even scored from second base on a sacrifice bunt in the first game.

Ferrick furnished homers #77, 130, 247, and 304. Each one of the four was hit while Ferrick was working for a different club—respectively the Athletics, Indians, Browns, and Yankees.

305 (#12) June 10 (second game) at Cleveland Stadium, Cleveland. Pitcher: George Zuverink (Cleveland Indians). RH. Age 26.

Top of the eighth inning. Three-run homer.

The Indians went down twice, 9-6 and 8-2. Williams had five RBIs, reaching exactly 50 on the season, two on a single to left field in the first game and three on his homer — also to left field — in the second. He hit the ball over the center-field fence. He was also credited with several fine fielding plays.

Zuverink was one of the tougher pitchers Ted faced. He was 2-for-20 against him, a .100 batting average — and the home run came in the very first at-bat. Over his next 19 at-bats, he was 1-for-19, a single in 1956. And the only two walks he got off him were ones ordered by the manager, intentional walks.

This was the only homer Ted hit off Zuverink. He had hit #87 off another pitcher whose surname started with the letters "Zu", though.

306 (#13) June 17 (second game) at Fenway Park. Pitcher: Al Widmar (St. Louis Browns). RH. Age 26.

Bottom of the first inning. Two-run homer. GAME WINNER.

The Red Sox swept their fifth doubleheader of the year, beating the Browns 5-4 (two of the runs were batted in by Ted Williams, his single driving in the game-winner) and 3-0 (all three of the runs were driven in by Williams, the two-run homer in the first being the game-winner.) The home run was another to left field, into the screen.

Ted hit three runs off Al Widmar — all three of them in 1951. They were #306, 311, and 322.

307 (#14) June 19 at Fenway Park. Pitcher: Bob Lemon (Cleveland Indians). RH. Age 30. Hall of Famer.

Bottom of the first inning. Two-run homer.

Chuck Stobbs threw a four-hitter and the Red Sox beat Bob Lemon and the Red Sox, 9-2. Ted hit two singles, drew a walk, "and turned in two spectacular catches." The home run went over the screen in left-center field, "a tremendous poke even for Ted." The Kid had four RBIs in the game. Manager Steve O'Neill enthused over Williams' fielding: "Ted made two of the greatest fielding plays I've seen a left fielder make—those sinking line drives he caught off Simpson and Easter. With any other left fielder, those would have been extra-base hits." (*Boston Traveler*)

Ted hit four homers off the future Hall of Famer. They were #307, 406, 435, and 442.

308 (#15) July 5 at Shibe Park, Philadelphia. Pitcher: Bob Hooper (Philadelphia Athletics). RH. Age 29.

Top of the seventh inning. Two-run homer.

"Williams' blow, his 15th of the year and first in 16 games, was a terrific belt over the right-field wall and the tall left-fielder added a wind-blown double and single to his hit collection." It was "far and high" over the wall. The Red Sox won the game, 8-3.

Ted's other two homers off Hooper: #294 and 335.

309 (#16) July 7 at Fenway Park. Pitcher: Spec Shea (New York Yankees). RH. Age 30.

Bottom of the sixth inning. Two-run homer.

The Red Sox scored six runs in the first inning, four of them on Clyde Vollmer's grand slam, setting the Sox well on the way to a 10-4 win over the Yankees at Fenway. Ted Williams added the last two runs with his homer five rows deep into the seats beyond the Yankees bullpen.

Shea served up five home runs: #198, 224, 309, 326, and 328.

310 (#17) July 14 at Comiskey Park, Chicago. Pitcher: Ken Holcombe (Chicago White Sox). RH. Age 32.

Top of the fourth inning. One-run homer.

Ted hit a solo line-drive home run into Comiskey Park's right-field seats in the top of the fourth inning. It was the only run the Red Sox scored until Clyde Vollmer drove in two more in the top of the ninth. Those won the game, 3-2.

Holcombe's other homers were #271 and 279.

311 (#18) July 16 at Sportsman's Park, St. Louis. Pitcher: Al Widmar (St. Louis Browns). RH. Age 26.

Top of the first inning. Two-run homer.

It was 104 degrees in St. Louis and Ted Williams got the Red Sox off to a good 2-0 lead when he homered an Al Widmar offering onto Sportsman's Park's right-field roof, scoring Dom DiMaggio ahead of him. A seven-run fifth inning for St. Louis gave the Browns a 9-5 win.

Ted hit three runs off Al Widmar—all three were two-run homers and they were all hit in 1951. They were #306, 311, and 322.

312 (#19) July 24 at Fenway Park. Pitcher: Harry Dorish. (Chicago White Sox). RH. Age 29.

Bottom of the second inning. One-run homer.

It was Johnny Pesky Night at Fenway Park with an overflowing crowd on hand. The Red Sox won 8-3, and Williams was 4-for-5. He'd singled and scored in the five-run bottom of the first inning, then homered leading off the second. The "scientific slugger" hit it over the left-center-field fence. Leo Kiely threw a four-hitter.

This was Ted's only homer off Harry Dorish. The two had been teammates in 1947-49 and were again in 1956.

313 (#20) July 26 at Fenway Park. Pitcher: Randy Gumpert (Chicago White Sox). RH. Age 32.

Bottom of the second inning. Two-run homer.

Ted hit a homer over the left-field wall in the second, but Clyde Vollmer hit three homers, helping out the Red Sox in the first, fifth, and sixth. Dom hit one, too, like Ted's a two-run HR. They were pretty much all necessary; the Red Sox scored 13 runs but the White Sox scored ten.

This was Ted's first homer off Gumpert in 1951. In 1949, he had hit another pair. The four home runs: 238, 261, 313, and 323.

314 (#21) July 29 at Fenway Park. Pitcher: Mike Garcia (Cleveland Indians). RH. Age 27.

Bottom of the third inning. Three-run homer.

Birdie Tebbetts had been sold to the Indians in December; he won this 5-4 game for Cleveland with a home run in the fourth and a well-executed bunt single as leadoff batter in the seventh. His homer was his second of the season. Ted Williams connected for #21 in the third for three runs, hitting it into the Red Sox bullpen.

Six homers given up by Garcia: #257, 284, 314, 325, 331, and 380.

315 (#22) August 1 at Fenway Park. Pitcher: Duane Pillette (St. Louis Browns). RH. Age 28.

Bottom of the first inning. One-run homer.

It was quite a demonstration of Fenway Park power in the first inning when Ted Williams "belted a towering drive deep into the right-field stands" and Vern Stephens followed with one over the wall in left field, and then Bobby Doerr dented the wall. Ted's homer was "parked...15 rows deep into the wing of the right-field grandstand." (*Herald*)

Ted's other homer off Pillette was #347. Duane's father Herm had been a teammate of Ted's in 1936 and 1937 on the Pacific Coast League's San Diego Padres.

316 (#23) August 9 (first game) at Fenway Park. Pitcher: Morrie Martin (Philadelphia Athletics). LH. Age 28.

Bottom of the first inning. One-run homer.

Ted's home run was hit into the Red Sox bullpen. Even with the three runs they scored in the bottom of the ninth, sending hopes soaring for the fans, Boston fell short, 6-5. At least he gave the 6,500 Little Leaguers present a thrill to remember. And for those who were able to stay for the full second game, they saw a 5-3 Red Sox win.

Ted also hit #412 off Morrie.

317 (#24) August 14 at Shibe Park, Philadelphia. Pitcher: Sam Zoldak (Philadelphia Athletics). LH. Age 32.

Top of the first inning. Two-run homer.

Ted's first homer, in the first, was "a high fly ball that just cleared the short but high right-field fence." Pesky was on board and the Red Sox scored the first two of their three first-inning runs. His second homer, in the fourth, gave him the league lead over Gus Zernial and an even 100 runs batted in.

Zoldak also allowed homer #214.

318 (#25) August 14 at Shibe Park, Philadelphia. Pitcher: Joe Coleman (Philadelphia Athletics). RH. Age 28.

Top of the fourth inning. One-run homer.

In the fourth inning, Williams made the score 7-1 in favor of the Red Sox when he "whipped a liner over the fence in right-center...This was a real rap." Billy Goodman had the chance to turn an unassisted triple play, but he went for the surer triple killing instead. He caught Hank Majeski's line drive and stepped on the bag, doubling off Allie Clark. He saw Gus Zernial coming at him, and only 20 feet away—he probably could have beaten Zernial by running him down on the way back to first but he simply threw the ball over to Walt Dropo on first base.

See earlier homers #167 and 194.

319 (#26) August 19 at Griffith Stadium, Washington. Pitcher: Joe Haynes (Washington Senators). RH. Age 33.

Top of the sixth inning. Two-run homer.

The Red Sox beat the Senators, 8-3, with a lead they'd achieved with five runs in the first inning. It was 6-3 when Williams came to the plate in the sixth inning. Pesky was on first base. Haynes threw Ted "a sort of blooper pitch" and "Ted just stepped into the arching slow curve and conked it as he did during the 1946 All-Star Game when Rip Sewell served the original model up at Fenway Park." He lofted it over the right-field wall.

Haynes had previously given up homers #110 and 211.

320 (#27) August 29 at Briggs Stadium, Detroit. Pitcher: Virgil Trucks (Detroit Tigers). RH. Age 34.

Top of the third inning. Three-run homer.

The Red Sox were five games out of first place, and still in the race, after winning this 7-5 game. The two runs they scored in the top of the ninth spelled the difference, breaking a 5-5 tie. Of course, they wouldn't have been tied without Williams' three-run homer back in the third inning. Ted also made "three brilliant catches" in left field; the *Herald* said it was one of the best games of his career in the field. His homer was a 335-foot drive into the right-field seats.

Ted's 12 homers off Trucks: 108, 115, 146, 174, 189, 226, 236, 243, 320, 342, 437, and 444.

321 (#28) September 5 at Yankee Stadium. Pitcher: Vic Raschi (New York Yankees). RH. Age 32.

Top of the third inning. One-run homer. GAME WINNER.

The Sox scored twice in the first inning when Billy Goodman doubled in Williams and Doerr. Ted's solo home run in the top of the third gave them a 3-0 lead in a game they eventually won, 4-2. The New York loss knocked the Yankees out of first place. Cleveland was on top and the Red Sox just four games behind. Williams had been out for a few days with the grippe, not having played since August 30. He was still weak, but asked into the game and said that manager O'Neill could take him out if he wasn't handling it. He walked twice, singled, and hit the game-winning homer, and got extra credit for his outfield play.

On Raschi's 1-1 pitch in the third, he "got a toehold…and it was a jackpot wallop. The ball bounced off a railing fronting the top deck of the three-tiered stand in right field." The ball was apparently hit right down the line.

Ted victimized Vic for five home runs in all, this one being perhaps the most painful: though a solo home run, it won the game. The five home runs: #250, 266, 292, 293, and 321.

322 (#29) September 14 at Fenway Park. Pitcher: Al Widmar (St. Louis Browns). RH. Age 26.

Bottom of the second inning. Two-run homer. GAME WINNER.

The biggest home run story of this game was when a sportswriter hit two home runs in his first two major-league at-bats; Bob Nieman was a 24-year-old journalism student at Kent State who homered in the third and homered in the fifth, both off Maury McDermott. Ted's two-run homer in the second gave the Sox and 7-2 lead. It was hit into the right-field stands over the St. Louis bullpen. He also singled in a run to boost his RBI total to 120. The Red Sox won, 9-6, but Ted was far from pleased when Satchel Paige struck him out his last time up, in the bottom of the eighth. Paige was 44 at the time, and he fooled Ted, who'd swung at a pitch outside the strike zone. Angry at himself, Williams "smashed his bat into pieces. He first whacked it against the railing of the runway leading to the dressing room. When that didn't suffice, Williams flung the bat towards the rack. He still wasn't satisfied, so he smashed it on the floor of the dugout. That ended the bat's worth for good. All the while Williams was doing his rail-splitting act, ol' Satchimo [sic] was laughing his head off on the mound."

Nieman had a good 12-year career as an outfielder, batting .295 overall with 125 home runs.

Ted hit three runs off Al Widmar — all three of them in 1951. They were #306, 311, and 322.

323 (**#30**) September 17 at Fenway Park. Pitcher: Randy Gumpert (Chicago White Sox). RH. Age 32.

Bottom of the eighth inning. One-run homer.

The Red Sox were only 2 ½ games out of first place after bearing the White Sox by a 12-5 score this day in Boston. Ted had driven in two of the previous 11 runs, part of a 4-for-4 day that followed an extra half-hour's batting practice in the morning. His homer as first batter up in the eighth provided the 12th run, hit into the Red Sox bullpen.

With 13 games remaining on the schedule, the Sox certainly had a shot at winning the pennant, but they lost all but one of those games and wound up 11 full games out of first.

This was Ted's second homer off Gumpert in 1951. In 1949, he had hit another pair. The four home runs: 238, 261, 313, and 323.

1952

324 **(#1 of 1952)** April 30 at Fenway Park. Pitcher: Dizzy Trout (Detroit Tigers). RH. Age 37.

Bottom of the seventh inning. Two-run homer. GAME WINNER.

The last one of Ted's six homers off Trout won the game. It came on "Ted Williams Day"—a day scheduled to say goodbye to Ted Williams as he left baseball to re-join the United States Marine Corps. Even though he was turning 34 and had a wife and child, he'd been recalled to service because of the shortage of Marine aviators at the time of the Korean War. He only had time to get into six games in 1952 before having to report for duty. In ten at-bats, Ted had four hits—a .400 batting average. He had two singles, a triple, and this home run, which won the game, his two-run homer with two outs in the seventh breaking a 3-3 tie. More than 45 years later, Williams remembered, "Dominic DiMaggio was on first and I launched, just launched, one into the right-field bleachers, against Dizzy Trout. Final score: Sox 5, Tigers 3." [62]

The *Boston Globe* reported that "Williams clipped a curve ball into the [right-field] grandstand section near the runway, about eight rows deep." The *Boston Daily Record* said "the sphere sailed majestically over Wertz's head and landed among a group of sailors seated in the right-field bend of the grandstand." It was caught by Mike Lopilato, a 36-year-old fruit vendor from Boston, and Ted swapped him a new signed ball for it after the game.

"How did it feel? How would you feel? It felt great, great! It was a curve ball, and I hit it pretty good. I figured he would curve me." (*Christian Science Monitor*) Was it his greatest thrill, to win a game with a home run his last time up before going off to war, perhaps never to play again? No, he answered honestly. "The home run I hit in the 1941 All-Star Game at Detroit had this one beat 10 to 1. I don't think anything will ever pass that."

Earlier Trout homers were numbers 107, 144, 164, 221, and 283.

Korean War service

What now? After breaking his elbow in 1950, what else could derail his career? Plenty, it turned out. He was very lucky ever to play baseball again. Though he was 34 years old, with an infant daughter, and though he'd already served three years in the military, he was called back to service. The story is exhaustively detailed in the book *Ted Williams at War*. This time, Ted wasn't going to play any baseball at all—not a single exhibition game. He was angry he'd been called back, but he went, and he declined any attempt there might have been for him to serve in morale-building p.r. events. If he were going back, this time he wanted to see combat.

Williams volunteered to fly jets—as in baseball and sport fishing, he always wanted the best equipment, and to be one of the best with the equipment. He'd only flown prop planes in World War II but had been made an instructor in aviation and in gunnery because he was so good. Now it was jet aircraft he wanted to fly and he was assigned to the most elite squadron in the United States Marine Corps, VMF-311. One of the other 32 men in the squadron was John Glenn.

Captain T. S. Williams flew 39 combat missions—most of them dive-bombing missions—and was shot down on just his third mission, crash-landing his plane at an Air Force base (he couldn't get back to his own base) and barely escaping with his life as the plane went up in flames. Less than 24 hours later, he was up on mission #4. His plane was hit by groundfire on at least one other occasion. With the war winding down, and Williams suffering from a number of ailments, including ear problems occasioned by a too-rapid descent, he was transferred back Stateside in time to throw out the first pitch at the 1953 All-Star Game.

1953

325 **(#1 of 1953)** August 9 at Fenway Park. Pitcher: Mike Garcia
(Cleveland Indians). RH. Age 29.

Bottom of the seventh inning. One-run homer.

Away from the game for more than 15 months, now a war veteran who had
flown 39 combat missions in Korea (and whose F-9F Pantherjet had indeed
been burnt beyond repair after he'd been shot down and crashed), Williams
was back home, signed a contract with the Red Sox to play what he could
during what remained of the season.

"My first day back I took some batting practice. Boudreau threw to me. Gee,
it felt so good to be swinging a bat again. About the eighth or ninth pitch I
hit one into the center-field bleachers. Cronin was watching. He said, "Ted,
nobody's hit one out there all year.' After I'd finished, we were standing at
home plate and I told Cronin I thought the plate was off line."[63] This was
a little more than halfway through the season and no player — Sox or visitors — had noticed it all year.

"I don't think he believed me. But he figured he'd humor Theodore Samuel
Williams. Sure enough, it *was* off. I took about a week to get into shape,
get my legs limber, take BP — hit some shots off Lou Boudreau, our new
manager, I'll tell you. I got into a game on August 6., Made an out. But

three days later I pinch hit a homer off Mike Garcia into the right-field seats — 420 feet."[64]

Ted hit this home run in his second plate appearance, pinch-hitting as he tried to work his way back into the game without benefit of play at a lower level. Contemporary news coverage put the homer in the center-field bleachers. "It felt like old times," said Red Sox clubhouse manager Johnny Orlando, showing off a black and blue mark on his left arm. Ted had reportedly been hitting Orlando on the arm after each home run — now 325 of them. "I knew he was happy. He took the same shot at me and said like he always had, 'Just like Joe Louis.'" The homer came on a 3-1 fastball, and landed several rows into the bleachers over the center-field end of the Red Sox bullpen. The game itself ended with the Indians on top, 9-3.

In Ted's first home run after returning from Korea, he hit the fourth of his career off Mike Garcia. He hit six in all: 257, 284, 314, 325, 331, and 380.

Ted Williams: "I had hit a home run the day I left [for the Korean War] and a home run my first day back...After that it seemed like every pitch that came in was as big as a grapefruit...For the next 37 games, I hit .407, including 13 home runs, a home run every seven times at bat. I had a slugging percentage of .901. Joe Cronin said I had set spring training back 20 years."[65]

326 (#2) August 16 (second game) at Fenway Park. Pitcher: Spec Shea (Washington Senators). RH. Age 32.

Bottom of the fifth inning. One-run homer.

It was Ted's first day starting game, after seven games in which he'd pinch-hit (with just the August 9 homer to show for his work.) He played in the second game of the doubleheader and was 2-for-3 with a double and a homer, collecting two of Boston's six hits. Washington won, 7-4. The Sox had won the first game, 4-1. Ted's home run was "pulled right down the line into the right-field grandstand." (*Herald*) It came in the bottom of the fifth, a solo homer, and landed as far as 40 feet beyond the foul pole. Ted left after the fifth, replaced in left field by Hoot Evers.

The following evening, Ted was officially welcomed home with a $100-a-plate dinner at the Hotel Statler, all of the money going at his request to the Jimmy Fund.

After Ted hit three home runs off Shea as a Yankee, he came back after the Korean War and hit two more off Shea as a Senator, in the course of one week. The total was five: #198, 224, 309, 326, and 328.

327 (#3) August 19 at Fenway Park. Pitcher: Charlie Bishop (Philadelphia Athletics). RH. Age 29.

Bottom of the seventh inning. Two-run homer. GAME WINNER.

The Red Sox were down, 4-3, when Ted came up in the bottom of the seventh. Al Zarilla had singled; there was nobody out. He hit a "410-foot smash far into the right-field stands"—maybe as far as 24 or 25 rows up into the Section 3 seats. It gave Boston the lead, which the Red Sox did not relinquish. It also provided a good memory for the 5,000 Little Leaguers who were guests of the Red Sox at the game.

This was the only homer Ted hit off Bishop.

328 (#4) August 21 (second game) at Griffith Stadium, Washington. Pitcher: Spec Shea (Washington Senators). RH. Age 32.

Top of the fifth inning. Three-run homer.

Ted just pinch-hit in the first game and popped up to the shortstop in the top of the seventh. The Sox lost, 9-1. He was a big part of the second game, his three-run homer tying the game 3-3 in the top of the fifth. He singled in a fourth run in the seventh—the winning run, as it proved—and then left for a pinch-runner. He still wasn't fully in condition, but he was hitting .474 in his first 19 chances. The Red Sox had hit seven home runs in August and Williams now had four of the seven. Some wondered how he'd do once he was truly back in shape. This day's homer went into the "distant right-center-field Washington bullpen." He now had six hits in a row off Shea, who said "the Marines should have kept Williams 20 more years."

This was the last of the five homers Ted hit off Spec Shea; the preceding ones were #198, 224, 309, and 326.

329 (#5) August 23 at Griffith Stadium, Washington. Pitcher: Sonny Dixon (Washington Senators). RH. Age 28.

Top of the seventh inning. One-run homer.

After Ted homered to tie the game, 4-4, in the seventh, he was replaced in left field by Karl Olson. In the top of the ninth, Olson doubled in Jimmy Piersall from first base for the go-ahead and winning fifth run. Ted swung at Dixon's first pitch and hit it over the high wall in Griffith Stadium's right field.

This was the only homer Ted hit off Dixon.

330 (#6) August 30 (first game) at Cleveland Stadium, Cleveland. Pitcher: Bob Feller (Cleveland Indians). RH. Age 34. Hall of Famer.

Top of the first inning. One-run homer.

Williams hit a solo home run in the top of the first inning; the *Cleveland Plain Dealer* said he was the first batter all year who hit one into the upper right-field deck. After the game, Ted said that Feller was the greatest pitcher of his lifetime. He added, "He doesn't have the fireball he used to, but he has a good sinker and is a cutie out on the mound." (*Boston Traveler*)

This was the sixth in the sequence of 10 homers hit off Feller: 131, 141, 203, 210, 227, 330, 351, 353, 374, 416.

331 (#7) August 31 at Cleveland Stadium, Cleveland. Pitcher: Mike Garcia (Cleveland Indians). RH. Age 29.

Top of the seventh inning. Three-run homer. GAME WINNER.

3-RUN HOMER BY WILLIAMS WINS FOR SOX—that kind of *Boston Globe* headline was always welcome. The story began, "Ted Williams lost 19 points off his batting average tonight but he won the game with his only hit. The score was 6-4." He'd been having a rough day, including a strikeout and hitting into a double play. But his home run into the second tier in right field gave the Red Sox a 5-1 lead at the time. The *Plain Dealer* had just noted the day before that he was the first one to hit one into the upper deck all year and now he'd done it two days in a row. It was only a few rows short of the August 30 homer. There were only 12,228 fans and "only a teen-aged youngster was within sections of the ball and he didn't even have to hurry to recover it as a souvenir." (*Herald*)

This was his second homer of the year off the Tribe's Garcia. The six Garcia granted him: #257, 284, 314, 325, 331, and 380.

Pitchers in those days were not always announced beforehand, so that the opposition had less time to prepare. Prior to this day's game, Dick Gernert said that Williams had asked the clubhouse boy to find out who the Indians would be starting. Told it was Garcia, his response was, "Sliders. I'm going to hit a slide out of here today." Dick Gernert saw Ted strike out, then ground into a double play, then ground out again. In the top of the seventh, he hit the three-run bomb. He told Gernert, "The fucken guy finally threw me a slider. I told you I'd nail it."[66] He'd waited for his pitch.

Gernert told Leigh Montville that Ted played every angle. Even after finishing batting practice, when most players were relaxing and waiting for the game, Williams would just change his shirt and run back on the field to watch the opposing pitcher warm up. He "would dissect the pitcher's curveball, point out what location the pitcher liked, how much the ball curved, what indications there were that the curve was coming...."[67]

332 (#8) September 6 (first game) at Shibe Park, Philadelphia. Pitcher: Marion Fricano (Philadelphia Athletics). RH. Age 29.

Top of the first inning. One-run homer.

The Red Sox swept two, 8-4 and 4-0. Ted's first-inning homer in the first game was "a towering homer over the right-field fence." John Gillooly of the *Record* pinned down the position a little more, dubbing it "a balloon which floated over the right-field wall and landed somewhere between 18th and 19th on Chestnut St." In the eighth inning, Williams was walked intentionally with no one on base.

This was Ted's only homer off Fricano.

333 (#9) September 7 (first game) at Fenway Park. Pitcher: Jim McDonald (New York Yankees). RH. Age 26.

Bottom of the first inning. Two-run homer.

The day after homering on the road in Philadelphia, Williams and the Red Sox were back in Boston hosting the Yankees and, once again, Ted hit a first-inning homer to kick things off. The two runs gave them a lead they never relinquished, the final score 7-4. The homer was hit "a third of the way up among the grandstand patrons in the right-field sector." (*Herald*) Boston Police sat near the Yankees bench due to a death threat mailed to Mickey Mantle—who also homered in the game.

Ted's other homer off McDonald came from when Jim worked for the Orioles; it was HR #378.

334 (#10) September 10 at Fenway Park. Pitcher: Early Wynn (Cleveland Indians). RH. Age 33. Hall of Famer.

Bottom of the fourth inning. Two-run homer.

Indians manager Al Lopez put on the most exaggerated "Williams Shift" yet positioned—the third baseman played right behind second base and the three outfielders were all moved to right and center. There was not even one defender on the left half of the field. Ted homered over them all—twice. Jimmy Piersall was on base in the fourth when Ted "lofted one into the [right-field] pavilion, not too deep, but deep enough to finish Wynn."

Eight round-trippers Ted hit off Wynn: #190, 334, 405, 433, 434, 447, 489, and 497.

335 (#11) September 10 at Fenway Park. Pitcher: Bob Hooper (Cleveland Indians). RH. Age 31.

Bottom of the sixth inning. One-run homer.

In 60 at-bats, Williams now had 11 home runs. "I hit those two homers today pretty good," he said. Especially the second one. That one felt real good." (*Herald*) It should have felt good; it went 15 rows up in the seats behind the Red Sox bullpen. The *Globe* let readers know that "Williams crossed home plate wearing a broad grin and chuckling both times." No shift was going to stop him if he could hit over it.

Ted's other two homers off Hooper: #294 and 308.

336 (#12) September 14 at Fenway Park. Pitcher: Mike Fornieles (Chicago White Sox). RH. Age 21.

Bottom of the eighth inning. Three-run homer.

Williams was wearing a bandage on his left wrist due to a sprain. It was a pinch-hit home run, hit on the first pitch he saw, and driven into Section 2 of the right-field grandstand. The White Sox erupted for eight runs in the top of the sixth, breaking open a 1-1 game, and even a three-run homer just brought Boston a little closer.

This was Ted's only homer off Fornieles. From 1957 to the end of Ted's career, the two were teammates.

337 (#13) September 17 at Fenway Park. Pitcher: Ned Garver (Detroit Tigers). RH. Age 27.

Bottom of the eighth inning. Two-run homer. GAME WINNER.

The former Capt. T. S. Williams popped his 13th post-Korea homer into the right-field grandstand, erasing and overcoming the 1-0 Detroit lead which had prevailed until that moment with two outs in the bottom of the eighth. It went about 15 rows up into the Section 1 seats in right field, Piersall crossed the plate ahead of Ted, and the Red Sox ultimately won the game, 2-1. "It was a slider, but I don't think that Ned got it where he wanted to. This one was over the plate. The two he got me out on were almost on my fists." A man in a brown suit caught the ball. Kinder's relief appearance in the game was his 67th of the season, breaking Ed Walsh's 45-year old A.L. record.

Ten homers Ted hit off Ned: #213, 245, 272, 282, 337, 375, 385, 422, 436, and 459.

Remarkably, Garver was trying to walk Williams at the time. The count was 3-1 and he didn't want to come in with anything good, figuring he'd take his chances. "I'm going to put him on base and pitch to George Kell...I just threw it in there plenty bad [very high and inside, and not a strike] and Williams stepped back and hit that sucker for a home run...I'm trying to walk him and he hits a home run to make it 2-1 and win the ball game."[68]

1954

Ted broke his collarbone on the first day of spring training—March 1. Consequently, he didn't get into a game until May 15, and he still had a pin holding things together when he did return. He had no spring training games or rehab work such as is often done in the 21st century.

338 (#1 of 1954) May 16 (second game) at Briggs Stadium, Detroit. Pitcher: Ralph Branca (Detroit Tigers). RH. Age 28.

Top of the third inning. One-run homer.

It was Ted's second day playing in 1954. He'd gone 0-for-2 on May 15, then gone 3-for-4 (all singles) with two RBIs in the first game of the May 16 doubleheader—and then he exploded, going 5-for-5 with two homers and five more RBIs in the second game. The Red Sox lost both games, 7-6 and 9-8 (in 14 innings). Ted's first homer was hit into the second deck—the upper right-field stands, a favorite landing spot for Williams home runs.

This was Ted's only homer off Branca.

339 (#2) May 16 (second game) at Briggs Stadium, Detroit. Pitcher: Ray Herbert (Detroit Tigers). RH. Age 24.

Top of the eighth inning. Two-run homer.

Climaxing an 8-for-9 day, with seven RBIs, was Ted's two-run homer in the eighth. The third deck in Detroit's right field was about 120 feet—in other words, about triple the height of Fenway's "Green Monster." This one was hit into the third deck, caught by a fan in the first row—with Harry Agganis on board—at about the 355-foot mark. Joe Cashman of the *Boston Record* called 500 feet a conservative estimate.

Herbert was hit for five Williams home runs over time—#339, 355, 391, 478, and 490.

"It hurt me all day," Williams said of the pin in his shoulder that held his collarbone together. The worst jolt came when I swung and missed the ball in the eighth inning of the second game."

Curt Gowdy had talked to Ted before the game and Ted told him, "I'm not swinging the bat well. I shouldn't even be playing but I'm going in."[69]

340 (#3) May 29 at Fenway Park. Pitcher: Harry Byrd (New York Yankees). RH. Age 29.

Bottom of the sixth inning. One-run homer.

The Yankees won this game, 10-2, but Ted Williams got a homer in the sixth, as one of only two hits by the combined tandem of starter Harry Byrd and reliever Johnny Sain. The homer was quite a blast—"a tremendous clout over the bullpens in right field. The ball landed 20 rows up and covered an estimated 430 feet."

This was another Harry Byrd, not the longtime United States Senator from the Commonwealth of Virginia. This Byrd pitched seven years in the majors and surrendered four homers to Williams. Ted had hit #268 off Byrd, and followed with numbers 360, 367, and 381.

341 (#4) May 31 (first game) at Fenway Park. Pitcher: Art Ditmar (Philadelphia Athletics). RH. Age 25.

Bottom of the first inning. Three-run homer.

The Red Sox scored 29 runs in just one day, with 20-10 and 9-0 wins over the visiting Athletics. Ted still wasn't back in shape; he played four innings in the first game and seven in the second. He was 3-for-6 at the plate, with four RBIs (all in the first game.) He was the one to get it all rolling, with his homer into the right-field bleachers accounting for all three runs in the first inning of the first game.

This was the first of four homers off Ditmar: #341, 368, 395, and 429.

342 (#5) June 3 at Fenway Park. Pitcher: Virgil Trucks (Chicago White Sox). RH. Age 37.

Bottom of the sixth inning. Three-run homer.

Both Harry Agganis and Ted Williams hit their fifth homers of the season in the same game, and yet the Red Sox still lost, 9-6, due to shaky defense. Manager Lou Boudreau was angry, saying "When we stop giving away runs we're going to win a lot of ball games." Ted's homer went into the visiting team's bullpen.

Trout had come to Chicago, but Ted still had three more homers to hit off him — this one and #437 and 444. Ted's first nine homers off Trucks: 108, 115, 146, 174, 189, 226, 236, 243, and 320.

343 (#6) June 25 at Comiskey Park, Chicago. Pitcher: Bob Keegan (Chicago White Sox). RH. Age 33.

Top of the ninth inning. Two-run homer.

Ted had been laid low with a virus and missed 21 games. He entered this game in the ninth inning as a pinch-hitter. The Red Sox were losing, 6-2, and there were two outs. Ted Lepcio was on board with an inning-opening single and he'd advanced to third base on two grounders. Williams took two balls and then a strike. "The fourth pitch Keegan fired was also low but Ted pickled it with a quick flip of the wrists and the ball soared over the head of [Jim] Rivera and into the [lower deck of the right-field] stands." (*Boston Herald*) It went 400-450 feet. The Red Sox lost, 6-4.

Keegan was the only pitcher who gave up three home runs to Ted, all on the same day: #425, 426, and 427. This was the first of seven in all, the other four being this one (343) and then 352, 364, and 414.

344 (#7) July 7 at Yankee Stadium, New York. Pitcher: Allie Reynolds (New York Yankees). RH. Age 37.

Top of the first inning. Two-run homer.

Williams started the game off right. He "belted a towering drive into the upper deck in right field. It landed halfway up in the seats...But Ted still insists that he is 'weak' from his bout with a virus in his lung." (*Boston Traveler*) The Yankees won the game, however, 17-9—and the game only lasted eight innings, due to rain.

In his last year in the big leagues, Reynolds allowed 13 homers. This was the last one he allowed Ted Williams. He had previously given up #199, 216, 251, 265, and 290.

345 (#8) July 11 (first game) at Connie Mack Stadium, Philadelphia. Pitcher: Dutch Romberger (Philadelphia Athletics). RH. Age 27.

Top of the sixth inning. Three-run homer.

Ted singled in the first, then walked in the third, the fourth (intentionally), and the fifth. Each time he walked, he scored. The Red Sox were doing pretty well in the game, ahead 14-0 at this point. Then in the sixth, Williams came up again—for the fourth inning in a row. Milt Bolling and Jimmy Piersall had both singled. There was nobody out. He made it 17-0 with a three-run homer. It was "a massive homer...over the clock atop the high wall in right-center. It prompted comparisons. Only Ruth and Foxx, said the elders, stroked them further." (*Record*) The Red Sox won the game (no surprise there), 18-0, and then took the second game, too, 11-1. Red Sox batters collected 40 hits.

This was the only homer Ted hit off Romberger. It was Romberger's only year in the majors, and one of only three he surrendered.

346 (#9) July 15 (first game) at Fenway Park. Pitcher: Steve Gromek (Detroit Tigers). RH. Age 34.

Bottom of the third inning. One-run homer.

Sammy White and Harry Agganis each registered a run batted in during the first inning. Ted's homer provided a little extra insurance in the third, leading to a 3-1 win over the Tigers. The homer was a huge one, landing 20 rows deep ("high as the Hancock Building in the background," wrote John Gillooly in the *Record*) in the right-field pavilion. Detroit won the second game of the day/night doubleheader, 4-2.

Gromek surrendered homers #115, 155, 205, 263, 437, and 354.

347 (#10) July 18 (second game) at Fenway Park. Pitcher: Duane Pillette (Baltimore Orioles). RH. Age 31.

Bottom of the fourth inning. One-run homer.

Russ Kemmerer threw a one-hitter in the first game, a 4-0 shutout. Only Sam Mele's seventh-inning single off the left-field wall marred Kemmerer's game. It was his first start in the major leagues. The O's won the second game, 4-1, with Williams' home run in the fourth being that one run. He hit it against the shift, "a loft into the left-field netting"—the screen on top of the wall.

The first homer Ted hit off Pillette was in 1951, #315.

348 (#11) July 19 (first game) at Fenway Park. Pitcher: Bob Chakales (Baltimore Orioles). RH. Age 26.

Bottom of the sixth inning. Three-run homer.

The Red Sox hit seven home runs in the day's two games, with Williams and Jackie Jensen each getting two. Mickey Owen's grand slam (just after Ted was walked intentionally) capped a six-run ninth inning that catapulted the Red Sox to a 9-7 win. Ted's first homer came in the sixth inning and provided all the runs the Red Sox had before the ninth. It wasn't much of a homer as homers go — "a little poke which landed just inside the foul pole in right field" — but it still counted for three runs. The *Daily Record* dubbed it "a Hong-Konger just beyond the foul pole in right, so small he'd throw it back if he were out fishing."

Chakales, a teammate of Ted's in 1957, allowed three home runs, this one and numbers 357 and 421.

349 (#12) July 19 (second game) at Fenway Park. Pitcher: Don Larsen (Baltimore Orioles). RH. Age 24.

Bottom of the fourth inning. One-run homer.

Ted's second home run of the day, in the second game of the day, was "a king-sized homer deep in the right-field grandstand." The two games were 9-7 and 8-5, both Boston wins.

The first of three homers hit off Larsen. Ted also hit #387 and #449.

350 (#13) July 21 at Fenway Park. Pitcher: Art Houtteman (Cleveland Indians). RH. Age 26.

Bottom of the third inning. One-run homer.

The Red Sox neither won nor lost this game, a 7-7 tie brought to an end by rains. It was the second Red Sox game in a row which ended in a tie; the game before was a 5-5 stalemate. The home run "bounced into the Indians bullpen" explained Bob Coyne's sports page cartoon in the *Boston Post*, but the text explained it had landed in the seats behind the bullpen, and then bounced back into the bullpen.

This was the sixth homer hit off Houtteman: #231, 239, 249, 275, and 285 were the first five.

351 (#14) July 22 (first game) at Fenway Park. Pitcher: Bob Feller (Cleveland Indians). RH. Age 35. Hall of Famer.

Bottom of the fifth inning. Two-run homer.

This was the seventh home run Williams hit off Bob Feller. It was a line drive right into the Cleveland bullpen and tied the score 3-3 at the time (the Indians won, 6-3.) The Indians also won the second game, 5-2. A week later, to the day, Ted hit another homer off Rapid Robert, this time in Cleveland. See #353.

#131, 141, 203, 210, 227, 330, 351, 353, 374, and 416.

352 (#15) July 24 at Fenway Park. Pitcher: Bob Keegan (Chicago White Sox). RH. Age 33.

Bottom of the seventh inning. One-run homer.

The Red Sox beat the White Sox, 5-3. Chicago had taken a 2-0 lead but an under-the-weather Jackie Jensen pounded a three-run homer to give Boston the lead. Ted hit one into the left-field netting in the seventh. Later in the seventh, Del Wilber of the Red Sox hit one, too. Ted was only nine home runs behind Joe DiMaggio for fifth all-time.

Keegan's seven home runs: #341, 352, 364, 414, 425, 426, and 427.

353 (#16) July 29 at Cleveland Stadium, Cleveland. Pitcher: Bob Feller (Cleveland Indians). RH. Age 35. Hall of Famer.

Top of the first inning. Two-run homer.

Harry Jones of the *Cleveland Plain Dealer* wrote that "Ted Williams became the first player this season to hit a ball into the upper right-field deck." On the very next pitch, Jensen hit one out to left. Jones also noted that Ted was walked four times in the game, twice intentionally, and that we was going to have a hard time qualifying for the batting title (which at the time only counted 400 at-bats and not a given number of plate appearances as the threshold) if he kept getting walked so much. Boston 10, Cleveland 2.

Jensen said, "Ted helps everyone on the team an awful lot with batting tips and hints. Stands at the cage every day and has some little thing to offer. His tips combined have been a great help to me." (*Boston Traveler*)

Just a week after #351 came #353. The other eight homers: #131, 141, 203, 210, 227, 330, 374, and 416.

Hall of Famer Richie Ashburn said, "There aren't that many hitters that players watch around the batting cage. We used to do that all the time. We'd gather around and watch him hit. He had great, great ability but he also had great discipline as a hitter. When he talked about the strike zone, he knew exactly what he could do with pitches in certain parts of the strike zone. I'm sure you've read his book. To me, it's the Bible of hitting. I don't know whether everybody understands it. I think there are a lot of major-league hitters who's read it and don't understand half of what he's talking about."[70]

One who did was Mike Piazza. Mike's father Vince invited Ted to see Mike when Mike was just 15. He watched him in the cage and then said, "Mike, there's only one thing I want you to think about. What I see in that cage is about 50 percent of what's required for you to be an extremely good hitter." Then he tapped Mike on the head and said, "This is the other 50 percent. If you can get this—the mental aspect of the game—you'll be one hell of a hitter. You'll hit 25 home runs in the major leagues."[71] Which, indeed, he did—nine different seasons.

354 (#17) July 31 at Briggs Stadium, Detroit. Pitcher: Steve Gromek (Detroit Tigers). RH. Age 34.

Top of the ninth inning. One-run homer.

Tom Brewer and Ellis Kinder (the youngest and oldest pitchers of the staff) combined to throw a 4-0 shutout in Detroit. The Red Sox scored one run in the top of the first on a Jimmy Piersall single, a semi-intentional walk to Williams, and a single to center by Jensen. They didn't score again until the top of the ninth, when Ted hit a solo homer and Grady Hatton hit a two-run homer. Ted hit a line drive on a 1-0 pitch into the lower right-field deck, according to the AP story which ran in the *Springfield Republican* and around the country.

Gromek surrendered homers #115, 155, 205, 263, 437, and 354.

355 (#18) August 1 at Briggs Stadium, Detroit. Pitcher: Ray Herbert (Detroit Tigers). RH. Age 24.

Top of the fifth. Two-run homer.

Ted Williams homered again and drove in four runs in all as the Red Sox beat the Tigers, 10-8. He asked Lou Boudreau if he could bat second in the order and his manager agreed. Ted said he figured he'd get ten more at-bats by the end of the season if he did and have a chance to qualify for the crown. "Ted thumped his homer into the upper deck in right field." He also doubled and singled. He batted second the rest of the season.

Herbert's five homers: #339, 355, 391, 478, and 490.

356 (#19) August 4 at Comiskey Park, Chicago. Pitcher: Billy Pierce (Chicago White Sox). LH. Age 27.

Top of the eighth inning. Three-run homer.

Batting with the White Sox up, 5-0, Ted hit "a high smash into the right-field stands" with two out and two on. (*Record*) Billy Pierce had a two-hit shutout going into the eighth but singles from Billy Consolo and Jimmy Piersall put two Red Sox on the sacks. Ted went for a pitch he perhaps shouldn't have swing at. Hy Hurwitz of the *Boston Globe* wrote, "He hit an inside and a bad pitch high enough and hard enough to home-run territory in right-center." The Red Sox scored two more runs in the top of the ninth, tying the score, 5-5, but lost it in the tenth.

Ted also hit #270 off Billy Pierce.

One wonders if Ted spent time beating himself up that night, knowing he'd swung for a bad pitch. "Giving the pitcher an extra two inches around the strike zone increases the area of the strike zone 35 percent. Don't believe it? Give a major-league pitcher that kind of advantage and he'll murder you."[72]

357 (#20) August 6 at Memorial Stadium, Baltimore. Pitcher: Bob Chakales (Baltimore Orioles). RH. Age 26.

Top of the tenth inning. Two-run homer. GAME WINNER.

It's maybe not a good idea to spark a fire in the heart of a hitter like Ted Williams. He'd had five official at-bats in Baltimore in 1954 and failed to get a hit. He'd never hit a home run in Baltimore, since the franchise had only relocated there the year before and Williams was in the Marine Corps. The Orioles dugout was giving him a hard time in the top of the tenth in a 1-1 game; he glared in, and dug in. Piersall was on base. It wasn't the smartest of moves; what was the percentage in heckling Ted? He hit a 1-1 pitch "with jet-like force" and "lashed a line drive about eight rows deep into the stands, two sections over from the foul line about 33 feet out." (*Globe*, then *Herald*) Both papers agreed that Ted had twice paused and looked directly at the Orioles dugout, and then "as Ted crossed home plate, he looked over at the Orioles bench, wearing a big grin." Red Sox Willard Nixon pitched the tenth inning, too, and had a 3-1 win.

This was one of three homers Chakales allowed: 348, 357, and 421.

358 (#21) August 11 (first game) at Fenway Park. Pitcher: Connie Marrero (Washington Senators). RH. Age 43.

Bottom of the first inning. Two-run homer. GAME WINNER.

Batting second, with Piersall on second, Williams hit a two-run homer in the bottom of the first inning and the Red Sox had a 2-1 lead. He hit this one off Connie Marrero into the right-field stands, into the lower seats of Section 2. All the rest of the runs scored (Boston won, 10-1) were superfluous, though naturally no one could know it at the time.

Ted had hit #302 off Marrero, then hit two in this game.

359 (#22) August 11 (first game) at Fenway Park. Pitcher: Connie Marrero (Washington Senators). RH. Age 43.

Bottom of the third inning. Two-run homer.

Ted's second homer of the game put him in a tie with "The Big Cat"—Johnny Mize—who'd retired after the 1953 season with 359 career home runs. The two sluggers were tied for sixth place, all-time. Marrero was still in the game; Ted hit this one into the center-field stands into the triangular section behind the Red Sox bullpen.

Ted's second two-run homer of the game. He'd hit #302 back in 1951.

360 (#23) August 22 at Fenway Park. Pitcher: Harry Byrd (New York Yankees). RH. Age 29.

Bottom of the third inning. Two-run homer.

The Red Sox were acting as spoilers, beating the Yankees, 8-2, and dimming their hopes of catching the Indians and winning yet another pennant. Cleveland held a 5 ½ game lead over New York, once this day was done. Ted's two-run homer with Billy Goodman on base was the first scoring in the game. He homered into the center-field bleachers. He later doubled off the left-field wall to drive in two more runs in the fifth, making it 4-0, the

1954 – batting against the Yankees

double being the game-winning hit. The homer was "far and high off Byrd. The ball went over the Red Sox bullpen and some 20 rows deep."

This was the middle one of five homers Ted hit off Harry. Earlier were #268 and 340 and later came 367 and 381.

361 (#24) August 26 at Fenway Park. Pitcher: Bob Turley (Baltimore Orioles). RH. Age 23.

Bottom of the eighth inning. One-run homer.

Home run #361 tied Ted with Joltin' Joe DiMaggio for fifth place. Unfortunately, the Red Sox lost the game, 5-3. For Baltimore, though, it was a big win, ending a 14-game losing streak. Bullet Bob Turley had a three-hit shutout going in the eighth and Ted actually tried to bunt not just once, but twice. Failing both times (he missed the first attempt entirely) and facing a 3-2 count, he homered into the right-field grandstand seats.

Bullet Bob Turley was another pitcher who gave up five homers to Ted Williams. His were #361, 376, 454, 479, and 488.

1954 – batting against the Yankees

362 (#25) September 3 at Connie Mack Stadium, Philadelphia. Pitcher: Arnie Portocarrero (Philadelphia Athletics). RH. Age 22.

Top of the third inning. Two-run homer. GAME WINNER.

Ed Rumill helped Ted Williams retrieve only the second baseball souvenir of his career. The *Christian Science Monitor* sportswriter said it was only the second baseball he ever asked for. There was the first homer he hit off Bob Feller, and this one which edged him past Joe DiMaggio into sole possession of fifth place of all homer hitters. In the third inning, "Ted lifted a high fastball right over the right-field wall, across 20th Street, and onto the roof of an apartment house. This writer arranged for a 20th Street resident to return the ball, in exchange for which he received a new ball autographed as follows: 'To Bill: this is in exchange for my record-breaking home run number 362. Thanks, Ted Williams.'" The Red Sox won the game, 11-1. "The pitch was a fastball, up high," Ted said, and he'd atypically stopped halfway to first base to watch it leave the ballpark.

"The ball carried over a 40-foot wall and landed on one of the chimneys that loom up like gravestones on the apartment houses on No. 20th Street. After hitting the chimney, it caromed off the roof of the home and bounced into the backyard of Bill Gillard, a middle-aged man who lives at No. 2743."

Williams had said he was retiring after the 1954 season, but some scribes had never believed it. He was asked about catching Lou Gehrig, which would rank him fourth. "Well, I have only 22 games to do it," he replied.

This was Ted's only homer off Portocarrero.

363 (#26) September 5 (first game) at Connie Mack Stadium, Philadelphia. Pitcher: Bill Oster (Philadelphia Athletics). LH. Age 21.

Top of the seventh inning. Two-run homer.

By scores of 12-5 and 7-3, the Red Sox took two from Philadelphia. Milt Bolling had five hits on the day, and Jackie Jensen hit two home runs. And Ted Williams hit one off the light stanchion in right field.

This was Ted's only homer off Oster. It was one of only two homers Oster sur-rendered and they both came in the same inning of the same game. Milt Bolling had hit a three-run homer, three batters earlier. He had recently joined the A's out of NYU. He only appeared in eight big-league games.

Oster struck Ted out on a curveball his first time up. His second time up, Ted told the catcher, "He's starting to tire" and flew out to center field. The third time up, he said, "The kid's lost it"—and hit the home run.[73]

364 (#27) September 12 (first game) at Comiskey Park, Chicago. Pitcher: Bob Keegan (Chicago White Sox). RH. Age 33.

Top of the seventh inning. One-run homer.

The Red Sox dropped two games, and dropped in the standings from fourth place to fifth place. Ted Williams had eight at-bats but only one hit—his home run in the seventh inning, a line drive into the lower deck in right field.

This was Keegan's third homer of the year—#341, 352, and this one. Keegan later served up four more: #414, 425, 426, and 427.

365 (#28) September 20 at Fenway Park. Pitcher: Johnny Gray (Philadelphia Athletics). RH. Age 26.

Bottom of the seventh inning. One-run homer.

There were only 1,555 fans who turned out for the game, but they saw the Red Sox beat the A's, 5-2. Farrell was Ted Williams led off the seventh inning with his home run, "a high drive which was escorted into the visiting bullpen by the wind."

This was Ted's only homer off Gray.

366 (#29) September 26 at Fenway Park. Pitcher: Gus Keriazakos (Washington Senators). RF. Age 22.

Bottom of the seventh inning. One-run homer.

Back in the spring of 1954, Williams had written a series of article for the *Saturday Evening Post* entitled, "This is My Last Year in Baseball." On September 26, he reiterated his intention to retire and in what might have been his last at-bat as a major leaguer, he led off the seventh inning with a home run. As it happened, the Sox scored four more runs and Ted got another at-bat in the eighth. He popped up to the shortstop. The home run was hit into the right-field grandstand seats and grabbed by Tufts College freshman Henry McKenna, who posed for a photo with Ted after the game. The Red Sox won, 11-2.

Williams may even have believed it was his last time at bat in the major leagues. Sportswriter George Sullivan said that in the clubhouse after the game, "it was the first time I'd seen him almost misty-eyed, very sentimental."[74]

This was Ted's only homer off Keriazakos.

1955

Williams' first game of the 1955 season didn't come until May 28. He'd meant it when he'd told people in 1954 that he was going to retire—and that's what he did. However, strange as it might seem to some, four days after his divorce from Doris Soule Williams became final and all the financial terms agreed to on May 9, he took up employment again. The next day, May 14, he took batting practice at Fenway and hit a few out off Boo Ferriss.

May 30 seemed late for Ted's first home run of the year in 1955. In 1956, his first homer didn't come until June 22. It was his 41st game of the season, and he was hitting .344 as of the day before. He just hadn't hit a home run yet. The latest he'd ever hit a homer before was in the ninth game of his season.

367 (#1 of 1955) May 30 (first game) at Fenway Park. Pitcher: Harry Byrd (Baltimore Orioles). RH. Age 30.

Bottom of the first inning. Three-run homer.

In the first game of the Memorial Day twinbill, Ted didn't waste time. After a walk and a walk, Ted homered for a quick three runs. The Orioles won, though, 8-6. Williams banged Byrd's ball into the right grandstand seats. Joking with Red Sox rookie Bill Klaus, Ted asked him how many homers he'd hit at Minneapolis in 1954. Klaus said he'd hit 21. Ted said, "Hmm. Hit 21 at Minneapolis, too—that was in 1938." Then he added, "And I hit 22 on the road." (*Washington Post*)

Byrd gave up five homers to Ted Williams: #268, 340, 360, 367, and 381.

Ted Williams: "I worked out for a few days, about 10 or 11, running hard to get my legs in shape and that year at the start I used golf gloves on both hands in batting practice so I wouldn't develop blisters. I was swinging a lot, trying to get ready in a hurry, and I couldn't afford to wait for the calluses. I hit a home run my first day back. I hit .356 for the season. Al Kaline won the batting championship with .340. I wasn't even close, because I only got up 320 times. Even if they hadn't walked me so much (110 times) I probably would not have made it that year anyway, but the rules committee finally saw the injustice of it and changed the rules. Now a batter needs only 502 physical appearances at the plate rather than 400 official times-at-bat to qualify for the championship."[75]

Ted was also the first hitter to use rosin to keep his hands dry, wrote Ed Linn, quoting Bobby Doerr, adding "And then he got the idea of mixing the rosin with olive oil to concoct a sticky substance to apply to the bat." Years before players began to use pine tar. [76]

Linn also details the kinds of exercise routines Ted developed for himself. And then pursued. Relentlessly.

368 (#2) June 4 at Municipal Stadium, Kansas City. Pitcher: Art Ditmar (Kanas City Athletics). RH. Age 26.

Top of the sixth. One-run homer.

Ted hit a single and a double and a home run, the homer breaking up a 0-0 tie in the top of the sixth. Two batters later, Jackie Jensen had singled and Norm Zauchin homered. It was a "well-hit ball that went over the right-field barrier (353 feet) with plenty to spare and came to rest half-way up the banking that surrounds this spanking new ballpark. The homer covered some 400 feet."

This was the second of four homers off Ditmar: #341, 368, 395, and 429.

369 **(#3)** June 10 at Briggs Stadium, Detroit. Pitcher: Duke Maas (Detroit Tigers). RH. Age 26.

Top of the first inning. One-run homer.

Coming off a heavy cold that had kept him out for a couple of days in Cleveland, Ted couldn't pass up the opportunity to hit in Detroit. He enjoyed his return to Briggs Stadium, hitting two homers—the first one, a solo home run with two outs in the top of the first. It was a line drive into the lower right-field seats.

Williams only hit two homers off Duke Maas. They both came in the same game, in the first inning and in the third inning.

370 **(#4)** June 10 at Briggs Stadium, Detroit. Pitcher: Duke Maas (Detroit Tigers). RH. Age 26.

Top of the third inning. Two-run homer. GAME WINNER.

His second time up in the game, Ted lined one deep into the upper deck in right. It was another two-out homer, but this time was a two-run homer, with Billy Klaus on board. Williams was responsible for the first three runs in a 5-2 win.

With his second homer of the June 10 game, Williams won the game over Duke Maas.

371 **(#5)** June 14 at Fenway Park. Pitcher: Tom Gorman (Kansas City Athletics). RH. Age 30.

Bottom of the seventh inning. One-run homer.

Ted's "high homer into the right-field grandstand" was just one of Boston's 12 hits and accounted for just one of the 12 runs the Red Sox scored while routing Kansas City, 12-4. The homer was the 12th run. He also hit a double, #400 of his career, which had driven in another. Ted had three RBIs in the game.

The first of four homers: #371, 400, 417, and 463.

372 (#6) June 16 at Fenway Park. Pitcher: Cloyd Boyer (Kansas City Athletics). RH. Age 27.

Bottom of the fifth. One-run homer.

Billy Klaus hit a walkoff home run in the ninth to give the Red Sox a 7-6 win. Ted's solo homer had tied the score earlier in the game, 2-2. It was "titanic…a tremendous homer into the area they once called Williamsburg." Ted deliberately placed a key hit down the third-base line to kick off the eighth, followed immediately by back-to-back homers from Jensen and Zauchin. Ted's hit to left was the talk after the game, but the *Herald's* Sampson called the homer "one of his King Size clouts, a towering smash soaring 20 rows deep into the bleachers beyond the visiting club bullpen."

This was Ted's only home run off Boyer.

373 (#7) June 19 at Fenway Park. Pitcher: Herb Score (Cleveland Indians). LH. Age 22.

Bottom of the fifth inning. One-run homer.

This was quite a day, to hit homers off both Herb Score and Bob Feller in the same game. The Indians were on top, 5-3, when Ted brought Boston a bit closer with his leadoff homer in the fifth. It was a 430-foot shot into the center-field bleachers. It "crashed against a bleacher plank in dead center." (*Herald*) He may have fired up the troops; the Sox scored four more runs in the inning, three on a Piersall home run.

Score struck out Ted in the first inning, the first time he'd ever faced him. Ted told his teammates, back on the bench, "If he throws me that pitch I struck out on again, I'll hit one today." Ted sat on the pitch, and homered in the fifth.[77]

Ted homered three times off fireballing rookie Herb Score in 1955, and once in 1956. Homers: 373, 382, 389, and 415.

374 (#8) June 19 at Fenway Park. Pitcher: Bob Feller (Cleveland Indians). RH. Age 36. Hall of Famer.

Bottom of the eighth inning. Two-run homer.

Total distance of Ted's two homers was reckoned at 830 feet on the day, with this 400-foot drive into the right-field grandstand making the score 10-7 in his team's favor. Sammy White's RBI double later in the inning produced the final run of the 11-7 win.

This was his penultimate homer off Feller. The other numbers were 131, 141, 203, 210, 227, 330, 351, 353, and 416.

Jimmy Piersall told a story: "Hitting was the name of his game. He went 5-for-5 against Feller one day and he was unhappy because they were all ground balls. He took in extra batting practice after the game. He was such a perfectionist."[78] There is a problem with Piersall's memory. Ted never had a 5-for-5 day against Feller, though he did have a 4-for-4 day once. One of the four was a home run. Regardless of the details, the story does give us an insight into Ted's character.

375 (#9) June 21 at Fenway Park. Pitcher: Ned Garver (Detroit Tigers). RH. Age 29.

Bottom of the eighth inning. Three-run homer. GAME WINNER.

"The moral of this story is, never take a chance on Ted Williams, regardless of the count." So wrote Bob Holbrook of the *Boston Globe*. Ted swung and connected on a 3-0 pitch and drove a home run into the right-field stands. After the game, Williams mostly complained that he hadn't hit it will, not like the two he'd hit on the 19th. Hitting a ball *well* was important to Ted Williams. "I didn't get a good pitch to hit all night," he grumbled. "I think it was supposed to be some kind of a breaking pitch. But it didn't do much." It was hit into "the extreme edge of the right-field grandstand." It wasn't hit deep. Right fielder Al Kaline leapt for it, but couldn't corral it.

It was a hard-hit ball, on a day where storms threatened and throughout the eighth inning, thunder was heard in Boston. Writers took advantage of the imagery, and Henry McKenna of the *Herald* began his story: "Lightning flashed across the skies, thunder roared and Ted Williams, like the mighty Zeus, tossed one of his famous thunderbolts into the firmament in another bristling, battling thriller last night at Fenway Park." The Tigers had just taken a 3-2 lead in the top of the eighth; Ted's home run made it 5-4, Red Sox. Detroit didn't score in the ninth.

#213, 245, 272, 282, 337, 375, 385, 422, 436, and 459. Ten Ted homers charged to Garver.

376 (#10) July 4 (first game) at Yankee Stadium. Pitcher: Bob Turley (New York Yankees). RH. Age 24.

Top of the fifth inning. One-run homer.

The Red Sox swept a doubleheader at Yankee Stadium, 4-2 in the first game and 10-5 in the nightcap. Ted's solo home improved his team's 3-2 lead by one run. Jensen hit a grand slam and Zauchin hit a three-run homer in the second game. It was "a towering shot which made the upper deck of the triple-tiered stadium about seven or eight feet from the foul pole." Premier Nu of Burma stopped in to watch some of the second game, but by arriving so late he missed seeing Ted Williams homer.

"Williams was the darling of the crowd," wrote the *New York Times.* "The slugger, in his first showing against the Yankees this season, drew cheers each time he batted. Each time Williams was walked, they jeered."

Turley's five Ted homers were #361, 376, 454, 479, and 488.

377 (#11) July 6 at Fenway Park. Pitcher: Dean Stone (Washington Senators). LH. Age 24.

Bottom of the fifth inning. Two-run homer.

The second game scheduled on the 6th was called off due to a downpour, but they got in the first game, a 7-5 win for the Red Sox. Even the first game had been delayed for more than an hour. Conditions were far from the best, but Ted's two-run homer in the fifth gave Boston a 5-4 lead. Hit on a 3-2 count, it was "a line shot into the center-field bleachers" with Billy Klaus aboard. Ted also hit a double (to left) and beat out an infield hit for a single.

1955-60 - Boston Red Sox Ted Williams (#9) with back to the camera chatting with two unknown Red Sox near the batting cage at Fenway Park. (The man looking away from Williams looks like manager Pinky Higgins.)

It was the sixth win in a row for the Red Sox, and they'd won 11 of 12 and were climbing in the standings, though still in fourth place and 6 ½ games behind the Yankees.

Williams hit one other home run off Dean Stone, #410.

378 (#12) July 10 at Fenway Park. Pitcher: Jim McDonald (Baltimore Orioles). RH. Age 28.

Bottom of the first inning. Three-run homer.

It was the last game before the All-Star Break and Ted Williams' three-run homer in the first gave the Red Sox an early 3-0 lead. It was, though, a lead which evaporated as the O's took a 4-3 lead in the third. That was promptly tied up, but when the Orioles scored three in the top of the eighth, they held a 7-4 lead—until Boston scored five runs in the bottom of the eighth to win, 10-7. There was supposed to be a second game, too, but that got washed out. Right fielder Dave Philley could have caught the ball; it landed in the first row of seats where a fan caught in and then dropped it. Philley had been playing toward the line but had been too shallow.

#333 was the other homer Ted hit off former teammate McDonald.

379 (#13) July 14 (second game) at Briggs Stadium, Detroit. Pitcher: Al Aber (Detroit Tigers). LH. Age 27.

Top of the seventh inning. Two-run homer.

Ted Williams didn't get the $5.00 he was after for hitting home run #379. Frank Lary shut out the Red Sox, 6-0, in the first game. Billy Klaus's two-run double in the fourth gave Boston a 4-3 lead in the second game. In the top of the seventh, Klaus walked and then Williams came to the plate. Before he'd gone to the on-deck circle, Ted turned to Sox pitcher Frank Sullivan and said, "I'll bet you five bucks I hit one out of here." Ted had been 0-for-4 in the first game and had taken a called third strike in the fourth against Aber. Sullivan told the *Boston Traveler*, "I wouldn't take the bet. He was due to connect and, besides, I don't have that kind of money to bet…But I guess I made him mad enough anyway. It sure pays to make him mad, sometimes." Ted hit Aber's 3-1 pitch into the upper deck in right field. Jackie Jensen followed Ted with a home run to left.

The other home run Ted hit off Al Aber is number #390.

380 (#14) July 17 (second game) at Cleveland Stadium, Cleveland. Pitcher: Mike Garcia (Cleveland Indians). RH. Age 31.

Top of the sixth inning. Two-run homer.

Williams was in a slump; the only hit he'd had in 20 at-bats was the homer he hit in Detroit on the 14th. That included the 0-for-3 in the first July 17 game (which Boston won 6-0; Tom Brewer took a no-hitter into the seventh) and the first two outs in the second game. In fact, he hadn't hit the ball out of the infield during the first two games in Cleveland. Finally, in the top of the sixth, with two outs and Klaus on first base, he hit a line-drive homer into the bottom deck of Cleveland's right-field seats for the first two Red Sox runs of the game; the game was a 6-5 loss.

Garcia gave up six homers to Ted Williams: #257, 284, 314, 325, 331, and 380.

381 (#15) July 23 at Comiskey Park, Chicago. Pitcher: Harry Byrd (Chicago White Sox). RH. Age 30.

Top of the second. Three-run homer.

Klaus was the table setter for Williams these days. In the second inning at Comiskey, two Billys were on board—Goodman and Klaus—when Ted swung and hit "a towering smash which landed on the double-decked right-field roof" (*Chicago Tribune*) to give the Red Sox an early 5-1 lead. He singled home a run in the top of the ninth (again with the same two men on base) and the Red Sox won, 9-7.

The final one of the five Byrd offered up; the first four were #268, 340, 360, and 367.

382 (#16) July 26 at Fenway Park. Pitcher: Herb Score (Cleveland Indians). LH. Age 22.

Bottom of the fifth inning. One-run homer.

Ted's solo home run, whacked into the right-field bleachers, gave Boston a 3-1 lead; they won, 5-1 and were climbing in the standings—in fourth place but just four games out of first. Ted praised Score: "He had great stuff. Everything he throws moves. But a hitter always gets his longest homers off a fastball pitcher. I caught one of his fastballs, that's all." (*Herald*)

Four Williams homers off Herb: #373, 382, 389, and 415.

383 (#17) July 29 at Fenway Park. Pitcher: Jim Bunning (Detroit Tigers). RH. Age 23. Hall of Famer.

Bottom of the first inning. One-run homer. GAME WINNER.

A one-run homer in the first winning a game? Yes. And it was the first of eight homers Ted hit off Bunning. Willard Nixon threw a four-hit shutout for the Red Sox. Ted's homer was hit "tight up the right-field line and well back into the stands." (*Herald*) The final was 5-0.

The eight homers Ted hit off the future United States Senator from Kentucky: #383, 439, 440, 451, 472, 498, 504, and 519.

384 (#18) July 30 at Fenway Park. Pitcher: Babe Birrer (Detroit Tigers). RH. Age 26.

Bottom of the fifth inning. One-run homer.

There was an "east wind that knifed in from right field" and Williams combined that with the thought of trying to show he could fight the shift (after grounding to first base for a double play in the first). He singled to left, then homered to left, and finally doubled to left. The Tigers still won, 5-2. Ted had been receiving some heavy heckling from the "wolves" in the left-field stands and he reportedly turned to the fans in the top of the fifth inning and pointed to the net atop of the left-field wall and said the next one's going there. And so it did, just barely, bouncing off the top of the wall and into the netting.

This was the only homer Ted hit off Birrer.

385 (#19) July 31 (first game) at Fenway Park. Pitcher: Ned Garver (Detroit Tigers). RH. Age 29.

Bottom of the fourth inning. Four-run homer. Grand slam #12. GAME WINNER.

He hit a grand slam, capping a six-run bottom of the fourth, driving in Piersall, Frank Sullivan, and Klaus and bringing the score to 7-2 at the time. It was his first grand slam since Korea. He hit it on a 2-2 pitch that eluded Tigers right-fielder Charlie Maxwell and landed in the Tigers' bullpen. He got a standing ovation for the home run and then again when taking his position in left field in the top of the fifth. The Sox won, 8-3, and a ninth-inning homer by Jimmy Piersall gave them a 3-2 win in the second game. All in all, a good day for the Red Sox.

Ted off Ned: homers #213, 245, 272, 282, 337, 375, 385, 422, 436, and 459.

Writing about pitchers who were stubborn in their approach, Williams said, "Ned Garver was another one. Sliders all the time, and you could anticipate when and where they'd be, usually inside. A guy who can swing a bat is going to hurt a pitcher who throws him inside — from them middle of the plate in. In a jam, I could always figure on a slider from Garver. I got to Garver pretty good." One could say that; Ted hit .417 against Garver, with all those home runs.

The battle between pitcher and batter was one Ted enjoyed. And Hank Aaron appreciated what Ted brought to it. "What made Ted so great was that he refused to think that a pitcher could get him out. I mean he just refused to buckle, and that's what it takes to be great. Somehow you've got to feel that you are the best. That's how he played the game, and that's how he left the game, as the best."[79]

386 (#20) August 15 at Fenway Park. Pitcher: Ted Abernathy (Washington Senators). RH. Age 22.

Bottom of the second inning. Four-run homer. Grand slam #13. GAME WINNER.

Ted had been hitting well enough; there were four two-hit games in between homers, but there was nonetheless a gap of a little over two weeks between homers #385 and 386. Both were grand slams and both were game-winners.

Ted Abernathy learned a lesson in this one. Pedro Ramos remembered that Abernathy had struck Ted out twice in the game. "He went by me to drink some water and he said, 'Pete, I got the Big Man twice.' I said, 'You better shut up because the Big Man has to come up at least one more time.' Oh, man, in the eighth inning the bases were loaded and the Big Man came up. Abernathy got two quick strikes, but then I could hear Ted christen his bat: he rapped the ball all the way into the bleachers. Lavagetto took Abernathy out and I reminded him of what I said. I can't repeat what Abernathy said."[80]

Williams drove the ball about 440-450 feet, ten rows up in the center-field bleachers. Leo Kiely pitched 6 1/3 innings of one-hit relief in the 8-4 win.

The ball and bat with which he had stroked his 2000th hit (on August 11) was given to the Jimmy Fund for a contest, the winner to be the person judged to have best completed, in 15 words or less: "I would like to help the Red Sox fight cancer in children because…."

This was the only homer Ted hit off Abernathy.

387 (#21) August 16 at Fenway Park. Pitcher: Don Larsen (New York Yankees). RH. Age 25.

Bottom of the sixth inning. Two-run homer.

The Yankees beat up the Red Sox pretty badly, 13-6, but fans had one consolation anyhow—seeing Ted Williams hit a home run. The score was already 10-2 at the time. It was a line drive homer into the Yankees bullpen. Mickey Mantle homered, too.

Larsen also surrendered #349 and #449.

Mantle later wrote, "Ted showed me what it was to be aggressive at the plate. When he decided to go after a ball, he really attacked it, as if he meant to demolish it entirely. There was never anything defensive about his ways at the plate, no halfhearted swings or pokes. He exploded at a ball, trying to drive it as hard and as far as he could. I know that is not the way for every batter. But it was the right way for Ted and me."[81]

388 (#22) August 20 at Griffith Stadium, Washington. Pitcher: Pedro Ramos (Washington Senators). RH. Age 20.

Top of the fourth inning. One-run homer.

Leading off the fourth inning, Ted Williams homered on a 2-0 pitch, sending the ball over Griffith Stadium's 41-foot tall scoreboard in right-center field. The homer tied the game at the time, but Washington went on to win, 6-2. Pitching was 19-year-old Pedro Ramos of Cuba who threw a seven-hitter for his first complete-game win.

Williams hit six home runs off Pedro: #388, 409, 418, 430, 482, and 520.

389 (#23) August 23 at Cleveland Stadium, Cleveland. Pitcher: Herb Score (Cleveland Indians). LH. Age 22.

Top of the third inning. Two-run homer.

With a home run and a double, Ted Williams drove in half of Boston's runs in the day's 8-3 victory over the Indians. The Red Sox were still in fourth place, but only 3 ½ games out of first in a very tightly bunched pennant race. Cleveland was in third place, just one game out. The homer was in the third inning and left the park "high over the right-field fence," according to the *Cleveland Plain Dealer.*

This tie-breaker was the third home run of the year Ted hit off Score. His other three homers: #373, 382, and (the following year) 415.

390 (#24) August 27 at Briggs Stadium, Detroit. Pitcher: Al Aber (Detroit Tigers). LH. Age 27.

Top of the ninth inning. Four-run homer. Grand slam # 14. GAME WINNER.

A grand slam in the ninth? There's a good chance it could be a game-winner. And this one was, but a bit of a shocker. Starter Frank Lary held a 3-0 lead after the third inning until the ninth. He'd walked three and given up six hits, but all nine batters had been stranded on the basepaths. In the top of the ninth, Lary gave up three singles—without a run coming across. He had two outs, but lefty specialist Al Aber was brought in to pitch to Ted Williams. Two outs, bases loaded—and then the complexion of the game changed in an instant.

Earlier in the game, he'd muffed a ball and allowed one of the three Tigers runs to score. On the 26th, he'd taken three called strikes in the ninth inning with the Red Sox down by one run. A ball, a strike Ted hit foul, another ball. A walk—intentional or otherwise—would have only given the Red Sox one run. But the next pitch was over the plate and Ted hit it 10 rows deep into the upper deck in right field. "Mighty Casey DID NOT strike out," wrote Arthur Sampson in the *Boston Herald.* The win allowed the Red Sox to gain a full game on the Yankees in the standings; they were now four games back.

It was his third grand slam of the year, ranking him fourth all-time. Ellis Kinder got the call, preserving the sudden 4-3 win for reliever Tom Hurd.

The slam was one of two homers Ted hit off Al Aber; his only other homer off Aber was #379.

Williams never really complained about balls and strikes, and never showed an umpire up. Right-hander Charlie Beamon explained, "If they happened to call something he didn't think was a strike, he never said anything. All he needed was one pitch anyway, you know!"[82]

391 (#25) August 28 at Municipal Stadium, Kansas City. Pitcher: Ray Herbert (Kansas City Athletics). RH. Age 25.

Top of the fourth-inning. One-run homer.

The Red Sox administered a 14-2 shellacking of the Athletics, and it was already 8-2 when Ted homered in the top of the fourth. Eddie Joost homered twice. Ted had singled in the first and scored on Grady Hatton's grand slam. He'd singled in the third and scored (from second base) on a passed ball. He had an RBI single later in the game, too. His homer departed over the wall in right-center field and up against the embankment. Despite missing all of April and almost all of May. Williams now had 25 homers in 1955.

Two earlier homers: #339 and 355. Two later homers: #478 and 490.

392 (#26) September 2 at Memorial Stadium, Baltimore. Pitcher: Ray Moore (Baltimore Orioles). RH. Age 29.

Top of the fourth inning. One-run homer.

Ted hit Ray Moore's fastball "into the far reaches of the right-field stands" for the first of eight runs the Red Sox would score on the day, against three for the Orioles. By hitting his homer in Memorial Stadium, Williams had hit for a cycle of his own—homering in every American League park in 1955. The homer landed at least half way up in the bleachers.

This and #399 were the only two homers Ted hit off Moore.

With this homer, "Ted Williams, el gran bateador de los Medias Rojas de Boston, ha conectado de jonron en todos los parques de la Liga en esta temporada, por sexta ocasion en su carrera."[83] For the sixth time in his career, he'd hit a home run in every park in the league.

393 (#27) September 3 at Memorial Stadium, Baltimore. Pitcher: Eddie Lopat (Baltimore Orioles).LH.Age 37.

Top of the sixth inning. One-run homer.

Relief pitcher Ellis Kinder's clutch single in the top of the 12th inning gave the Red Sox the run they needed to go for a 2-1 win. The one run that been scored earlier in the game, by Boston, was the solo home run Ted hit off Eddie Lopat in the sixth. Baltimore's run had come off Sox starter Ike Delock, on a seventh-inning Gus Triandos homer. Kinder had only allowed one hit over 4 ½ innings. Ted's homer was "a towering drive better than halfway up in the right-field bleacher," hit on a 2-2 count right after Lopat thought he had the Big Guy struck on the previous pitch—only to see the umpire rule it a little low.

Ted hit homer #264 off Lopat, back when he was with the Yankees.

Ted befriended umpires and chatted them up whenever he could; after all, they had a wonderful perspective on what a pitcher was throwing and often shared some of that with him. "The umpires make the strike zone," he said. "Who knew better than the umpires who was sharp and who was losing his fast ball and all the rest of it?" So, Ed Linn said, "he studied the umpires almost as closely as he studied the pitchers. On his first time at bat he was looking not only for what the pitcher was throwing but also for where the umpire's strike zone was going to be."[84]

394 (#28) September 20 (first game) at Fenway Park. Pitcher: Bill Wight (Baltimore Orioles). LH.Age 33.

Bottom of the fifth inning. One-run homer.

The Red Sox lost two games in one day, dropping a doubleheader to the Orioles at Fenway Park, 3-2 and 7-4. The team had dropped to 11 games out of first place, enmired as they were in a seven-game losing streak. Ted's homer in the fifth inning of the first game had given Boston a 2-1 lead after it bounced off the roof of the Baltimore bullpen. But two sacrifice flies by Newburyport's Angelo Dagres bumped Baltimore up on top.

A former teammate who was pitching for his sixth team, Ted had hit homer #237 off Wight before joining the Red Sox and this one after the two were teammates.

1956

On the first day of spring training, Ted bet $25 to a new writer, wagering that he could hit a homer on one of the first five pitches he saw. Frank Sullivan, in on it, served them up. Ted hit the fourth one out over the center-field fence. "There, right into that lousy trailer camp," said Ted. He hit the fifth one out, too.[85]

395 (**#1 of 1956**) June 22 at Municipal Stadium, Kansas City. Pitcher: Art Ditmar (Kansas City Athletics). RH. Age 27.

Top of the sixth inning. One-run homer.

Ted Williams' long home-run drought finally ended with a solo home run off Art Ditmar in Kansas City. It was a 385-foot drive over Municipal Stadium's right-field fence in a game played in oppressive humidity. The two-run homer (Piersall was on base) were two of Ted's three RBIs. Don Buddin homered, too, and the Red Sox won, 6-3. Surprisingly little had been written about the lack of Williams homers, though Harold Kaese's column in the June 15 *Globe* said he'd been hitting to left field, against the shift, about 50 percent of the time—and with success (if not power), given the .344 average he had through June 21. He was focused on a batting title, Kaese suggested, and home runs would be incidental. There had been four of them held up by contrary winds "but when he was younger, he sometimes hit 'em through the wind."

Opening Day, 1956 – batting practice

This was the third of four homers off Ditmar: #341, 368, 395, and 429.

Four months in which Ted failed to homer: Ted had played in 41 games before he hit his first home run of the year. A number of those games (19) were in pinch-hitting roles, but he nonetheless racked up 93 at-bats before he finally homered. Throughout his career, there were only four months in which he failed to hit a homer. One was April 1956 (10 at-bats); his 21 at-bats without a homer in May 1956 reflect the most at-bats in a homerless month. The other two months in which he failed to homer were September 1959 (13 at-bats) and May 1960 (11 at-bats). Given 22 or more at-bats, there was never a month in which he failed to hit a home run.

396 (#2) June 24 at Municipal Stadium, Kansas City. Pitcher: Alex Kellner (Kansas City Athletics). LH. Age 31.

Top of the first inning. One-run homer.

Ted Williams hit a homer an estimated 400 feet to the right of the scoreboard in right-center field, in the top of the first—but there was nobody on base and the Red Sox only managed one more run. Kansas City scored five times. It was "a bullet-like drive straight over the fence." (*Boston Record*)

This was the only homer Ted hit off Kellner.

397 (#3) July 1 at Memorial Stadium, Baltimore. Pitcher: Connie Johnson (Baltimore Orioles). RH. Age 33.

Top of the third inning. Two-run homer.

Ted singled in the first inning and Orioles' Billy Loes started heckling him from the Baltimore bench. "Why don't a strong guy like you pull the ball instead of settling for those lousy taps to left?" (*Record*) It's not clear that Connie Johnson appreciated Loes' effort. In the top of the third, with Bob Porterfield on base, Ted hit "a hoist into the right-field stands" scoring both. Porterfield homered later in the game, but Johnson won, 5-2. (*Boston Record*)

Connie Johnson was tagged for #397 and #407.

398 (#4) July 4 (first game) at Fenway Park. Pitcher: Johnny Kucks (New York Yankees). RH. Age 22.

Bottom of the seventh inning. Three-run homer.

Ted's homer into the Red Sox bullpen gave the Red Sox a 5-2 lead in the seventh inning, but the Yankees scored four times in the ninth to take the lead. Boston got one back and it was tied until the bottom of the 11th, when Jimmy Piersall singled in the winning run, 7-6. Ted was a little down after the 9-4 second game which saw a lot of fans leaving in the sixth and seventh innings. He perked up when receptionist Helen Robinson relayed a message to him that Archbishop Cushing of Boston had called to congratulate him on the home run. It was his first homer of the year at home.

Kucks was tagged for #398 and 470.

399 (#5) July 8 (first game) at Fenway Park. Pitcher: Ray Moore (Baltimore Orioles). RH. Age 30.

Bottom of the first inning. Two-run homer. GAME WINNER.

Frank Sullivan threw a 9-0 shutout, so when Ted Williams hit a two-run homer into the right-field bleachers right over the Red Sox bullpen in the bottom of the first, it was the game-winner. It was Ted's 399th home run—he was right on the brink of 400. He also had a single, a double, and a bases-loaded walk in the game—a 3-for-3 day with four RBIs. He was 1-for-5 with an RBI in the second game, an 8-4 win for the Red Sox. The single in the second game drove in the 1,500th RBI of his career.

Ted was involved with another Sullivan this day—CBS television's Ed Sullivan. Ted Williams was national campaign chairman of Boston's Jimmy Fund and he appeared in the three-minute cut-in on the show. At the end of his remarks on fighting cancer in children, he took a moment to ask the kidnaper of 5-week-old Peter Weinberger of Long Island to return the child to his parents. Tragically, Angelo LaMarca killed the young boy. He was himself executed at Sing Sing in August 1958.

Ted also hit #392 off Ray Moore.

1956 All-Star Game—Tuesday, July 10, 1956 at Griffith Stadium

Mantle, Mays, and Williams—Willie Mays hit a two-run homer off of Whitey Ford in the top of the fourth, and Ted Williams hit a two-run homer off Warren Spahn. It was Ted's fourth in All-Star play, tying a record for the most homers in Midsummer Classic games. The NL beat the AL, 7-3, the other AL run coming on a solo home run by Mickey Mantle. Ted's homer was hit into the right-field bullpen.

400 (#6) July 17 (second game) at Fenway Park. Pitcher: Tom Gorman (Kansas City Athletics). RH. Age 31.

Bottom of the sixth inning. One-run homer. GAME WINNER.

"MOVE OVER BABE, JIM, MEL, LOU!"—*Boston Globe* headline.

Hitting homer #400 put Ted Williams into a very exclusive club. At the time, he was only the fifth man to hit 400 or more home runs. Babe Ruth (714), Jimmie Foxx (534), Mel Ott (511), and Lou Gehrig (494) were the ones who preceded him. It occurred in a scoreless game, and was the only run of the game, winning the 1-0 game for Bob Porterfield. At the moment of impact, there was "no doubt about the destination of his smash. He hit Gorman's first toss high into the air and it sailed into the bleachers a half dozen rows up behind the visiting bullpen." There was "quite a scramble" for the ball in the bleachers. It wound up in the hands of 24-year-old Peter Hickey of Winthrop Street, Waltham. Bullpen coach Mickey Owen and a couple of ushers approached Hickey and he got to meet Ted, get a couple of autographed balls and a pair of tickets to a future game in exchange for the memento. He said he would save one of the autographed balls for his son, Jimmy Hickey.

The Red Sox shut out the Athletics in the first game, too, 10-0, a four-hit shutout by Tom Brewer.

After the game, Ted said, "I didn't think I'd ever get it. It was a long time coming. But it sure felt good."

Mickey Vernon said that Ted "was so intent that 'as I put out my hand to congratulate him he didn't even see me.'"[86]

This was the second of his four four-baggers off Gorman. The other three were: #371, 417, and 463.

401 (#7) July 19 at Fenway Park. Pitcher: Wally Burnette (Kansas City Athletics). RH. Age 27.

Bottom of the eighth inning. One-run homer.

Kansas City 8, Boston 4—despite home runs by both Ted Williams and Jimmy Piersall. Both Boston homers were solo ones. Ted's went into the Kansas City bullpen and Jimmy's sixth-inning homer had gone over the wall in left field.

This was the only homer Ted hit off Burnette.

402 (#8) July 21 at Fenway Park. Pitcher: Walt Masterson (Detroit Tigers). RH. Age 33.

Bottom of the seventh inning. Two-run homer.

The Red Sox beat the Tigers, 8-3, with half of the runs (that would be four runs) driven in by Tempestuous Ted Williams. He singled in two in the third inning (the game-winning hit), doubled off the wall in left in the fifth inning, and hit a two-run homer in the seventh — into the left-field screen. Tempestuous Ted? The day before, he'd had another episode of spitting toward the press box, calling them "gutless" and saying, 'Nobody's going to make me stop spitting. The newspaper guys in this town are bush and some of the fans are the worst in the world." (*Washington Post*)

Why hadn't Williams hit a homer off Masterson since 1948? Walt pitched for the Red Sox from 1949 through 1952. He did hit five in all: #6, 42, 197, 218, and then — after the interval — this one, #402.

403 (#9) July 26 at Municipal Stadium, Kansas City. Pitcher: Bobby Shantz (Kansas City Athletics). LH. Age 30.

Top of the tenth inning. Two-run homer. GAME WINNER.

Long relief was much more common years ago, and Ike Delock had already worked three innings in a 3-3 game in relief of Frank Sullivan. The game went into extras, playing in 100-degree heat. Ted Lepcio pinch-hit for Billy Klaus, leading off the top of the tenth. He didn't get a hit, but he did draw a base on balls. Ted Williams was up next and he got to a 3-2 count, too. Then a "flick of Williams' wrists…clipped the next pitch right on the button" produced "a lofty smash that cleared the center-field wall better than 400 feet from the point of origin." It was 5-3 and Delock put down the A's 1-2-3 for the win. The ball "soared so far over the regular fence a little bit to the right of dead center that it landed at the base of the huge electric scoreboard that was transported from Braves Field." (*Herald*) After he'd crossed the plate, a fan in a white t-shirt jumped out of the stands, ran to shake Ted's hand, and then kept running and hopped back into the stands on the other side.

The other homer Ted hit off Shantz was #279.

404 (#10) August 1 at Briggs Stadium, Detroit. Pitcher: Paul Foytack (Detroit Tigers). RH. Age 25.

Top of the first inning. Three-run homer.

Ted hit double digits—his tenth homer of the year—and put the Red Sox out in front early with a three-run homer in the top of the first, "a rising line drive against the empty chairs in the upper deck of the right-field stands." (*Herald*) The Sox held a 5-2 lead after seven, and survived single runs scored by the Tigers in the eighth and ninth.

Ted hit four homers in the 400's off Foytack: #404, 438, 450, and 462.

405 (#11) August 4 at Cleveland Stadium, Cleveland. Pitcher: Early Wynn (Cleveland Indians). RH. Age 36. Hall of Famer.

Top of the first inning. Two-run homer.

This game went into extra innings, the Red Sox emerging victorious in ten, 6-5, another win for Ike Delock after another four-inning effort in long relief. Ted had given the Red Sox a quick, early lead with his two-run homer (on a 3-2 count) "deep into the lower right-field stands" in the top of the first. But the game was tied after nine. Don Buddin singled, Delock sacrificed him, and Billy Goodman singled Don home.

Of the eight homers Ted hit off Early Wynn, who broken in way back in 1939, six of them were in the 400's: 405, 433, 434, 447, 489, and 497. Two earlier ones were #190 and #334.

406 (#12) August 5 at Cleveland Stadium, Cleveland. Pitcher: Bob Lemon (Cleveland Indians). RH. Age 35. Hall of Famer.

Top of the sixth inning. One-run homer. GAME WINNER.

With a walk and a triple, Dave Sisler gave up one run in the bottom of the first but threw a four-hitter against the Indians. Jackie Jensen hit a solo homer leading off the fifth and Ted Williams hit a solo homer with two outs in the sixth. "He didn't leave much doubt about his homer he drove deep in the right-field lower stands." (*Globe*) That was all the scoring in the game, Ted's home run the game-winner. A violent storm ended the game after seven innings, completely washing out the planned second game, too.

Ted hit four homers off the future Hall of Famer. They were #307, 406, 435, and 442.

Unfortunately, we can't pin down which of the homers hit off Lemon was the one he described when talking about how he felt it was good policy for a batter to (almost) always take the first pitch. "Despite taking that first pitch, I was still pitched to carefully—an indication of respect, I guess, or maybe that the pitchers didn't trust me. (I hit a home run off Bob Lemon on a first pitch one time, and he yelled, 'What the hell are you doing?' He was one guy I didn't want to get ahead of me.)"[87]

407 (#13) August 8 at Fenway Park. Pitcher: Connie Johnson (Baltimore Orioles). RH. Age 33.

Bottom of the sixth inning. One-run homer. GAME WINNER.

Red Sox owner Tom Yawkey had reportedly fined Williams $5,000 for spitting toward the fans and the press, but some fans were said to be raising money to help him pay the fine (despite him being one of the most highly-paid people in America.) An advertising firm has reportedly called the park and inquired about renting a billboard and posting a message of support. There was a lot of backing for "our Teddy."

The "splendid spigot" hadn't exactly been contrite. (The phrase was Gillooly's in the *Record*.) Before the game, he said, "I'd do the same thing again if I get mad enough. I was right." The *Globe*'s Clif Keane went out to watch the game from left field, and all but a very few hecklers were solidly in Ted's corner. He was cheered when he first came out on the field. It was a huge Family Night crowd and the score 2-2 entering the bottom of the sixth. Ted was the leadoff batter. He'd grounded out twice, to this point in the game. Then he hit a "long, tie-breaking homer into the wings of the right-field grandstand" and—after shaking hands with third-base coach Jack Burns, on-deck Mickey Vernon, and the batboy, clamped his right hand over his mouth in a gesture to indicate his mouth was clamped shut. A smile had been seen, though, by those close enough to see. "Everybody in the park was watching intently and this action produced a park-rocking roar of laughter."

(*Herald*) Fans left home happy, too, when Parnell kept the door shut and the Orioles scored no more. Williams singled in the bottom of the eighth to help score four more insurance runs and put the game away.

Ted had also hit #397 off Connie Johnson.

Ted Williams: "Actually, Mr. Yawkey never did take it out of my pay. He kept me hanging for a while, then he said, 'Aw, Ted, we don't want your money.'"[88]

Did Ted hit better when he was angry? Biographer Michael Seidel said he once asked Williams why more pitchers didn't brush him back from the plate. The succinct response: "They knew I hit better mad."[89] And he told Jimmy Piersall, "Kid, there's only one way for you to become a hitter. Go up to the plate and get mad. Get mad at yourself and mad at the pitcher."[90] He even told Ted Ashby of the *Boston Globe*, straight out: "I hit better when I'm mad. I'm sharper. My reactions are quicker. My sensibilities keener."[91] The use of "bulletin board material" to motivate ballplayers is an old one. Williams used to use it on himself. Roger Birtwell of the *Globe* reported that he'd overheard Dom DiMaggio calling him out on part of his technique: "You buy every newspaper you can get your hands on and spend half your time reading them—just to find someone to get mad at."[92]

408 (#14) August 10 at Griffith Stadium, Washington. Pitcher: Chuck Stobbs (Washington Senators). LH. Age 26.

Top of the first inning. One-run homer.

The "bad boy" Ted Williams story was a national one and he "received a fine ovation as he came to bat for the first time" and promptly "whacked his 14th homer into the Washington bullpen." Senators manager Charlie Dressen wanted to make it clear he wasn't trying to belittle Williams but he did say that he believed his reflexes weren't what they once were, suggesting that a long fly ball Ted had hit to center field in the eighth inning would have gone out a few years earlier. He granted, however, that "even if his reflexes are not so sharp as they were a few years ago, he still has the power to keep going." (*Boston Traveler*) The day's homer was indeed powered out—a "450-foot drive that bounced off the center-field wall behind the Nats bullpen."

(*Herald*) Sammy White hit a homer and Dick Gernert hit a homer and the Red Sox won the game, 3-2.

This was the only homer Ted hit off Chuck Stobbs. The two had been teammates from 1947 (when bonus baby Stobbs joined the Red Sox at age 17) to 1951.

409 (#15) August 11 at Griffith Stadium, Washington. Pitcher: Pedro Ramos (Washington Senators). RH. Age 21.

Top of the sixth inning. One-run homer.

The *Globe's* Kaese suggested that Williams should quit—"for his own good—to avoid taking punishment that is much more wracking than most people think, because much of it is self-inflicted." He added, however, "Any high-strung athlete who stays in there and competes, fights, wins, loses, and keeps coming back to try again has more guts than those of little imagination who do not compete and never win or lose anything."

The story didn't want to seem to die. A couple of St. Petersburg sportswriters sent Williams a cuspidor with a custom plaque affixed. When Ted let loose his anger, it sometimes spurred him to busting out on the field—and he hit another homer on August 11, already his sixth of the month. The game was a lost cause, a 6-1 Washington win, Ted's homer obviously accounting for the only Red Sox run. The homer was "a smash, sailing into an unoccupied part of the new 'beer pen' in left center."

Williams hit six home runs off Pedro: #388, 409, 418, 430, 482, and 520.

410 (#16) August 18 at Fenway Park. Pitcher: Dean Stone (Washington Senators). LH. Age 25.

Bottom of the third inning. Two-run homer.

The Red Sox were in third place, but 11 games behind the Yankees. They would have been a real long-shot to win the pennant, but were only a game and a half behind the second-place White Sox. Every win counted. And Ted Williams hit two homers on August 18 to try and do his part, going 3-for-5 with four RBIs. The first homer came in the third inning, with two outs and Klaus on board, "a hard wallop that went into the near rows of the right-field pavilion above the Red Sox bullpen."

Ted's other homer off Stone was #377.

411 (#17) August 18 at Fenway Park. Pitcher: Bud Byerly (Washington Senators). RH. Age 35.

Bottom of the ninth inning. One-run homer.

Ted Williams' second homer came in the bottom of the ninth, bringing the Sox a run closer—"a vicious line drive that rocketed into the visitors' bullpen just above Jim Lemon's outstretched glove."

"Little Ted" hit two homers, too—Ted Lepcio. But despite four homers hit by Sox players named Ted, the Senators still won, 9-7.

This was the only homer Ted hit off Byerly. It provided a late thrill for the Fenway fans who stuck around to see Williams get one more at-bat.

"To hit a bullet line drive is one thing; to hit it hard in the air is another thing. I've criticized some hitters who had extreme power and they'd hit line drives and blue darters through the infield—as hard as anybody could hit it—and they've singles or potential double-play balls. That never meant much to me, a hard-hit ball through the infield. Nice. Felt great off the bat. But I'd get to first base and say, 'Boy I wish I'd have got that in the air.'

"Home runs come from striking the ball in the right place with a slight uppercut on the ball, which is enough to get it in the air but still get top spin to it. But occasionally you'll get under it and get the under spin with all the power you needed, and it just keeps going, and then if you get a little wind behind it, it goes a ton."[93]

412 (#18) September 1 at Fenway Park. Pitcher: Morrie Martin (Baltimore Orioles). LH. Age 33.

Bottom of the eighth inning. Two-run homer. GAME WINNER.

SOX WIN, 4-2, ON TED'S 2-RUN HOMER. The *Globe* headline reeled readers into the story of Frank Sullivan winning his first game since August 9 and Ted Williams hitting "a low line drive into the right-field grandstand with Billy Klaus aboard to break up a 2-2 tie in the eighth." The Orioles had just tied the game up in the top of the eighth and one of the better catches of Ted's career interfered with Baltimore's plans to score more; with runners on first and second, he reeled in a hard-hit ball off George Kell's bat.

After Klaus singled to lead off the Boston eighth, Orioles manager Paul Richards brought in the left-hander Morrie Martin to replace starter Zuverink. "At the time I thought it was the right move," Richards said after the game. "George has had trouble with left-handers. But it didn't work out." (*Herald*) Ted hit the homer on a 1-1 pitch.

Ted had also hit #316 off Martin.

413 (#19) September 8 at Memorial Stadium, Baltimore. Pitcher: Billy Loes (Baltimore Orioles). RH. Age 26.

Top of the first inning. Three-run homer. GAME WINNER.

This is the same Loes who had been taunting Ted in the July 1 game (it was clear that Loes was good-natured in his ribbing). Ted got him nonetheless. Tommy Brewer threw a four-hitter for the Red Sox, with the only Oriole run scoring in the bottom of the seventh on a walk, single, and sacrifice fly. By then the Red Sox already had their six runs. The first three came on Ted's four-bagger after singles by Goodman and Klaus. Every batter in the lineup had at least one base hit. Of the game-winning hit, "Ted jumped on a one-ball, two-strike pitch and lashed it into the right-field bleachers." (*Herald*)

TSW later hit homer #420 off Loes.

414 (#20) September 11 at Comiskey Park. Pitcher: Bob Keegan (Chicago White Sox). RH. Age 35.

Top of the fifth inning. One-run homer. GAME WINNER.

This was the third of three game-winning homers in a row, and the 20th home run of the season for a guy who hadn't hit the first one until June 22.

Willard Nixon started and there was a little see-saw action going on in the early innings, with the score 3-3 after four innings. Ted Williams was the first man up in the top of the fifth and he clobbered "a vicious line drive that carried 430 feet and bounced off the Red Sox bullpen roof in center field." *(Herald)* The final score was 7-3, so Ted's tie-breaker turned out to be the game winner.

Keegan's seven home runs: #341, 352, 364, 414, 425, 426, and 427.

415 (#21) September 14 (first game) at Cleveland Stadium, Cleveland. Pitcher: Herb Score (Cleveland Indians). LH. Age 23.

Top of the sixth inning. One-run homer.

The Indians won, 10-2. Ted Williams was on base all the time, but the rest of the team sort of took the first game off. Ted was 2-for-2 with two bases on balls. The only other Red Sox hits were a single by Jackie Jensen and a double by Pete Daley. One of Ted's hits was his sixth-inning homer into the right-field stands.

In the second game, Boston turned the tables. The Indians were up, 3-1, through eight, but Ted pinch-hit in the top of the ninth and doubled in Piersall and Mickey Vernon to tie the game, then left for pinch-runner Milt Bolling, who scored on a Sammy White single to center. It was a welcome rally for rookie Dave Sisler who'd lost a no-hitter in the bottom of the eighth and seen those three runs score—but Sisler had finished out the eighth and got the win. (He did pitch the ninth, too.) Ted's three hits boosted him to .353, two points above Mickey Mantle for the league lead.

The fourth and last homer Ted hit off Herb Score. The earlier three: #373, 382, and 389.

Ted faced Score in a game at Tucson the following spring, on March 29. Bob Holbrook of the *Globe* billed it as the "world's fastest pitcher" against the "world's greatest hitter." "Jesus, Ted went after that challenge like you wouldn't believe. Ted worked him to 2 and 2. Then he got the next pitch and hit it. The last time it was seen, it was going over McDill Air Force base, some place on the California border. Oh shit. All he did was chug around the bases. 'How do you like that, you son of a bitch?'"[94] The ball was hit over the 30-foot fence in center field.

On the day of the 14th, Cleveland slugger Rocky Colavito credited Ted Williams with helping him—an opposing batter. Referring to the last time the Indians had visited Fenway, Colavito said, "He came out and stood with me by the backstop for about half an hour…He kept firing things at me that he thought would be helpful…Imagine him giving me all that time and taking such an interest in me. I doubt if there is any other player in baseball who would have done that." [95]

He helped Al Kaline. He helped Harvey Kuenn. Moose Skowron said, "He's helped every young kid who ever went to him. He has the respect of all the players. I learned more about hitting by talking to Ted for ten minutes than I'd learned in my entire career."[96]

416 (#22) September 15 at Cleveland Stadium, Cleveland. Pitcher: Bob Feller (Cleveland Indians). RH. Age 37. Hall of Famer.

Top of the sixth inning. Three-run homer.

It wasn't a game-winner but it was a very important home run. The Indians held a 3-0 lead through the first five. The Red Sox got a couple of men on base and then Ted "banged the one-and-one pitch over the fence in left-center, 365 feet from the plate." That tied the game.

With the bases loaded and one out in the top of the ninth, Sammy White singled and drove in two and the Red Sox were on their way to a 5-3 win.

It was Feller's last year in the majors. This was the 10th homer Ted had hit off him (the full list being 131, 141, 203, 210, 227, 330, 351, 353, 374, and this one, 416.) This was the first one that drove in three runs. Not one of the 10 was a game-winning homer.

417 (#23) September 18 at Municipal Stadium, Kansas City. Pitcher: Tom Gorman (Kansas City Athletics). RH. Age 31.

Top of the seventh inning. One-run homer.

Ted's homer produced the first run as the Red Sox rallied from being down 4-0, starting with Williams' leadoff homer in the seventh—"a wallop over the 387-foot sign in right-center." (*Boston Post*) The Sox even briefly took a 5-4 lead, but single Kansas City runs in the bottom of the eighth and ninth gave them a 6-5 victory.

Four-baggers Williams hit off Gorman: #371, 400, 417, and 463.

418 (#24) September 25 at Fenway Park. Pitcher: Pedro Ramos (Washington Senators). RH. Age 21.

Bottom of the second inning. Three-run homer. GAME WINNER.

A second-inning three-run homer hit over the visiting bullpen provided runs four, five, and six in a 6-0 lead. The final score, giving Dave Sisler a win, was 10-4, Red Sox. Pedro Ramos had already beaten the Red Sox six times in 1956; it was good for the team to get one.

Williams hit six home runs off Pedro: #388, 409, 418, 430, 482, and 520. The first two were warmups, but each one of the last four were game-winners.

1957

A homer in Hollywood

Ted Williams' first home run of 1957 was hit in Hollywood, during a March 25 spring training game against the Hollywood Stars at Gilmore Field. It was a 3-0 win for the Red Sox. With one out in the third inning, he hit one and "the ball went over the fence in right-center like a cannon. It was one of Ted's towering types which was almost as high as the light tower."

419 (#1 of 1957) April 21 at Fenway Park. Pitcher: Tom Sturdivant (New York Yankees). RH. Age 27.

Bottom of the sixth inning. One-run homer.

Ted's first home run of a season that in some ways could be said to be his most impressive came against the Yankees in the fourth game of the year, a solo homer in the sixth. It was a homer "from Santa Claus. Ted lofted a high drive towards medium right. Hank Bauer came in to catch it but the wind escorted the ball into the right-field grandstand." The *Daily Record* said, "He never got a cheaper one." It went about one yard past the foul pole and into just the second row of seats. The *Boston Herald* ran a photo of David L. Plummer of Beacon Hill catching the ball with his bare hand; Plummer said he would auction it off for the Jimmy Fund.

In the eighth, he hit a ball harder and further, "off the base of the center-field bleacher for one of the longest singles possible."

Many consider 1957 to be Ted's best season. The year he turned 39, he hit .388. This was the first of his 38 home runs. He later hit #455 off Tom Sturdivant, the 37th of those 38 home runs.

420 (#2) April 23 at Fenway Park. Pitcher: Billy Loes (Baltimore Orioles). RH. Age 27.

Bottom of the first inning. One-run homer.

Frank Sullivan threw a four-hit, 3-1, win. Ted drove in two of the runs — the first and the third — the first one coming in the bottom of the first. It was a curve ball, low and inside, and "the big guy really unloaded on it and drilled the ball into the center-field bleachers, 435 feet away."

Homer #413 had been hit off Loes in September 1956.

421 (#3) April 24 at Griffith Stadium, Washington. Pitcher: Bob Chakales (Washington Senators). RH. Age 29.

Top of the eighth inning. One-run homer.

Boston took a 2-0 lead, then fell behind, 3-2. In the top of the eighth, Ted tied it up with a bases-empty home run "over the 31-foot high fence in right field, 360 feet out from home plate." (*Herald*) The Red Sox won the game, 4-3, in the tenth on a hit by Jackie Jensen. The game might not have been tied after nine, but Senators starting pitcher Pedro Ramos was called out for failing to touch third base on his way to the plate in the bottom of the fourth inning. It would have given Washington a 4-2 lead.

Five days after allowing this home run, Chakales was traded to the Red Sox, with Dean Stone, for Milt Bolling, Russ Kemmerer, and Faye Throneberry.

422 (#4) April 30 at Municipal Stadium, Kansas City. Pitcher: Ned Garver (Kansas City Athletics). RH. Age 31.

Top of the eighth inning. One-run homer.

Willard Nixon threw a three-hitter and the Red Sox won, 3-1, on homers by Jackie Jensen and Ted Williams. Ted's eighth-inning four-base hit was a "line drive boring into the dirt banking outside the right-field fence." (*Herald*). He also "made one of the most sensational catches of his long career in the seventh when he robbed Simpson of what seemed like a sure double." It was such a dramatic catch that veteran *Herald* scribe Arthur Sampson devoted three paragraphs to it. Ted also singled and doubled.

#213, 245, 272, 282, 337, 375, 385, 422, 436, and 459.

423 (#5) May 1 at Municipal Stadium, Kansas City. Pitcher: Tom Morgan (Kansas City Athletics). RH. Age 27.

Top of the first inning. One-run homer.

The A's won, 7-5, dropping Dave Sisler to 0-4 against Kansas City—even though he was 4-0 against the Yankees and Indians. Williams gave him a one-run lead with his home run in the first—as the day before, hit over the right-field fence—but Kansas City scored twice in the bottom of the first. The Red Sox scored four more run in the top of the second, but the Athletics responded immediately with four of their own. Ted hit a 387-shot later in the game but the wind held it up and kept it in the park.

#452 was the other homer Ted hit off Tom Morgan.

424 (#6) May 7 at Comiskey Park, Chicago. Pitcher: Dick Donovan (Chicago White Sox). RH. Age 27.

Top of the ninth inning. Two-run homer. GAME WINNER.

Ted gave the team and Tom Brewer a 4-3 win (Brewer threw a three-hitter) with his ninth-inning homer. Teddy Ballgame figured in all four Red Sox runs, with a single and three intentional walks putting him on base five times in five plate appearances. The single (through the vacated shortstop hole, with a shift on) drove in a run back in the first inning. His homer was "a terrific shot into the lower deck of the extreme edge of the right-field stands." (*Globe*). The *Herald* said it "traveled like a bullet into the stands beyond the Red Sox bullpen." Larry Doby's two-run homer in the bottom of the ninth brought the White Sox tantalizingly close, but one run short.

Donovan's 16-6 record tied him with Tom Sturdivant for best in wins percentage in 1957, but this homer cost him one of his six losses. It was the only homer Ted Williams hit off him.

Ted hit .310 off Donovan (18-for-58), with four doubles. He wrote, "Most pitchers are hardheaded enough not to realize you have figured them out. Dick Donovan of the White Sox was a good pitcher and should have been one of the best. He had an exceptionally good slider. He got everybody out on it, but he threw it too often, and for six or seven years I laid for that one pitch and hit a tune on it. Then one day he threw me a big, slow-breaking curve and I looked so bad on it it must have woke him up, because after that the threw me more curves and became a tougher pitcher for me."[97]

425 (#7) May 8 at Comiskey Park, Chicago. Pitcher: Bob Keegan (Chicago White Sox). RH. Age 36.

Top of the first inning. One-run homer.

Before the game, Jackie Jensen bet Ted Williams he couldn't hit a ball out of the park during batting practice. Ted "swung at three balls and the best he could do was hit a ground ball." (*Record*)

Frank Sullivan four-hit the White Sox, while Ted Williams three-homered them. It was only the second time Ted had hit three homers in a game, the other being on July 14, 1946. The first of three homers came in the first, on a 3-2 count, when he "ripped a Keegan slider into the right-field seats for a 1 0 Red Sox lead." (*Globe*) The *Herald* offered a more dramatic assessment: "a smash that almost scaled the roof of the park's high grandstand."

This wasn't Keegan's best day. This was the first of three Ted hit off him in just the one game. See #427 for a full list of the homers Ted hit off Bob Keegan.

426 (#8) May 8 at Comiskey Park, Chicago. Pitcher: Bob Keegan (Chicago White Sox). RH. Age 36.

Top of the third inning. One-run homer. GAME WINNER.

Ted doubled the Red Sox score, taking it to 2-0 when he came up for his second time in the game, in the third frame. "Keegan threw Williams an outside fast ball on the first pitch and Ted lofted a high drive to left field which the favoring wind wafted into the bottom row of the grandstand." The *Chicago Tribune* said it had come on a 2-0 count.

Ted had reached base 11 times in succession, but in the sixth inning he broke the number one of the cardinal rules of hitting. "I went for a bad ball…and I popped it up. When you go for a bad ball, you seldom hit it good. That's why I lay off 'em. But I didn't today." He may have spent as much time beating himself up over not waiting for a good pitch to hit than he did celebrating hitting three homers in the game (of course, it's possible he might have hit four.)

This is the one that won the game, which ended with a 4-1 Red Sox win.

427 (#9) May 8 at Comiskey Park, Chicago. Pitcher: Bob Keegan (Chicago White Sox). RH. Age 36.

Top of the eighth inning. Two-run homer.

Keegan was still pitching well, having only given up two runs through the first seven innings—the two Ted Williams solo home runs. He was still in there, and served up another. This one, Hy Hurwitz wrote, was Ted's "best homer of the day. The ball landed deep in the upstairs section of the grandstand in right-center." When Ted came up in the ninth, he was walked intentionally. Frank Sullivan said after one of the best pitching performances of his career, "Let Ted Williams hit three homers every time I pitch and get the headlines, as long as I win the game."

Ted was walked intentionally his last time up and thus deprived of the chance to hit four home runs in the game. White Sox pitcher Bill Fischer said that Chicago manager Al Lopez had said, "No one guy is ever going to hit four home runs against my team."[98]

In back-to-back games, despite being walked intentionally four times, Ted had hit four homers and driven in seven of the eight Red Sox runs.

Four other Red Sox batters had enjoyed three-homer games—Doerr, Tabor, Vollmer, and Zauchin—but now Ted became the only Sox slugger to have done it twice. And on June 13, he did it again. It's become more common since, with 17 more times someone's done it—and Jim Rice, Mo Vaughn, and Nomar Garciaparra have each done it twice. No one else has done it thrice, and no Red Sox batter has ever hit four in a game.

The Kid was 38 years old. After the game, he said, "At my age, I can only try my best to help the Red Sox as much as I can. There are times when it is foolish to go for home runs and there are other times when it is foolish to hit through an over-shifted defense. The score, the type of pitching you are facing, the wind and other factors govern what a batter should do at the plate." (*Herald*)

The seven home runs he surrendered to Ted Williams in the course of his career: #341, 352, 364, 414, 425, 426, and 427.

428 (#10) May 22 at Fenway Park. Pitcher: Cal McLish (Cleveland Indians). RH. Age 31.

Bottom of the sixth inning. One-run homer.

Ted's home run was just one of four Red Sox homers in the bottom of the sixth inning. Joining him in hitting them out were Gene Mauch, Dick Gernert, and Frank Malzone. Final score, 11-0. Mauch's was first, into the net on top of the wall in left. Ted's came next, "a long home run into the right-center-field bleachers about 15 rows high." Jensen walked and Gernert hit one over everything in left. Malzone's was hit into the net, like Mauch's. At that point, Indians manager Kerby Farrell decided it might be time to make a change. The *Herald* pegged it at 420 feet, but a photo in the *Boston Traveler* showed fans scrambling for the ball, hit high up toward where the red seat stands today.

It was only the second time the Red Sox had hit four homers in one inning; they'd done it before in September 1940 when Williams, Foxx, Cronin, and Tabor had done it on the 24th of the month.

The Oklahoma-born Calvin Coolidge Julius Caesar Tuskahoma McLish also gave up home run #465.

Bud Daley had been the starter in the game. He'd walked Ted the first time he faced him, but with two strikes on him, he'd thrown a fastball right down the middle of the plate. Ted took the pitch and umpire Jim Honochick called it a ball. When Daley came up to bat in the third, he asked Honochick, "Hey, what was the matter with the pitch to Williams? It was right down the middle." Honochick answered, "Son, let me tell you. People don't come here to see him strike out, they come here to see him hit."

Paul Foytack's take: "Umpires had a tendency to sometimes give him a ball call when it was a strike only because he didn't swing at it. I said that's okay with me — don't ever swing at it!"[99]

429 (#11) May 28 at Fenway Park. Pitcher: Art Ditmar (New York Yankees). RH. Age 28.

Bottom of the ninth inning. One-run homer.

The Red Sox had trailed by as much as four runs during the game, but pulled into a 5-5 tie when Ted hit one off Art Ditmar. But the Yankees scored three times in the top of the tenth, and — even though the Sox got two baserunners on before making their first out in the bottom of the tenth, they made three outs before they could get any one of them home.

This was the fourth of four homers off Ditmar: #341, 368, 395, and 429.

430 (#12) June 2 at Griffith Stadium, Washington. Pitcher: Pedro Ramos (Washington Senators). RH. Age 22.

Top of the eighth inning. Three-run homer. GAME WINNER.

"Like the jets he used to fly, the ball tore on a line to deepest center, landing in the Nats' warm-up enclosure, and sending the occupants thereof scattering in all directions." (*Record*) Ted's three-run homer erased a 3-2 Washington lead and gave Boston a 5-3 edge. That was the way it ended. It was a slow curve, said manager Higgins. It hit the wall behind the Washington bullpen, about 450 feet from home, said the *Traveler.* The *Herald* put it at 440, a "viciously stroked liner."

Williams hit six home runs off Pedro: #388, 409, 418, 430, 482, and 520.

431 (#13) June 9 (first game) at Municipal Stadium, Kansas City. Pitcher: Gene Host (Kansas City Athletics). LH. Age 24.

Top of the ninth inning. One-run homer.

The Red Sox won two games, 8-4 and 9-5, in part on a barrage of homers, seven from the Sox and four from the Athletics. Ted hit two—Ted Lepcio, that is—and Jimmy Piersall hit a pair, too. Mr. Williams hit just one, a one-run homer that was icing on the cake in the first game. Klaus and Gernert homered in the second game. Ted's was hit, like Kansas City's Bob Cerv's, over the center-field scoreboard. It was a tremendous clout in any language and was estimated at 400 feet.

This was the only home run Host permitted Mr. Williams.

432 (#14) June 11 at Cleveland Stadium, Cleveland. Pitcher: Dick Tomanek (Cleveland Indians). LH. Age 26.

Top of the first inning. Three-run homer.

The Red Sox jumped out to a quick and substantial lead on the strength of Ted Williams' three-run homer in the top of the first, hammered "over the fence in left-center" field. (*Cleveland Plain Dealer*) Piersall was on base, due to an error, and Klaus, thanks to a walk. They doubled their runs by adding three more in the third and led the Indians, 6-1, but wound up losing the game, 7-6, on a come-from-behind Chico Carrasquel home run in the eighth. Gene Woodling's spectacular catch—his back against the left-field fence—reeled in a Jackie Jensen drive with two aboard in the top of the ninth and may have saved the game for the Clevelanders.

This was the only homer Ted hit off Tomanek, but it's surprising how many times the guy who hit third in the order hit a three-run homer in the top of the first.

433 (#15) June 13 at Cleveland Stadium, Cleveland. Pitcher: Early Wynn (Cleveland Indians). RH. Age 37. Hall of Famer.

Top of the second inning. Three-run homer. GAME WINNER.

Just as Ted Williams had hit homers #7, 8, and 9 of the season just about five weeks earlier, now he hit #15, 16, and 17, all three of them off future Hall of Famers. The day hadn't started well; he was "so disgusted with himself in pre-game hitting practice that he threw his bat 50 feet in the air." Oddly, he then swapped bats with Bobby Avila of the Indians, going for Avila's lighter-weight bat. "That fat job is getting too heavy for me," he said. (*Boston Traveler*) Avila hit a double in the game, using Ted's war club. Williams became the first player in league history to have two three-homer games in the same season. The score was tied, 1-1, with both Piersall and Klaus on base, when Williams swung at a 2-2 pitch and "unloaded a line drive over the right-center-field fence."

The fourth and fifth of Wynn's eight homers both came on the same day. This one set the stage and the next one (#434) won the game. See #434 for the full list.

Appreciating the benefits of a lighter-weight bat ever pre-dated Ted's time in the big leagues. "I switched to a light bat as early as 1938, when I was with Minneapolis, the year before I went up with the Red Sox. It was in late August, and the weather was awful — hotter than I had ever seen it on the West Coast. I was having my first real good year in professional baseball, leading the American Association in batting, home runs, runs batted in, everything. But I was on base so much, swinging and running and sweating, that I felt wrung out.

"One night we were in Columbus, another hot muggy night, and I happened to pick up one of Stan Spence's bats. What a light bat. A toothpick, the lightest in the rack. It was real pumpkin wood, too…It felt good in my hands. I'd been swinging a 35-ouncer, so I asked Stan if I could use it.

"First time up, bases loaded, a little left-hander pitching, and the count went to 3 and 2. As I usually did in those cases, I choked up and said to myself, 'I'm not going to strike out now, I'm going to get some good wood on that ball,' and he threw me a good pitch, low and away but just over the plate. I gave this bat a little flip, and I could hardly believe it — a home run to center field. Not the longest poke in the word, only 410 feet, but long enough…I always used light bats from then on. I kept six or seven bats ready all the time, some as light as 32 ounces, but never over 34 ounces."[100]

In fact, Ted confessed, he'd actually started 1957 with a 34 ½ ounce bat and was doing very well with it against the shift—since he couldn't get around as fast with it. When the opposition noticed him beating the shift, they stopped using it and he switched back to a lighter bat.

434 (#16) June 13 at Cleveland Stadium, Cleveland. Pitcher: Early Wynn (Cleveland Indians). RH. Age 37. Hall of Famer.

Top of the fifth inning. One-run homer.

Ted's second home run of the day was on a 1-0 pitch and left the park, "a high blast over almost the same spot as the first." It gave the Sox an insurance run—but the Sox weren't finished yet in the fifth. Malzone doubled in two and Mauch brought in another on a sacrifice fly. The final score was 9-3. "I wanted to come out after my second homer. It was a cold, crummy night. 'Come on, Mike, take me out.' 'What for? You might hit another one.' Pinky Higgins, my manager, talked me into staying in the game. I got homer number three and a place in the record books." [101]

The full list of Ted's eight homers off Early Wynn: #190, 334, 405, 433, 434, 447, 489, and 497.

435 (#17) June 13 at Cleveland Stadium, Cleveland. Pitcher: Bob Lemon (Cleveland Indians). RH. Age 36. Hall of Famer.

Top of the ninth inning. One-run homer.

Ted's third homer was on a 2-1 pitch. "This was a long wallop over the right-field fence that narrowly missed going into the pavilion where it is marked 435 feet. The smashes got progressively longer."

Ted was, quite naturally, happy to hit homers any time, and three in one game was a bonanza. After saying he couldn't believe it had never been done twice in an American League season before, he recalled the three he'd hit off Keegan in May. "All I know is that when I hit the three homers the other time this year, I got a terrible writeup in one of the Boston newspapers. The story said I hit the three homers off a sore-armed pitcher whom nobody ever heard of. Well, let's see what happens this time." (*Traveler*)

Ted made it clear to the United Press that "batting isn't a matter of eyesight alone. I know a lot of morons in this racket with better eyes than I have who can't hit a lick. I make a study of hitting and pitchers. I have a checklist when I'm not doing well. I check my stance, the arc of my swing, the pitchers giving me trouble." And, we say now looking back a half-century later, all without access to videotape and computers.

Three homers off two future Hall of Famers in one game! Ted had hit two off Early Wynn earlier in the game, and then this one in the ninth.

"A trip to the plate was an adventure for me, one that I could reflect on and store up information. I honestly believe I can recall everything there was to know about my first 300 home runs—who the pitcher was, the count, the pitch itself, where the ball landed. I didn't have to keep a written book on pitchers—I *lived* a book on pitchers. I was a guy who practiced until the blisters bled, and then practiced some more. When I was a kid I carried my bat to school with me. I'd run a buddy's newspaper route if I could get him to shag flies for me. When I played for the San Diego Padres I *paid* kids to shag flies on my days off." [102]

436 (#18) June 23 (first game) at Fenway Park. Pitcher: Ned Garver (Kansas City Athletics). RH. Age 31.

Bottom of the first inning. Two-run homer.

There were two ten-run games this day, as the Sox slammed 31 hits and won both halves of a doubleheader, 10-6 and 10-1. "Ted's first time at bat set the pattern for the entire afternoon since he smashed one of Ned Garver's change of pace offerings into the center-field bleachers with Jimmy Piersall on base." (*Herald*) It gave the Sox a 2-0 lead. They added five runs in the second and three in the third and then the offense took the rest of the game off.

#213, 245, 272, 282, 337, 375, 385, 422, 436, and 459—all ten homers Ted got from Garver.

437 (#19) June 23 (second game) at Fenway Park. Pitcher: Virgil Trucks (Kansas City Athletics). RH. Age 40.

Bottom of the sixth inning. One-run homer.

Ted hit a home run in the second game, too, "a twin of his first homer." Manager Pinky Higgins said, "Those two homers of Ted's seemed to land within a few feet of each other." He almost hit a third one out to center, but the ball "curved just enough to crash against the high wall for a double." (All quotes from the *Boston Herald*.)

"Fire" Trucks was now with the Athletics, and Ted hit his 11th and 12th homers off Trucks during Ted's spectacular 1957 season. This was the year Ted turned 39. Trucks was a year older. Ted's 12 homers off Trucks: 108, 115, 146, 174, 189, 226, 236, 243, 320, 342, 437, and 444.

NOTE: Ted appreciated Trucks as a "great fastball pitcher" and wrote, "If I just said to myself, 'I'll watch for the fast ball,' and waited for it, I didn't get the results I wanted. I had to anticipate — to start my swing where I thought Trucks was prone to throw it — about crotch high, and up, and if I got started somewhere in between I could adjust in time to get in front of the ball. Otherwise, being as fast as he was, I wouldn't have been able to pull the ball."[103]

438 (#20) June 30 at Fenway Park. Pitcher: Paul Foytack (Detroit Tigers). RH. Age 26.

Bottom of the seventh inning. Three-run homer.

There were two outs and nobody on the bases in the bottom of the seventh. The Red Sox held a slim 4-3 lead, all four runs coming on a Jackie Jensen grand slam in the third inning. Then Jimmy Piersall singled. He stole second. Billy Klaus walked. And then Ted Williams — who'd earlier singled and doubled off the wall in left, hit a home run to more or less straightaway center, right into and down the exit stairs that led from the bleachers down to the concourse below. The *Herald* said it was about a 450-foot drive. The inning wasn't over yet. The Red Sox went on to add three more runs before making the third out.

Ted hit four homers in the 400's off Foytack: #404, 438, 450, and 462.

439 (#21) July 12 at Briggs Stadium, Detroit. Pitcher: Jim Bunning (Detroit Tigers). RH. Age 25. Hall of Famer.

Top of the first inning. One-run homer.

TED HITS TWO OFF BUNNING BUT SOX BOW — *Boston Globe* headline. It was a 5-3 Tigers win, and Frank Sullivan lost his sixth game of the season, four of the losses at the hands of the Tigers. Ted did his best, driving in three runs. The rest of the Red Sox drove in none. Ray Boone drove in three for the Tigers, and Al Kaline and Dave Philley each drove in one. The Red Sox scored first; Williams "belted one and it struck the third level of the right-field grandstand." The *Record* dubbed it a "screaming line drive that dented the front wall of the upper deck in right."

The first homer Ted hit off Bunning (#383) won the game. Then he hit two in the same game, this one and #440. Five more followed: #451, 472, 498, 504, and 519.

440 (#22) July 12 at Briggs Stadium, Detroit. Pitcher: Jim Bunning (Detroit Tigers). RH. Age 25. Hall of Famer.

Top of the third inning. Two-run homer.

With two out in the third inning, Billy Klaus beat out an infield hit. Ted worked a 3-2 count, then fouled off three balls. "The next one he lined vigorously toward the right-field stands. It was still on its way up when it struck the front of the second deck in right field. This drive was one of the swiftest and hardest Ted has hit in a long while."

See #383 for a list of all eight of Ted's homers off Jim Bunning.

Ted Williams: "Jim Bunning of the Tigers struck me out three times one day in June and it was a front-page banner: 'TED FANS THREE TIMES.' Not the score, not who won, not whether there was an earthquake somewhere or a war, but 'Ted Fans.' It was one of the few times I had struck out three times in one game in 20 years. (I got a little satisfaction in July. We went to Detroit and Bunning tried those high sliders again — unlike most sliders, Bunning's tended to rise, he kind of slung it sidearm — and I hit the first one on the roof of the upper desk and the second one into the right-field stands."

It had totally rankled Ted that he'd been struck out three times. Leigh Montville writes that Ted's batting cage chatter incorporated a new element for a few weeks, calling out situations as he so often did before the next batting practice pitch: "Bottom of the ninth, two on, two out, Briggs Stadium in Detroit, Jim Bunning on the mound...."

And there was money riding on this day's game. Ted had bet Red Sox PR man Joe McKenney 25 cents that he'd homer off Bunning. "The ball came up and in on a slider from Bunning, instead of down. That gave me trouble. I'd be looking for it and swing from my ass and be, ugh, just underneath it. I was missing the fucken sliders and he had that little extra speed. I made up my mind I was going to swing to get on top of the fucken ball. Pssssshhh! That's what I did."[104]

441 (#23) July 13 at Briggs Stadium, Detroit. Pitcher: Lou Sleater (Detroit Tigers). LH. Age 30.

Top of the seventh inning. One-run homer.

"Williams homered into the second deck of the right field seats," bumping up the Red Sox lead from 4-2 to 5-2. The Sox added one more run and (on his third try) Tom Brewer had his tenth victory of the season, a 6-2 win. Ted had previously walked three times, but with two out and nobody on base, Detroit decided to pitch to him.

Ted also hit #298 off Sleater.

442 (#24) July 14 (first game) at Cleveland Stadium. Pitcher: Bob Lemon (Cleveland Indians). RH. Age 36. Hall of Famer.

Top of the sixth. One-run homer.

The Red Sox played two games in Cleveland and lost them both, despite Ted Williams homering once in each game and going 4-for-4 on the day. The score was 1-1 at the time, so Ted's four-base hit leading off the sixth inning ("a wallop over the fence in left-center"— *Cleveland Plain Dealer*) gave Boston a narrow lead. The ball landed in the bullpen. The Indians scored twice in the bottom of the ninth, to walk off with a win.

This was the fourth homer hit off Lemon. The first three: #307, 406, and 435.

443 (#25) July 14 (second game) at Cleveland Stadium. Pitcher: Stan Pitula (Cleveland Indians). RH. Age 26.

Top of the seventh inning. Two-run homer.

Ted's home run in the day's second game was a pinch-hit homer, batting for pitcher George Susce and driving in two runs. The Sox were down, 8-2, at the time. Ted's two runs narrowed the lead to 8-4, but then the Indians poured on nine runs in the bottom of the eighth, effectively putting the game away. Ted had fouled a ball hard off his foot and after the home run was forced to limp around the bases. His homer was "a high drive which landed on the canopy bullpen roof" and reporters agreed it had more or less duplicated his homer in the first game, though the first one hadn't hit the roof. It was his seventh home run of the year off Indians pitching, taking him to 15-for-33 against the Tribe in 1957. This made Ted 9-for-14 since the All-Star Game; he'd added ten points to his batting average in just one day—not an easy thing to do as late as mid-July.

This was Pitula's only year in the majors; he allowed eight homers but just this one to Ted Williams.

444 (#26) July 16 at Municipal Stadium, Kansas City. Pitcher: Virgil Trucks (Kansas City Athletics). Age 40.

Top of the ninth inning. One-run homer.

The Red Sox were down 2-1 after eight innings, with Virgil Trucks throwing a four-hitter (he'd walked Ted Williams twice.) In the top of the ninth, Ted hit a solo home run, tying the game. Then he walked Mickey Vernon on four straight pitches. Completely a string of six unfortunate pitches in a row, Trucks threw another one over the plate and Jackie Jensen slammed a two-run homer, giving Boston a 4-2 lead. Ted now had six home runs over the last five games, one shy of the record. This game's homer was "smashed on a line over the right-field wall and into the banking behind the fence." (*Herald*)

The last one of the 12 homers Ted hit off Trucks. The full list: 108, 115, 146, 174, 189, 226, 236, 243, 320, 342, 437, and 444.

445 (#27) July 19 at Comiskey Park, Chicago. Pitcher: Paul LaPalme (Chicago White Sox). LH. Age 33.

Top of the eighth inning. One-run homer.

Williams' eighth-inning homer added a "superfluous run" but a useful insurance run in a 5-2 win. It was "lined…into the lower right-field stands." (*Chicago Tribune*) This was Ted's 100th base hit of the season. It was Ted Lepcio's three-run homer in the third inning which was the game-winner.

This was LaPalme's only homer allowed Ted Williams.

446 (#28) July 27 at Fenway Park. Pitcher: Ray Narleski (Cleveland Indians). RH. Age 28.

Bottom of the first inning. One-run homer.

The son of former Sox player Bill Narleski, Ray was a reliever who was getting a start with the Indians—and won the 7-2 game, improving his won-loss record to 7-1. Ted Williams kicked off the scoring with a solo home run in the bottom of the first, hit into one of his favorite spots at Fenway, "thumping the ball behind the back wall of the visiting bullpen onto the ramp in right field between the grandstand and bleacher."

This was the first of three homers Narleski gave Ted Williams. See also #460 and 484.

447 (#29) July 28 at Fenway Park. Pitcher: Early Wynn (Cleveland Indians). RH. Age 37. Hall of Famer.

Bottom of the first inning. One-run homer.

"If Williams can hurt you, walk him." So said Ned Garver, a day or two before this game. Williams homered in the first inning, but it was a solo home run so the damage was limited to just the one run. He came up for a second time in the bottom of the third inning, with one out and runners on first and second—so Indians manager Kerby Farrell had him walked, and it worked out when Jensen hit into a double play. But the Red Sox fell behind in the game, 6-1. The one run was the homer ("a towering drive"—*Herald*) Ted had hit into the bleachers just over the Red Sox bullpen. But Rocky Colavito hit two homers and so did Vic Wertz. The Indians scored eight runs in all. The Sox were down, 6-1, at the seventh-inning stretch, when Ted came up with the bases loaded. Rather than walk him and settle for one, he was pitched to, doubled, and drove in two. Boston scored four runs in the seventh and four more in the eighth, winning the game, 9-8, and Ted was 4-for-4 on the day, scoring three times.

This was Ted's third homer of the year off Wynn. His other seven: #190, 334, 405, 433, 434, 489, and 497.

448 (#30) August 2 at Fenway Park. Pitcher: Jim Wilson (Chicago White Sox). RH. Age 35.

Bottom of the fifth inning. Three-run homer.

Sammy White singled, Frank Sullivan sacrificed Sammy to second, then Jimmy Piersall singled, and Frank Malzone singled—driving in White. And then Ted Williams homered on a 1-1 pitch, the four Sox batters combining to erase a 2-0 White Sox lead and convert it to a 4-2 Red Sox lead. It was, the *Globe* averred, "a jumbo-sized homer between the bleachers and the right-field grandstand." Had it landed in the seats, it would have landed about ten rows up. The Red Sox won the game, 5-4.

Wilson also gave up #223 and 477.

449 (#31) August 14 at Fenway Park. Pitcher: Don Larsen (New York Yankees). RH. Age 27.

Bottom of the second. Three-run homer. GAME WINNER.

It was said to be the second largest turnout for a day game in Fenway Park's 45-year history, some 36,207 fans. Ted Williams did not disappoint, hitting a three-run homer into the left-field screen in the second inning, enough to boost the score to 5-0 and provide the winning run in the eventual 7-4 triumph over the visiting Yankees. Ted singled in the game, too, and boosted his mid-August batting average up to .390. He also starred on defense, expertly playing a Hank Bauer ball hit off the wall, and throwing Bauer out at second base to secure an assist.

Larsen gave up #349 and then #387.

450 (#32) August 27 at Briggs Stadium, Detroit. Pitcher: Paul Foytack (Detroit Tigers). RH. Age 26.

Top of the fifth inning. Two-run homer.

Comedian Jerry Lewis was in town and worked out with the Red Sox before the game, inviting them to his show in town after the game. Ted's fifth-inning home run landed in the upper deck in right field. The game ran 11 innings, and the Red Sox won, 7-5.

The third of the four Ted hit off Paul Foytack. The other three were #404, 438, and 462.

451 (#33) August 28 at Briggs Stadium, Detroit. Pitcher: Jim Bunning (Detroit Tigers). RH. Age 25. Hall of Famer.

Top of the seventh. One-run homer. GAME WINNER.

Jim Bunning squared off against Frank Sullivan in a pitchers' duel and neither team had scored a run through six innings. In fact, Ted Williams hadn't even swung his bat—he'd walked on five pitches in the first, without taking a cut, then struck out in the fourth, again without swinging. He let the count go to 3-0 in the seventh and still hadn't swung at a pitch. Then he did. The count built to 3-2 when he whipped his bat and slugged one, "the ball landing in the upper deck in deep right-center field, considerably beyond the 400-foot mark in the distance." (*Christian Science Monitor*)

Another one-run homer off Bunning that was a game-winner. See the first one—#383. And his other six: #439, 440, 472, 498, 504, and 519.

452 **(#34)** September 17 at Fenway Park. Pitcher: Tom Morgan (Kansas City Athletics). RH. Age 27.

Bottom of the eighth inning. One-run homer.

"The 39-year-old slugger, ill for the past 16 days, emerged from the dugout in a pinch-hit appearance against the Kansas City A's and smashed one of the longest home runs of his brilliant career in the eighth inning as the Hose trailed, 8-7. His 34th home run, hoisted majestically some 25 rows deep into the extreme corner of the right-field stands, barely missing the runway" tied the game at 8-8. It was estimated to have traveled 440 feet before striking a seat and bounding higher into the seats in Section 1, "high into the back of the stands." *(Herald)* Then Piersall beat out a bunt, took second on a wild pitch, and scored on Billy Klaus's single, and the Red Sox won, 9-8. Ted had been out with a chest infection since September 1.

#423 was the only other homer Williams hit off Morgan; it came on May 1, 1957.

453 **(#35)** September 20 at Yankee Stadium, New York. Pitcher: Whitey Ford (New York Yankees). LH. Age 28. Hall of Famer.

Top of the ninth inning. One-run homer.

The Yankees were closing in on the pennant, with a 7-0 lead through eight innings. In the top of the ninth inning, Ted pinch-hit for Murray Wall—just as he had done on the 17th—and again he homered in place of Wall. He hit a 2-2 pitch off Whitey Ford into the upper deck in Yankee Stadium's right-field, at least giving the Red Sox one run in the game. He may have inspired his teammates; three more runs followed the first one, but the game still ended with an "L" for the Red Sox, albeit by a more respectable 7-4 score. Ted's blow "was a tremendously high hoist that must have reached the top of the stadium because from our perch we lost it temporarily in the lights above the upper deck. Then it came down and settled in the first few rows of the upper deck." *(Herald)*

This was the only home run that anyone nicknamed "Whitey" ever accorded Ted Williams.

Ted Williams: "I have to say Ford was one of the five toughest pitchers I ever faced. Toughest for me....Most of the hits I got off Ford were to center and left-center. He made very few mistakes, a tough little guy, and smart. The home run I hit was a mistake. He threw a curve in the ninth inning of a game he was leading by seven runs, but he hung it high and I hit it into the right-field seats at Yankee Stadium. It was the only high curve Ford ever threw me."[105]

454 (#36) September 21 at Yankee Stadium, New York. Pitcher: Bob Turley (New York Yankees). RH. Age 26.

Top of the second inning. Four-run homer. Grand slam # 15. GAME WINNER.

Ted Williams faced 15 pitches on the day, and only one was thrown over the plate. The Yankees needed just one win to clinch the pennant but they had to delay any celebration for another day after Ted Williams hit his 15th grand slam in the second inning, part of a six-run Red Sox rally that led to an 8-3 Red Sox win. It was his third home run in three consecutive official at-bats. "The towering smash sailed fairly deep into the lower pavilion in right field...the Yanks walked him three other times. In fact, they are so frightened of Williams at the moment that the only pitch he got to swing at all day was the grand-slam home run."

Ted hit homers #361, 376, 454, 479, and 488 off Bob Turley.

455 (#37) September 22 at Yankee Stadium, New York. Pitcher: Tom Sturdivant (New York Yankees). RH. Age 27.

Top of the fourth inning. One-run homer.

Four at-bats in a row, and four times Ted Williams homered. The story of the game could have been how Dave Sisler walked eight Yankees, who won the game (5-1) and clinched at least a tie for the pennant, but in Red Sox territory it was Ted going 2-for-2, homering the first time — making it four home runs in four consecutive at-bats, with a bunch of bases on balls mixed in. He'd now reached base 11 times in a row, one way or another. He singled later in the game. The homer was, simply, "a drive into the lower stands in right." (*Herald*) Yogi Berra's comment, reported in the *Globe*: "Ted looks better after he's had a rest, doesn't he?"

Sturdivant led the league in wins percentage in 1957 (16-6, tied with Dick Donovan—see HR #424) and Williams led the league in batting average, with .388. Sturdivant had served up Ted's first homer of the year, #419 overall. Both were solo homers.

Ted said: "It's a lot tougher to hit four home runs in a row this way than in a single game. You're playing at night, during the day, different places, four different pitchers. It's a lot tougher than doing it in four at-bats against the same pitcher on the same day."[106]

456 (#38) September 24 at Griffith Stadium, Washington. Pitcher: Hal Griggs (Washington Senators). RH. Age 28.

Top of the fourth inning. One-run homer. GAME WINNER.

After a record-breaking stretch of reaching base 16 times in a row—a record still standing more than half a century later—Ted was retired when Washington's Hal Griggs got him to ground out in the first inning. His next time up, though, Ted homered—"a line drive over the right-field fence" at Griffith Stadium. (*Herald*) And the homer won the game, to boot—a 2-1 win for Fran Sullivan. A Sullivan single and a Piersall triple scored the first Red Sox run; Ted's homer provided the second. Frank Malzone tied an American League record in the game with ten assists from third base.

Ted's last home run of 1957 was the first of three hit off Griggs. The other two were #458 and #468.

1958

457 **(#1 of 1958)** April 21 at Yankee Stadium, New York. Pitcher: Bob Grim (New York Yankees). RH. Age 28.

Top of the seventh inning. One-run homer.

The Yankees won, 4-1, the one coming on a homer by Ted Williams, who "in the seventh crashed a solo homer deep into the right-field stand." (*New York Times*) The *Boston Herald* agreed: "deep into the stands in right field." It was all that Red Sox fans could crow about, and that wasn't much.

Before being traded to Kansas City, Grim granted Williams this one home run.

458 **(#2)** April 26 at Fenway Park. Pitcher: Hal Griggs (Washington Senators). RH. Age 29.

Bottom of the fifth inning. Two-run homer.

For $3.49, one could purchase a zipper jacket with an image of Ted Williams on the front. For $1.19, one could buy a t-shirt. And every purchase from Leopold Morse Co. on Washington Street came with a Ted Williams autograph, per an advertisement in the *Sunday Herald*. In Saturday's game, Don Buddin walked and Ted Williams "rapped a long homer into the right-field bleachers." (*Washington Post*) But the Senators scored seven runs to five from the Red Sox.

This was one of three Ted hit off Griggs. See also #456 and 468.

459 (#3) April 30 at Fenway Park. Pitcher: Ned Garver (Kansas City Athletics). RH. Age 32.

Bottom of the ninth inning. Two-run homer.

The Kansas City Athletics swamped the Red Sox, 11-4, but those who remained saw Ted Williams hit his third home run of the season in the bottom of the ninth, a two-run homer that was his 1,000th extra-base hit. Pete Runnels had singled and was on base, when Ted "hit a lowish pitch into the right-field extension of the grandstand." Garver said, "It was a slider, inside." Williams was the tenth player to reach 1,000 extra-base hits.

Ted Williams, who turned 40 later in the year, had been hitting homers off Garver for ten years, since Garver was 22. The ten homers in ten years: #213, 245, 272, 282, 337, 375, 385, 422, 436, and 459.

460 (#4) May 20 at Cleveland Stadium, Cleveland. Pitcher: Ray Narleski (Cleveland Indians). RH. Age 29.

Top of the third inning. One-run homer.

Riverboat Smith threw a three-hitter for the Red Sox, who won the game by a 6-1 score. With two out in the bottom of the third, Pete Runnels hit a ball that glanced off Rocky Colavito's "upflung glove and went into the right-field seats...Williams hit a 350-footer—ten feet farther than Runnels—into the right-field seats for a third Sox run." Piersall homered, too. Ted's home run came on a 3-2 pitch, "350 feet out, somewhat down the line but well out from the foul pole." (*Herald*)

Though a little late to the party, Narleski gave Ted three homers—#446 in 1957 and #484 in 1959.

461 (#5) May 22 at Municipal Stadium, Kansas City. Pitcher: Jack Urban (Kansas City Athletics). RH. Age 29.

Top of the fourth inning. Four-run homer. Grand slam #16. GAME WINNER

The *Kansas City Star* ran a headline on May 22: "What's The Matter With Ted Williams?" The Red Sox were down by a run when Ted came up to bat with two outs and the bases loaded in the bottom of the fourth. He fouled off Jack Urban's first pitch, and then the second pitch, and then the third pitch. The fourth pitch he hit "over the 11-foot right-field fence—363 feet from the plate. Fifteen farther on, and up an embankment, it hit the base of a light tower." It caromed off the concrete base of the tower and bounded back toward the field. It also gave the Red Sox a 6-3 lead, on their way to an 8-5 win.

The only homer Ted ever hit off Urban was a grand slam. One can wager it's one Urban never forgot.

462 (#6) May 27 at Briggs Stadium, Detroit. Pitcher: Paul Foytack (Detroit Tigers). RH. Age 27.

Top of the fourth inning. One-run homer.

The Tigers staved off a ninth-inning rally by the Red Sox for a 3-2 win, but Ted Williams placed another home run in his Detroit collection with a solo home run in the fourth inning. Ted had "hoisted a high drive to right that just did clear the barrier and fall in the stands for a round-tripper." (*Record*) It was the only hit the Red Sox had for the first eight innings, save for a Ted Lepcio single in the second.

Four homers off Foytack: #404, 438, 450, and 462.

463 (#7) June 14 at Fenway Park. Pitcher: Tom Gorman (Kansas City Athletics). RH. Age 33.

Bottom of the second inning. Three-run homer.

The Sox won, 7-1, with both Williams and Piersall homering, the infield executing four double players, and Frank Sullivan holding the A's to six hits. Frank Malzone hit a 420-foot triple that didn't miss by much leaving the ballpark; it was his fifth consecutive hit. Ted's homer? "Williams lofted one into the stiff southerly breeze and it sailed into the right-field grandstand for a three-run homer." Piersall's was a ground-rule homer, bouncing off the left-field wall and into the bleachers and then back out on the playing field.

Previously, Ted hit #371, 400, and 417 off Gorman.

464 (#8) June 18 at Comiskey Park, Chicago. Pitcher: Gerry Staley (Chicago White Sox). RH. Age 37.

Top of the eighth inning. Two-run homer.

The White Sox pitching staff had thrown 33 consecutive scoreless innings. Manager Higgins gave Piersall a rest and put in bonus baby Marty Keough, who hit a home run and a key two-run, game-winning triple helping administer a 13-9 defeat to Chicago. Boston scored six runs in the eighth. Ted's was hit "high into the upper deck in right." (*Herald*)

Staley gave up 186 home runs in the big leagues, but just this one to Ted Williams.

465 (#9) June 26 at Cleveland Stadium, Cleveland. Pitcher: Cal McLish (Cleveland Indians). RH. Age 32.

Top of the ninth inning. One-run homer. GAME WINNER.

"No. 9 hit No. 9 in the ninth to beat the Indians here today, 2-1."— Roger Birtwell, *Boston Globe*. It was Ike Delock's first start of the season and he scattered five hits while striking out 12 Indians. Dick Gernert hit a solo homer for the Sox in the sixth inning. The score was tied, 1-1, when Williams came up to bat in the top of the ninth. He was leading off the inning and, on a 1-0 count, he "bombed a drive 10 rows up in the upper deck in right field, only a few feet inside the foul pole. That was the ball game."

McLish had been hammered for #428 in early 1957. He had a lot of middle names.

466 (#10) June 27 at Briggs Stadium, Detroit. Pitcher: Frank Lary (Detroit Tigers). RH. Age 28.

Top of the first inning. Two-run homer.

Ted's two-run homer provided half of the four runs the Red Sox scored to kick off the game. Two upper-deck shots produced those runs. After Marty Keough singled, Williams hit one "eight rows up in the upper deck in right." And after Frank Malzone singled, Jackie Jensen hit another homer "ten rows up in the upper deck in left." The Red Sox never scored again, while the Tigers pushed seven runs across, coming from behind with four in the seventh. For Jensen, it was #20 on the season; for Williams, it was #10.

This was the only homer Ted hit off Lary.

467 (#11) June 29 at Briggs Stadium, Detroit. Pitcher: Bill Fischer (Detroit Tigers). RH. Age 27.

Top of the eighth inning. Three-run homer. GAME WINNER.

The Sox were down to Detroit, 5-2, after five innings. In the top of the sixth, Jensen hit a three-run homer that tied the score. In the top of the eighth, the Red Sox rallied for four more, Pete Runnels singling in the tie-breaker and then Ted Williams unloading with a three-run homer. It was "one of the more spectacular home runs of his career—a soaring drive that landed on top of the right-field roof and bounded back on the field....Williams once hit one over the roof in Detroit, but it was considerably nearer the foul line Today's was farther away, out toward right center." (See HR #3 on May 4, 1939 for the one hit over the roof. This homer sounds very much like #2.) Later in the game, Gene Stephens, who'd come in to sub for Ted, also hit one onto the roof.

A month later, Ted hit homer #473 off Fischer, too. Both were three-run homers and they both won games.

468 (#12) July 1 at Fenway Park. Pitcher: Hal Griggs (Washington Senators). RH. Age 30.

Bottom of the third inning. Two-run homer.

The Jensen/Williams duo dealt again, each homering in a game, a 10-5 win over Washington. Ike Delock's record improved to 6-0. Over a five-game stretch, Jackie had homered five times and Ted had homered four. Ted's came on a 1-1 pitch and "was hit into the last section of the right-field grandstand about 10 rows high." Jensen's went into the screen in left. Every homer hit by the Red Sox resulted in a donation made to the Jimmy Fund by the *Boston Daily Record* newspaper, on a sliding scale. With his first ten homers, Ted had prompted $500, while his 11th and 12th each prompted $75 apiece.

This was the third of the trio hit off Hal Griggs. #456 and 468 were the first two.

469 (#13) July 2 at Fenway Park. Pitcher: Camilo Pascual (Washington Senators). RH. Age 24.

Bottom of the ninth inning. Two-run homer.

With this homer hit in the bottom of the ninth, Williams had homered in five consecutive starts (there was one pinch-hitting appearance in one of the games in Detroit). Ted had driven in Boston's only run in the seventh inning with a sacrifice fly. He came up with Runnels on base in the ninth and "hammered Camilo Pascual's first pitch 12 to 15 rows deep into the center-field bleachers...It wafted high and far over the 420 mark, must have carried 450 feet at least and chased Pascual to the showers." *(Herald)* Then Malzone singled and Jensen walked. The Sox were down, 5-3. Dick Gernert fouled out and then Sammy White fouled out. Pinch-hitter Lou Berberet hit a fly ball long and deep, one which would have won the game, but for Faye Throneberry, who slammed up against the bullpen wall with his glove held high and caught the ball before it went in, ending the game.

The first of a pair of homers hit off Pascual; the second one was in early 1960 — #493.

470 (#14) July 6 at Yankee Stadium. Pitcher: Johnny Kucks (New York Yankees). RH. Age 28.

Top of the eighth inning. One-run homer.

Red Sox 10, Yankees 4. Sox fans are always pleased to see a score like that. Ike Delock improved to 7-0. Ted had two singles and a home run. The home run came in the eighth, the score already 8-2 in Boston's favor. It was "a towering drive into the upper deck in right field." (*Herald*) He also reached base with a walk, and scored two runs.

Earlier, in 1956, Johnny Kucks had served up #398.

471 (#15) July 19 at Fenway Park. Pitcher: Hank Aguirre (Detroit Tigers). LH. Age 27.

Bottom of the 12th inning. Two-run homer. GAME WINNER.

The game was tied, 5-5, after 11 innings, and then the Tigers scored once run in the top of the 12th. It wasn't looking good for the Red Sox. Earlier in the game, Ted Williams had received some catcalls. He'd misplayed a ball in the eighth inning that led to the fourth Detroit run, giving them a 4-3 lead. Misplaying the ball may have been kind; the *Globe* wrote that he achieved "the unusual feat of fielding a one-hop line drive with his posterior" (unfortunately, there are no online video replays). The Tigers were ahead 5-3 in the ninth, but the Red Sox scored twice to tie. Ted came up with two outs and runners on first and third. He grounded out to first base, unassisted. That got him a few more jeers.

It was Ted who came up in the bottom of the 12th, with one on and one out—and swung at the first pitch. He "smashed a soaring two-run homer into the right-field grandstand." (*Herald*) The Red Sox won the game, as the jeers changed to cheers.

It was so stunning a reversal that the Tigers seemed unable to believe it. "I never saw anything like it," said manager Pinky Higgins. "I had to look at the scoreboard to make sure we weren't tied. That Detroit team didn't move from the field. It was the doggonedest thing."

After grounding out in the ninth, Williams had told Higgins that Aguirre's ball was sailing in on him and that, in the manager's words, "he'd have to move back in the box to get a good shot at it." Williams said, "I don't know really what I did hit. Ask Aguirre. That guy has been really tough on me. It's about time I hit one." Of Ted's homer #471, the *Globe* noted, "He's getting closer to Lou Gehrig." Lou had 493 career home runs.

Aguirre gave up a pair to Williams: #471 and #499.

472 (#16) July 29 at Briggs Stadium, Detroit. Pitcher: Jim Bunning (Detroit Tigers). RH. Age 26. Hall of Famer.

Top of the third inning. Four-run homer. Grand slam #17.

Ted Williams started the scoring—big-time—with a grand slam in the top of the fourth inning, giving the Red Sox a 4-0 lead. He also ended the scoring—big-time—with a three-run homer in the 11th. (We'll get to the second one in the next entry.) Facing the future Hall of Famer, and recent no-hit maestro, Jim Bunning, Williams came up in the third with three men on base. He was 0-for-9 against Bunning in 1958, and Ted was hitless in his prior seven at-bats. He hit a grand slam, the 17th of his career, tying him with Babe Ruth for second place all-time. Lou Gehrig ranked first, with 23 grand slams. This was the last slam of Ted's career. He swung at Bunning's first pitch and hit a long foul into the upper deck—just foul. He took a ball, then swung at the 1-1 pitch and this one stayed fair, hit into the upper deck in right, not far from the foul pole. The Tigers scored four runs of their own later in the inning. Each team scored once in the fourth and each team scored three runs in the seventh.

Bunning's eight homers: 383, 439, 440, 451, 472, 498, 504, and 519.

473 (#17) July 29 at Briggs Stadium, Detroit. Pitcher: Bill Fischer (Detroit Tigers). RH. Age 27.

Top of the 11th inning. Three-run homer. GAME WINNER.

The tandem scoring begun with Williams' grand slam had the game tied through the tenth inning, 8-8. When he came up in the top of the 11th, it was with two men on base (singles by Lepcio and Runnels.) Williams slugged a "line-drive wallop into the lower deck that hit a girder and caromed back on the playing field." (*Herald*) Unlike the third, fourth, and seventh inning—each of which saw the Tigers match the Red Sox for runs scored—this time Ted's three-run homer gave Boston an 11-8 lead, and reliever Tom Brewer put down the Tigers 1-2-3.

With a three-run and a four-run homer, Williams had seven RBIs, and won the game.

On June 29, Ted had his homer #467 off Fischer. They were the only homers he ever hit off Fischer but both ones won a game.

474 (#18) August 3 (first game) at Cleveland Stadium, Cleveland. Pitcher: Gary Bell (Cleveland Indians). RH. Age 21.

Top of the ninth inning. Two-run homer. GAME WINNER.

And here is another game-winner, this one in the top of the ninth, boosting Boston to come from behind and win the game, 3-2. (The Sox won the second game, 4-2, on Pete Runnels' two-run double.) Gary Bell was pitching the first game and had been miserly, only allowing the Sox one run on three hits. Runnels led off the ninth. The two had conspired to win the game, Ted telling Runnels, "If you get on, Pete, I'll hit a homer." Runnels responded, "I couldn't let a promise like that go by." (*Boston Traveler*) He singled over second base. Ted ran the count to 3-2, fouling off a couple, then hit the third pitch high into the upper deck of right-field seats. The win snapped a five-game losing streak.

Bell also gave up #487, the following year.

475 (#19) August 5 at Fenway Park. Pitcher: John Romonosky (Washington Senators). RH. Age 28.

Bottom of the eighth inning. One-run homer.

21-year-old Bill Monbouquette from Medford, Massachusetts, earned his first major-league victory with a 7-1 seven-hitter against the visiting Senators. It was his fourth start. Jimmy Piersall's three-run homer was the biggest bang. Ted's homer was not necessary but homers are always nice for the team that benefits. This one went into the third row of the right-field seats in mid-right field "just to the left of the bullpen dividing line." The *Herald* saw a slightly different landing spot, and wrote that the ball actually went into the Red Sox bullpen.

When Ted went out to take his place in left field at the beginning of the seventh inning, the Associated Press reported, "he saw a spectator running after him. Williams broke out into a big grin and began running full speed. When Williams reached his post the fan caught up to him, put an arm around him and exchanged words. Then the spectator walked into the arms of pursuing policemen.

"The man was not booked by police, and Williams was not available for comment afterward. However, one Red Sox spokesman said the fan had a $70 check for the Jimmy Fund (a children's cancer research foundation drive, of which Williams is the chairman), which was one reason for the fan's impromptu appearance — that and the fact one of his friends bet him a $200 Jimmy Fund check he wouldn't run after Williams."

This was one of the two homers Williams hit off Romonosky, both in 1958. The other was #481.

476 (#20) August 7 at Fenway Park. Pitcher: Tex Clevenger (Washington Senators). RH. Age 25.

Bottom of the sixth inning. One-run homer.

Williams reinjured his right wrist sliding into third base in the second inning, but it wasn't so bad that he had to come out of the game nor was it so bad that it prevented him from hitting a tape-measure home run in the sixth that "soared about 25 rows up in the bleacher behind the visiting bullpen." The *Record* said it went "at least 20 rows up" and the *Herald* also cited 20.

His bases-loaded single in the second inning had been the game-winning hit, driving in two runs; the Red Sox won, 8-4. Don Buddin homered in the game, too. Ted's homer was #20 on the season, so every future homer would result in another $100 being donated to the Jimmy Fund by the *Boston Daily Record.*

"I hit this one pretty good," said Ted with a smile after the game, "but I don't think I hit it any better than the home run I hit into the third deck in New York off Johnny Kucks or the one I hit onto the roof of the upper deck in Detroit off Bill Fischer. Those balls were well-tagged, too." Then he added, "I would like to hit 500 homers before I quit, but I am still 24 shy of that mark, and it begins to seem a long way off. I can see the ball just as well as ever, I think, but I've got to admit that I get awfully tired. When I do, I don't seem to have quite the punch I used to have. I didn't get tired two years ago, but I do now. I have to get about twice as much rest as I used to." (*Boston Herald*) It was just over three weeks to Ted's 40th birthday.

This was the only homer Williams hit off Clevenger.

477 (#21) August 20 at Fenway Park. Pitcher: Jim Wilson (Chicago White Sox). RH. Age 36.

Bottom of the fifth inning. Three-run homer.

The White Sox won, 10-8. They'd jumped out to a 7-1 lead, so the outcome was not surprising but the Red Sox had made a fight of it. Ted Williams' three-run homer in the fifth had cut the deficit to 7-4. The ball was hit "well up into the right-field section of the grandstand." Boston scored four times in the sixth, to take the lead, but Jim Landis homered for Chicago in the top of the seventh and put his team ahead for good.

Wilson's two earlier home runs: #223 and 448.

478 (#22) September 17 (first game) at Municipal Stadium, Kansas City. Pitcher: Ray Herbert (Kansas City Athletics). RH. Age 28.

Top of the sixth inning. One-run homer.

Pete Runnels was 4-for-8, giving him a few points in the lead over the 2-for-4 Ted Williams in the race for the American League batting crown. Runnels homered in the top of the sixth and three pitches later, so did Ted Williams, "Williams' homer went 380 feet, 25 feet beyond the right-field fence and up an embankment." Ted sat out the second game. From August 24 to September 9, he'd been laid up with a virus and was still not at 100%.

Ted also hit #339, 355, 391, and 490 off Herbert.

479 (#23) September 23 at Fenway Park. Pitcher: Bob Turley (New York Yankees). RH. Age 27.

Bottom of the fourth inning. Two-run homer.

Roger Birtwell of the *Globe* started his story, "Repentant Ted Williams last night swung his bat instead of throwing it. He did it with deadly effect. Twice—before 21,552 at Fenway—he made hits that carried the Red Sox from behind and tied the Yankees. And on the second occasion he set up the run that carried the Red Sox to victory, 9 to 8." The fourth-inning homer had tied the game, 7-7. He hit Turley's first pitch after Piersall doubled; "it cleared the Yankee bullpen and went two rows up in the right-field stands." Ted had three hits and four RBIs.

The reference to bat throwing was to the famous incident where he hurled a bat in anger after striking out—and then in horror saw it sail into the stands and strike an older woman. She providentially happened to (a) not get seriously hurt, (b) be Joe Cronin's housekeeper, and (c) also be a big Ted Williams fan. Gladys Heffernan said, "He didn't mean it." Tom Yawkey nonetheless fined Williams $5,000.

Five homers that Ted hit off Turley: #361, 376, 454, 479, and 488.

480 (#24) September 26 (first game) at Griffith Stadium, Washington. Pitcher: Vito Valentinetti (Washington Senators). RH. Age 29.

Top of the fifth inning. Two-run homer.

The Red Sox won both games of the doubleheader, Ted playing in the first game and singling and homering in three at-bats. His homer was hit on the first pitch and was sent over the right-field wall. At the end of the day, Ted and Pete Runnels were tied for the batting crown; both had .322580645161 marks (Williams was 103-for-403 and Runnels 180-for-558.)

This was the only homer Williams hit off Valentinetti.

481 (#25) September 27 at Griffith Stadium, Washington. Pitcher: John Romonosky (Washington Senators). RH. Age 28.

Top of the fourth inning. One-run homer.

The competition for the batting title continued, and Pete Runnels added three hits in this game—a triple, a single, and a homer. Ted Williams walked and singled, and—two pitches after Runnels' home run—he hit one, too, "to almost exactly the same spot." They remained neck-and-neck, but Runnels had taken a slight decimal point edge. The lead flipped in the sixth when Pete grounded into a double play and Ted singled. Both flied out—both to center field—in the eighth, and Pete made another out in the ninth, leaving Ted in the on-deck circle, but Ted was now .327 and Pete .324.

Where did the fourth-inning homers come down? "After Buddin walked, Runnels hit a soaring smash which cleared the 30-foot right-field fence, 350 feet from the plate...Williams hit the ball over the right-field fence in almost the identical spot."

This was one of the two homers Williams hit off Romonosky, both in 1958. The other was #475.

482 (#26) September 28 at Griffith Stadium, Washington. Pitcher: Pedro Ramos (Washington Senators). RH. Age 23.

Top of the seventh inning. One-run homer. GAME WINNER.

Forty-year-old Ted Williams closed out his 1958 season hitting home runs three days in a row. His solo home run dealt defeat to Washington for its 13th loss in a row—a terrible way for any team to end a season. Seven of the 13 losses came at the hands of the Red Sox. They'd actually held a slim 4-3 lead after five, but Ted Lepcio homered in the sixth to tie it and Ted Williams homered in the seventh to make it 5-4, Boston. Sammy White homered in the eighth for an insurance run. Williams was 2-for-4 and ended the season batting .328, six points above Runnels' .322. He'd hit .500

over his final 28 at-bats. He'd hit .403 over his last 55 games. It was his sixth batting crown, achieved at the age of 40.

There was so much attention paid to the batting race that newspapers almost forgot to tell readers where Williams' home run went, but the words the *Globe* allotted Lepcio's homer provide the answer: "Lepcio hit a 400-foot homer to the left of center — almost to the same spot Williams later hit his, but a bit farther up." The *Herald* said Ted's homer was about halfway up in the stands.

This was the third consecutive game-winner Ramos allowed Williams. He gave up six homers in all: #388, 409, 418, 430, 482, and 520.

Ted's 26 homers raised $1,850 for the Jimmy Fund, thanks to the preseason pledge from the *Boston Record-American*. Fortunately for the Jimmy Fund, Jackie Jensen hit more homers than Ted Williams — his 35 homers raised $2,750 for the cause. In all, the Red Sox as a team hit 155 homers and the newspaper donated $9,725 to help finance children's cancer research.

 Ed Linn writes that during 1958 Williams "ran into a terrible streak of bad luck where by actual count, outfielders reached into the distant right-field bullpen at Fenway Park to take home runs away from him seven separate times in less than two months." [107]

1959

483 (#1 of 1959) May 30 (second game) at Fenway Park. Pitcher: Jerry Walker (Baltimore Orioles). RH. Age 20.

Bottom of the seventh inning. Two-run homer. GAME WINNER.

Williams suffered a really bad crick in his neck during spring training and didn't get into a game until May 12, when he went 0-for-5. The neck problem was so bad, it still lingered into 1960. He only cracked .200 during the Memorial Day doubleheader, going 2-for-4 in each game, and he hit a two-run homer (first of the season) in the second game—winning the game in the process. The score was 8-3; the Red Sox won the first game, 5-4. It wasn't a majestic home run—"it was a 310-foot shot that curled around the right-field foul pole"—but it was most welcome nonetheless.

Even though he broke in during July 1957 and pitched in 1958 and 1959, too, this game was Walker's first loss in the big leagues. He'd been 5-0 to this point.

The Sox had been short of outfielders, so Ted did play both games. It was the first time in three years he'd played in both halves of a doubleheader. The four hits brought his career hit total to 2,499. A double on June 2 got him to 2,500 (and drove in a run.)

This was the only homer Ted hit off Jerry Walker.

484 (#2) June 11 at Fenway Park. Pitcher: Ray Narleski (Detroit Tigers). RH. Age 30.

Bottom of the sixth inning. One-run homer.

The only run the Red Sox scored in an 8-1 loss to Detroit was Ted's solo home run in the sixth. The game had been quite close, with no scoring through five innings. The Tigers scored once off Boston pitcher Ted Wills in the top of the sixth, and then Ted Williams tied it in the bottom of the sixth. Three runs in the seventh and four more in the ninth spelled victory for the Tigers. The Ted Williams homer was, like #483, not a powerful smash, but was hit "into the right-field grandstand, not far from the foul pole." Ted was now 10 career home runs behind Lou Gehrig, and 16 from reaching 500.

Narleski also supplied #446 and 460.

485 (#3) June 23 at Briggs Stadium, Detroit. Pitcher: Dave Sisler (Detroit Tigers). RH. Age 27.

Top of the eighth inning. One-run homer.

When batting practice began, Williams lingered in the outfield as long as it was Frank Sullivan throwing b.p. As soon as Jim Busby took over for Sullivan, Ted ran in and promptly hit four out of the park. He got one in the game, too, off a former teammate—Dave Sisler. It was a solo homer in the top of the eighth, hit on a 1-1 count. It banged off the façade of the second deck in right field. Frank Malzone homered later in the inning, and Jackie Jensen in the ninth; Boston won, 10-4.

This was the only homer Ted hit off Dave Sisler. Sisler had been traded to the Tigers by the Red Sox on May 2, 1959.

Detroit writer Joe Falls remembered another late-career batting practice in the Motor City. There was already a large crowd in the park. Ted stepped into the cage to take his seven swings. "The first one he lines down the right-field line just inside the foul pole. Crash! Home run into the upper deck. The second one went a little further into the upper deck. The third one a little further. And now the crowd starts to pick up on this. The fourth one—BOOM, a little further. He did it seven straight times—seven times in the upper deck, each one a little longer than the last one and by the time the seventh ball went out, the place was up in uproar. I'd say 25,000 were roaring because they saw what he was doing. He turned around, went back to the dugout, went down the steps, didn't say hello, good-bye, kiss my ass, tip his hat, nothing."[108]

486 (#4) June 27 at Cleveland Stadium, Cleveland. Pitcher: Mudcat Grant (Cleveland Indians). RH. Age 23.

Top of the fifth inning. Two-run homer. GAME WINNER.

The Sox had a 2-1 lead after four. Runnels doubled in a third run, and then Ted Williams homered into the right-field seats to make it 5-1. Jensen homered right after Williams. The final score was 6-4. Frank Sullivan got the win; it had been two years and ten days since he'd beaten the Indians.

Williams also hit #507 off Grant.

487 (#5) June 28 (first game) at Cleveland Stadium, Cleveland. Pitcher: Gary Bell (Cleveland Indians). RH. Age 22.

Top of the third inning. One-run homer.

The Red Sox lost two games to the Tribe, 5-4 and 1-0, the second game being a two-hitter thrown by Herb Score, in which Williams pinch hit (and struck out.) His homer was his "first Williamsesque home run of the season." (*Herald*) The *Globe* called it "a towering smash into the upper deck in right field") came in the first game, a weird game in which second baseman Granny Hamner played 2B-SS-2B-SS-2B-SS-2B-SS-2B-SS-2B-SS-2B-SS-2B-SS-2B-SS (shortstop Woodie Held—who had more range—switched to play second base every time either Williams or Marty Keough came up to bat). The fourth homer of the month represented the most Williams hit in any month in 1959.

Bell also gave up #474, the preceding year.

488 (#6) July 9 at Fenway Park. Pitcher: Bob Turley (New York Yankees). RH. Age 28.

Bottom of the second inning. One-run homer.

Red Sox 14, Yankees 3. It was the first game the Red Sox played under new manager Billy Jurges. Both Williams and Wertz hit second-inning solo homers to get things going. Bobby Avila's three-run homer was the game-winner. Ted's homer was "ripped…on a line over the visitors' bullpen and into the bleachers, his longest smash of the year." Later, he hit another long ball, a two-run double that just missed the left side of the flagpole in center field, about six feet from the top of the fence, caromed off the wall and rebounded off the back of the pole itself, dropping to the ground.

This was the last of five homers that Ted hit off Bob: #361, 376, 454, 479, and 488.

489 (#7) July 22 at Comiskey Park, Chicago. Pitcher: Early Wynn (Chicago White Sox). RH. Age 39. Hall of Famer.

Top of the sixth inning. One-run homer.

The White Sox won, 5-4, but at least Ted Williams broke an 0-for-12 slump with a solo homer in the sixth. He broke it, and what was a 2-2 tie at the time, banging the ball "off the scoreboard affront the upper right-field deck." (*Record*) Pitcher Jerry Casale hit a home run for the Red Sox in the seventh.

The eight home runs Ted hit off Wynn: #190, 334, 405, 433, 434, 447, 489, and 497.

490 (#8) July 26 at Municipal Stadium, Kansas City. Pitcher: Ray Herbert (Chicago White Sox). RH. Age 29.

Top of the second inning. Two-run homer.

Stories were being written every week, saying that Williams was done and that this would be his last year. The *Globe* even mentioned that "strange news reports" had him "miraculously" back from Chillicothe, where he was supposedly on his way home. What the story authors may have failed to take into account were two things — his pride and wanting to go out the right way, not hitting well under .300, and his quest for 500 home runs. He didn't talk about it to the sportswriters, but those who knew him better—like Ed Rumill of the *Christian Science Monitor*—knew it had been on his mind since returning from the Korean War late in 1953. This homer left him 10 short of the mark.

The game was discouraging, though, the team's sixth loss in a row, this one 5-4. Ted's homer had given the Red Sox an early 2-1 lead, hit "over the 375-foot mark in left-center."

Oddly, during some of the visit to Kansas City, Williams sat out in the bullpen rather than in the dugout, when the Red Sox were up at bat. He played in all three games.

One of only ten homers Ted hit in his "down" year of 1959, it was the fifth off Ray Herbert in the course of his career. The first four: #339, 355, 391, and 478.

491 (#9) August 22 at Briggs Stadium, Detroit. Pitcher: Don Mossi (Detroit Tigers). LH. Age 30.

Top of the fourth inning. One-run homer. GAME WINNER.

This homer put Ted Williams within two home runs of tying Lou Gehrig's mark—though some tabulations at the time had Gehrig with 494. Williams was getting close, but home runs were coming few and far between. He hadn't hit one for almost a month. Frank Baumann threw a six-hit, 7-1 win for Boston, and Ted's solo home run in the fourth inning scored the second run of the game—the one needed to win the game. It was hit off Mossi's first pitch "high up into the back of the second deck of seats in right field." It landed about 15 rows up in the seats.

This was the only homer Ted hit off Mossi.

492 (#10) August 27 at Comiskey Park, Chicago. Pitcher: Barry Latman (Chicago White Sox). RH. Age 23.

Top of the ninth inning. One-run homer.

The only run the Red Sox scored came in the top of the ninth, hit by Ted Williams into the upper deck in right field. But the White Sox had already scored five runs. They were leading the league, on their way to the American League pennant.

Before the game, Williams had said, "I've had it!" What he might have meant was never fully explained. He was only hitting .236 at the time and couldn't have been feeling good about himself. He pinch hit and doubled in a run on August 28, but then didn't play again until September 11. His next eight games were all in pinch-hitting roles; he had hits in four of the eight. He ended the season hitting just .254, almost a full 100 points below what had been his lifetime batting average.

This was the first of a pair of homers Williams hit off Latman; the other was #512. It was only August but the last home run Ted hit in his most discouraging season.

1960

Ted Williams: "I didn't hit any big home runs in spring training—in fact, I didn't hit any home runs at all—but I didn't have as much restriction in my swing either. The pain in the neck was still around but I could live with it."[109]

493 (#1 of 1960) April 18 at Griffith Stadium, Washington. Pitcher: Camilo Pascual (Washington Senators). RH. Age 26.

Top of the second inning. One-run homer.

Ted Williams got off to a much better start in 1959, playing in and homering in the season opener. It was the fourth time he'd played in a game attended by the President of the United States. He'd done so in 1940 (FDR) and twice before Harry Truman (homering in the 1946 game). This day, he added Dwight D. Eisenhower to his list. Before the game, Vice President Nixon was overheard telling Ike, "This is probably his last season. Let's root for him." Eisenhower replied, "That's a good idea." (*New York Times*)

They didn't have to wait long. In his first time at bat in the new year, he hit one of the longest home runs of his career, a "450-foot smash over the lofty barrier in center field." Homer #493 tied him with Lou Gehrig, for fourth all-time. It came on a 3-2 pitch and brought an applauding President Eisenhower to his feet. The ball left the playing field, over the 35-foot wall in center field, a little to the right of the flagpole. The field was marked 438 feet to the edge of the bullpen and it traveled over that. The *Daily Record* wrote, "The tape-measure round-tripper…was estimated to have traveled close to 500 feet."

Senators pitcher Camilo Pascual allowed two scratch singles to other Sox batters (Pumpsie Green and Gary Geiger) but that was all the hitting; Pascual struck out 15 Red Sox. Washington won, 10-1.

The second of a pair of homers hit off Pascual; the second one was in July 1958 — #469.

494 (#2) April 19 at Fenway Park. Pitcher: Jim Coates (New York Yankees). RH. Age 27.

Bottom of the eighth inning. One-run homer.

After the one game in Washington to open the season, the Sox traveled to Boston and lost another one, this time to the Yankees, 8-4. Ted surpassed Gehrig's mark and ranked fourth all-time. Both had had careers curtailed, Williams losing most of five seasons to military service and Gehrig's to ALS. The score stood 8-2 in favor of the Yankees when Williams batted in the eighth. Fans had stuck around to see him hit one last time, and — once he did — "thousands" made for the exits. He hit the ball "down the line and into the stands." (*New York Times*) It was the first time Ted had hit a homer in both openers — home and away. And the first time he'd homered in the two first games of a season.

Roger Maris hit a single, a double, and two home runs, driving in four. The crowd was thought to be the second-largest Opening Day crowd in Boston baseball history.

Ted said he was still feeling the negative effects of his neck problem from a year earlier, and now had a pulled muscle in his leg. "My neck is somewhat better," he said, "But I still don't know how long I can keep this up." Then he explained, "There are a lot of reasons for hitting home runs. The speed the pitcher throws the ball is one. The speed you swing the bat is another. The wind is also a factor." (*Traveler*) Whatever his ailments, he made two plays in left field, a leaping catch up against the wall and a well-fielded ball off the wall, both of which impressed Casey Stengel.

With a 13-3 record, Coates had the best winning percentage in the AL in 1960. This was the only homer Williams hit off him.

495 (#3) June 5 (first game) at Yankee Stadium. Pitcher: Ralph Terry (New York Yankees). RH. Age 24.

Top of the seventh. Two-run homer.

After hitting homers in the first and second games of the season, Ted played the next 17 games in a row without hitting any—15 of those, however, were pinch-hitting appearances. The physical ailments hampered him throughout the full month of May and some on either side. In the June 5 game, the Yankees were leading, 5-0, but then Bobby Thomson singled, Marty Keough doubled, and Pete Runnels singled—and Williams "belted his third homer of the campaign into the right-field stands." (*Record*) The rally stopped there, though, one run short. The *Globe* put the ball "400 feet into the seats in the right-field side of right-center" while the *New York Times* extended it a bit, to a "longer-than-400-foot homer."

This was the only homer Williams hit off Ralph Terry.

496 (#4) June 10 at Fenway Park. Pitcher: Russ Kemmerer (Chicago White Sox). RH. Age 28.

Bottom of the sixth inning. One-run homer.

With 18 hits and 13 runs, the White Sox easily manhandled the Red Sox, who only scored three times—twice in the first and then once more on Ted Williams' homer in the sixth. The homer "dropped in the Boston bullpen in right center." (*Chicago Tribune*) The *Boston Herald*: "Ted's blast into a chilling east wind came in the sixth inning, carried into the Red Sox bullpen and produced an ovation for the 41-year-old slugger."

Kemmerer told Dave Heller, "He was going around first base and he was clapping. Of course the sportswriter don't know what he's saying; neither does the press or anybody else. But when he got to first base, he looked at me and said, 'Hey bush, I got you in my book.' He called everybody bush-leaguer. 'You're in my book, I got you in my book, baby.' He clapped all the way around." The next day, Kemmerer said, "I haven't thrown a slow breaking ball in like two or three years, and you hit the damn thing like you knew it was coming." Ted said, "I did…When you got right to the top of your windup, you did a little something that you don't normally do, and I knew you were going to throw me an off-speed pitch."[110]

This was the only homer Williams hit off former teammate Kemmerer.

497 (#5) June 11 (first game) at Fenway Park. Pitcher: Early Wynn (Chicago White Sox). RH. Age 40. Hall of Famer.

Bottom of the sixth inning. Two-run homer.

The Red Sox were down by two runs, but in the bottom of the sixth, Runnels singled off the left-field wall. Ted Williams came up. He'd fouled out twice. He "smashed Wynn's 1-1 pitch six rows up in the right-field seats — over the bullpen — to tie the score. The ball went 400 feet." The author of this book was sitting in the seats not that far away and asked to touch the ball, which permission was granted by the fortunate fan who'd captured it. One later run gave the Red Sox a 5-4 win.

The full list of eight homers Ted Williams recorded off Early Wynn: #190, 334, 405, 433, 434, 447, 489, and 497.

498 (#6) June 14 at Briggs Stadium, Detroit. Pitcher: Jim Bunning (Detroit Tigers). RH. Age 28. Hall of Famer.

Top of the sixth inning. One-run homer.

Jim Bunning pitched a whale of a game, for a 2-1 win, marred only by the solo home run he surrendered to Ted Williams in the top of the sixth. He struck out 13. Bill Monbouquette was pitching even better; he'd held the Tigers scoreless until the bottom of the eighth. There was hope Ted's home run (hit on a 1-1 pitch into the lower right-field seats) would win the game. Alas, the Tigers scored a pair and they were the team that won the tight 2-1 game.

In Ted's last season, he hit three of his final 29 home runs off Jim Bunning. Prior homers were #383, 439, 440, 455, and 472, and the two later ones were 504 and 519.

499 (#7) June 16 at Briggs Stadium, Detroit. Pitcher: Hank Aguirre (Detroit Tigers). LH. Age 29.

Top of the ninth inning. One-run homer.

Another Ted Williams homer, but in another one-run loss. This time the final score was 6-5. There was one down in the ninth, with the score 5-4 (Tigers on top) and Ted tied it, 5-5, sending the game into the tenth. The baseball was sent "into the upper stand in right field." It was hit on a 1-0 count, the *Herald* wrote, "a 400-foot smash, eight rows deep…[hit] with such finality and drive that there never was a doubt of its destination." Williams was leaving his favorite park in which to hit but all he needed was one more home run to reach the coveted #500. He only had to wait until the next day.

Aguirre gave up a pair to Williams: #471 and #499.

500 (#8) June 17 at Cleveland Stadium, Cleveland. Pitcher: Wynn Hawkins (Cleveland Indians). RH. Age 24.

Top of the third inning. Two-run homer. GAME WINNER.

What a milestone—this is the one which made Ted Williams part of the very exclusive "500 Home Run Club." And it won the game, to boot. In the top of the third inning, the score was tied, 1-1. The count was 0-2. "Williams boomed a Wynn Hawkins pitch toward the six-foot screen at the 365-foot mark in mid-left field. Left fielder Tito Francona ran back to the fence, edged against it, got ready to leap. Then he saw it was no use. The ball sailed five feet over his head." It actually landed in the Red Sox bullpen. Willie Tasby scored ahead of Ted, and neither team scored again for the remainder of the game. Only Babe Ruth (714), Jimmie Foxx (534), and Mel Ott (511) had ever hit more.

He was presented the ball and asked what he was going to do with it. "Well, I've never made a habit of collecting baseballs, but I might like to keep this one. I have a ball autographed by Babe Ruth. I have another autographed by five .400 hitters and the first one I hit off Bob Feller. Yes, I'd maybe like to keep this last one, but if someone came along and offered me some real

money for it, I'd be tempted to accept and turn it over to the Jimmy Fund."
(*Christian Science Monitor*)

He'd almost passed on playing in this day's game. "Before the game I told
Mike Higgins I was too stiff to play. He told me to try it and I did. How
tickled I am that I did." (*Hartford Courant*)

He said he knew he'd hit it, the moment the bat struck the ball. "It felt
wonderful." Frank Sullivan was happy, too. He'd been 1-6 going into the
game, but struck out 12 and held the Indians to just the one run.

Tickled though he was, he didn't show it as he rounded the bases. He "displayed absolutely no outward animation"—quite a change from the youthful
Kid who pranced around the bases after hitting the game-winning homer
in the 1941 All-Star Game, which he said was still his greatest thrill in baseball. (The characterization was Henry McKenna's, in the *Boston Herald*.)

"Ted didn't say anything much after he hit it," said Higgins, "but you could
tell he was overjoyed." He was amped up, though, and the *Herald* said he
"raced to his position like a colt the rest of the game [and] almost knocked
Tasby down in the throwing practice."

Homer #500 was the only one Williams hit off Wynn Hawkins.

Ted Williams: "That night I went to Mike Higgins and said, 'Mike, how
about taking me out of the lineup. It's a lousy night. I could use the rest.' He
said, 'Gee, Ted, I just handed the lineup card in. Go on and play tonight;
I'll take you out tomorrow.' I was thinking, What the hell difference does it
make if he did turn in the card? He could take me out of the lineup as easy
as he put me into it."[III]

501 (#9) June 19 (first game) at Cleveland Stadium, Cleveland. Pitcher:
Jim Perry (Cleveland Indians). RH. Age 24.

Top of the seventh inning. Three-run homer.

Only two days later, Teddy Ballgame hit #501. Eddie Mifflin had long since
let him know that Mel Ott's 511 home runs were in sight, and perhaps
reminded him that Jimmie Foxx's 534 were there if Ted could play through
1961. There was a doubleheader in Cleveland and the Red Sox won both

games. Game one starter Bill Monbouquette no doubt appreciative of the three insurance runs Ted's three-run homer provided in the top of the seventh. It took Ted two tries to get the home run; on two consecutive pitches he hit what appeared to be two home runs in one at-bat. Umpire Bill McKinley called the first one a foul ball. The pitches appeared to be identical, but the results differed. The first was hit into the upper right-field deck; the second, a little less loft to it, went into the lower deck. "The first, which sailed over the top of the foul pole, was judged foul. The second, farther into fair territory, was Home Run No. 501." The *Plain Dealer* said the first one was foul by a matter of feet.

Jim Perry was the last pitcher victimized by Ted hitting a trio off him — and all three were hit in 1960: #501, 508, and 511. Perry led the American League in games won in 1960.

502 (#10) June 21 at Municipal Stadium, Kansas City. Pitcher: Bud Daley (Kansas City Athletics). LH. Age 27.

Top of the fourth inning. One-run homer.

Ted hit two in one day, but not for the last time. The Royals had scored five runs in the first inning, and it was still 5-0 after three. Bud Daley was perhaps feeling he had some room and when Williams came up in the top of the fourth with no one on base and two outs, Daley beckoned catcher Harry Chiti out to the mound and said, "Hey, I've never thrown a slider and I've been working on it. Let's throw him a slider."

Daley was a gracious server. "Ted rattled one over the 387-foot marker in right-center field."

He hit it on a 1-2 pitch. Daley won the game, giving him a league-leading ten wins at this point in the season.

This wasn't the last time Ted hit two off a pitcher in the same game; he did it twice in 1960. See also HR's 514 and 515.

503 (#11) June 21 at Municipal Stadium, Kansas City. Pitcher: Bud Daley (Kansas City Athletics). LH. Age 27.

Top of the sixth inning. Two-run homer.

In the sixth inning, Daley told Chiti, "I'm going to try that slider again." The *Globe* reported that Williams "lashed a two-run blast off the banking behind the right-field fence at the 353-foot marker in the sixth." Chiti came back out and suggested, "I think you better work on that pitch some more."[112]

Even with his two homers and four RBIs (he also singled home Willie Tasby, the Sox were outscored, 11-7. By virtue of his 10th and 11th home runs of the 1960 season, Ted had already hit more homers than in all of 1959. The game was only his 18th start of the season—the rest of his appearances were in pinch-hitting roles—but he had now homered 11 times. He had six homers in the nine games on the road trip in progress. What a difference between the two years. In 1959, he'd hit ten home runs in 272 official at-bats. In 1960, he'd now hit one more in 71 at-bats.

The second one off Bud this day.

Ted emphasized being alert to *everything*—even the batter's box itself. "Fans think they're all alike, and most batters probably do. They're all 4 feet by 6, and they look alike. But it isn't so. I know for a fact that the batter's box in Boston was a fraction higher in the back than in the front. I always felt I had a better hold with my back foot when I swung there. In Kansas City, I felt the box slanted the other way—I felt as if I were hitting uphill. I told the groundskeeper about it, and the next time we came into Kansas City it was level. I hit two home runs that day, and when the Kansas City manager learned what had happened, he almost fired the groundskeeper."[113]

504 (#12) June 29 at Fenway Park. Pitcher: Jim Bunning (Detroit Tigers). RH. Age 28. Hall of Famer.

Bottom of the first inning. Two-run homer.

When Williams got back from the road trip and checked into his residence at Boston's Hotel Somerset, he was presented a cake in honor of his 500th home run by chef Louis Turco, the hotel GM, and two bellmen. The

Boston Traveler ran a photo and noted that Ted sent the cake to Children's Hospital. In the game, on a 2-2 pitch in the bottom of the first inning, with Pete Runnels on base, "Williams whacked a 1-1 pitch from Jim Bunning over the Red Sox bullpen and about a half dozen rows up into the bleacher." It was about a 440-foot drive. The Tigers tied it until Ted got on base in the sixth and Russ Nixon hit one up that came down in the visiting bullpen. Monbouquette got a 4-2 win.

The seventh of eight homers hit off Bunning in Ted's last six years in baseball. The eight home runs: #383, 439, 440, 455, 472, 498, 504, and 519.

505 (#13) June 30 at Fenway Park. Pitcher: Bob Bruce (Detroit Tigers). RH. Age 27.

Bottom of the fourth inning. One-run homer.

After three innings, Detroit had a 5-0 lead, thanks to two homers by Rocky Colavito which drove in every one of the five runs. The first batter up in Boston's fourth was Ted Williams, who hadn't homered since the day before. He rectified that shortcoming with a solo home run and Don Buddin drove in two. Two more in the fifth tied it, and after the Tigers took a 7-5 lead in the top of the seventh, the Red Sox scored six times in the bottom of the eighth to put the game away. It was just Bruce's second big-league start. Before the game, Clem Labine said to Bruce, "Do you realize you and I are the only pitchers on the Detroit staff that Williams does not have in his book?" Ted hit the ball "14 rows deep into section 1 of the grandstand." (*Herald*) After the game, Bruce said to Labine, "It didn't take him long, did it?" Before the month was out, Ted hit #510 off Labine.[114] Twelve-year-old Bobby Jo Williams saw this one from a box near the Red Sox dugout; she was in town for "her annual visit with her famous Dad." (*Traveler*)

This was Ted's only homer off Bob Bruce.

506 (#14) July 3 at Fenway Park. Pitcher: Dick Hall (Kansas City Athletics). RH. Age 29.

Bottom of the fifth inning. Two-run homer.

Ted Williams homered, Willie Tasby hit a grand slam, and Vic Wertz homered. The Red Sox manhandled Kansas City, 13-2 — a nice way to break out of a bit of a losing stretch, the Sox having dropped four of the previous five. Hall figured he'd start off Ted with a high fastball, but missed with the pitch and threw it too high "up and even with his chin. He was famous for never swinging at bad pitches, but this time, because he was obviously (by hindsight) looking for a high fastball, he swung at it. Problem: He hit it over their part of the bullpen for a home run."[115] Ted surprised Hall by swinging at the first pitch and struck "a towering 390-footer…which fell five rows up in the right-field pavilion just right of the K.C. bellpen." (*Record*)

Before the game, Ted presented both the bat he used and the ball he hit for home run #500 to William S. Koster of the Jimmy Fund, to be auctioned off as a fundraiser to fight cancer in children.

This was Ted's only homer off Dick Hall.

On July 10, 1960, John James of the Yankees pitched to Ted Williams and walked him, the one and only time he faced him. He said, "I walked him on five strikes." Home plate umpire Ed Hurley was tough on rookies and, as we've learned, if Ted Williams didn't swing at the pitch, it was a ball. The only strike in the at-bat was when Ted swung and missed — a little hard to call that one a ball. James said before the at-bat, "I probably had the same thing going through my mind as any rookie pitcher who ever faced Ted Williams for the first time. You are thrilled to be doing it, and you don't particularly care if you get him out. Take that with a grain of salt because you *do* want to get him out, but the main thing is that you want to face him in Fenway Park so you can tell the story to all the guys you played ball with when you were younger, 'How I pitched to Ted Williams in Fenway Park.'"

Then there was the time, also in 1960, when Marty Kutyna told umpire Nestor Chylak that he'd called a ball on a pitch that was a strike. He couldn't get a strike called a ball after that. "I shook my head and looked at Williams at first. Ted looked at me from first base and shouted, 'They were all strikes, rookie!'"[116]

507 (#15) July 22 at Fenway Park. Pitcher: Mudcat Grant (Cleveland Indians). RH. Age 24.

Bottom of the first inning. One-run homer.

This was the game in which "Ted Williams" became the answer to a trivia question that endured for many years—name the only major-league ballplayer to steal a base in four different decades. (Since that time, Rickey Henderson, Tim Raines, and Omar Vizquel have joined the list.) Tasby was on third base in the bottom of the seventh, but it wasn't a double steal. With two outs, Ted just took advantage of Dick Stigman and got himself in scoring position—but Gary Geiger flied out to end the inning.

Ted's home run came in the first, on a changeup. "It was a low thump into the right-field section of the grandstand, a few feet inside the foul line." The Red Sox did win the game, 6-4.

Williams also hit #486 off Mudcat.

508 (#16) July 23 at Fenway Park. Pitcher: Jim Perry (Cleveland Indians). RH. Age 24.

Bottom of the fourth inning. One-run homer.

When Williams came up in the bottom of the eighth, the Indians were ahead, 4-2, and there was one out. Willie Tasby was on base, so Ted represented the tying run. Cleveland left fielder Jimmy Piersall moved over into center field and started "running around and dancing like a dervish just before—and during—right-handed pitcher Jim Perry's delivery." He was warned, persisted, and was ejected from the game, and then came perilously close to threatening the umpire. Once order was restored, Williams hit a fly ball out to right field.

Earlier, Ted had "crashed a Perry pitch high into the grandstand seats in right field—well inside the foul pole." It was, the *Herald* wrote, "a long, long home run."

Ted also hit #501 and 511 off Perry, both in 1960, too.

509 (#17) July 27 at Fenway Park. Pitcher: Bob Shaw (Chicago White Sox). RH. Age 27.

Bottom of the fifth inning. One-run homer.

Under threatening skies, Ted Williams and Gary Geiger went back-to-back in the fifth, and the Red Sox took a 4-2 lead, but Chicago piled on runs in the later innings and won with ease in the end, 10-4. Ted's homer was "a mighty 440-foot blast, several rows up in the center-field stands not far from the flagpole." (*Record*) There was a large crowd of Aleppo Temple Shriners in attendance and they'd come prepared with a large banner reading "509". Joe Reichler of the Associated Press put the distance at 450 feet. The sports cartoon in the *Record* showed it landing many rows up in the bleachers, just about on the dividing line between the populated seats and the seats left empty for a better hitting background during day games.

This was the only home run Ted hit off Shaw.

510 (#18) July 31 (first game) at Fenway Park. Pitcher: Clem Labine (Detroit Tigers). RH. Age 33.

Bottom of the ninth. Two-run homer.

The Tigers dominated the Red Sox in the early going, leading 7-1 in the fourth. The Red Sox just made it look a little better, with four runs in the bottom of the ninth (the final score was 9-6). Half of those ninth-inning runs were scored by Ted Williams, with his 510th home run, leaving him just one homer behind Mel Ott and two months remaining in the season. "That wallop, over the visitor's bullpen into the bleachers off reliever Clem Labine, removed much of the bad taste." (*Herald*)

The only homer Ted hit off the veteran Labine, because Labine pitched 499 of his 513 games in the National League.

511 (#19) August 9 at Cleveland Stadium, Cleveland. Pitcher: Jim Perry (Cleveland Indians). RH. Age 24.

Top of the fifth inning. One-run homer.

It was a weird way to lose a game. Boston and Cleveland were tied at midpoint, 3-3, tied thanks to Ted Williams' home run in the top of the fifth. Bill Monbouquette was pitching for the Red Sox and the Indians had Ken Aspromonte on first base with two outs. Vic Power hit a ball to deep right field and Lu Clinton ran in pursuit. "The ball hit the fence, near the top, then — to most of a night crowd of 8,752 — seemed to disappear for a moment. Then, suddenly, it reappeared on the other side of the fence. What happened was this. The ball hit the five-foot wire fence — near the top — and the ball came right down at the right foot of the rushing Clinton. Clinton's foot met the ball and kicked it over the fence for a two-run homer." The Red Sox argued the ball had hit the ground first and been a ground-rule double. The Red Sox lost that argument.

Ted Williams' home run was almost lost in the oddity of the game-winning homer. He had hit #511 and tied Mel Ott. His homer "was a hard drive, on a low trajectory, over the 365-foot mark in right center. Piersall and Kuenn took only half a stride each, then watched it go over."

A very brief story ran in the *Globe*, datelined Cleveland but without a byline or attribution. In full, it read: "Ted Williams had little comment to make after his 511th homer to tie Mel Ott for third place among the all-time major-league sluggers." He did make one significant remark, however, when he said, "I hope I get the 512th in a hurry, before I collapse. They're hard coming."

Again, he intended the ball for charity. "I just gave the ball to Jack Fadden to keep for me. No, it's not going to the Hall of Fame at Cooperstown. I'm going to a big dinner when we get back home and I'm sure we can auction this off for $100 for the Jimmy Fund.

"I hit the hell off that ball. My neck's been bothering me lately, all through the Detroit series. I just haven't been able to get that little extra on good pitches." (*Herald*)

The third of the three Ted hit off Jim Perry. #501 and 508 both came earlier this same year. A news story on September 7 said that the ball actually was donated to the Hall of Fame.

512 (#20) August 10 at Cleveland Stadium, Cleveland. Pitcher: Barry Latman (Cleveland Indians). RH. Age 24.

Top of the fifth inning. One-run homer.

Williams was starting to get that little extra on pitches now, and hit two home runs in this game the very next day. He did hit #512 in a hurry, and #513, too. He was now only 21 behind Jimmie Foxx but, having passed Ott and in sole possession of third place all-time, he said he was definitely retiring at the end of the season.

Homer #512 was hit on the first pitch—"a high opposite-field fly that carried through a strong opposing cross-wind and landed in the lower deck of the left-field stands." (*Record*) Ted couldn't remember having hit one to left in Cleveland Stadium.

The sportswriters aboard the flight to Baltimore were almost speechless when flight attendants handed glasses to everyone on board—players, coaches, and the writers. "What are these for?" one of the writers asked traveling secretary Tom Dowd. "Champagne. Compliments of Ted Williams." (*Boston Globe*)

This was the first of a pair of homers Williams hit off Latman; the other was #492.

513 (#21) August 10 at Cleveland Stadium, Cleveland. Pitcher: Johnny Klippstein (Cleveland Indians). RH. Age 32.

Top of the ninth. Two-run homer.

Red Sox starting pitcher Earl Wilson was on base and there were two outs in the top of the ninth. Once more, Williams swung at the first pitch—twice in one game, surely a record in itself—and hit his second home run of the game. "In this instance, Theodore the terrific propelled a Johnny Klippstein pitch a country mile over the barrier in right-center. The ball must have traveled more than 425 feet." (*Record*)

"I wasn't going for the long hit either time," he told reporters. "I was simply looking for a base hit through the middle." The first one was hit to left field and the second one hit to right. "I got to know Mel Ott while he was traveling as a broadcaster with the Tigers. We used to talk hitting a lot. I can hardly believe that I have finally hit more homers than he did. I never thought as a young player that I had a chance of doing it. Why, when I broke in, Mel already had hit, I think, more than 400.

"I'll keep on playing for the rest of this season. I hope I can hit some more homers to help the club. But I have no more home run goals. When this season is over, I will have had it. I won't be back next year. I came back this year only because I had such a poor record last season. I wanted to go out with a good season. I felt certain that I'd have that good season this year if my neck didn't bother me. I'm mighty thankful that I've done as well as I have. I've proved to myself that I could do it. That's all I wanted to do. So this is my last year." (*Record*)

Ted's farewell homer in Cleveland, and the only one he hit off Klippstein.

514 (#22) August 20 (first game) at Fenway Park. Pitcher: Chuck Estrada (Baltimore Orioles). RH. Age 22.

Bottom of the fourth. Three-run homer.

It was never a personal goal, but instead a by-product of what he'd been told by Rogers Hornsby and always tried to put into practice—patience. "Get a good pitch to hit." In the August 20 game, Ted Williams drew base on balls #2,000. Only one player had ever walked more—Babe Ruth, who'd earned 2,056 walks. Ted got #2,000 in his 2,260th game; he wasn't far off from averaging a walk a game. Indeed, Ted Williams still remains—more than half a century later—the player with the highest walks percentage in baseball history: 20.75%. More than once in every five times to the plate, he got a free pass to first base.

Of course, it wasn't the walks that got Ted a standing ovation when he came to the plate in the eighth inning. It's because he'd already hit two three-run homers in the game, the first in the fourth and the second one in the sixth. The Orioles took a 3-0 lead in the first; Ted's homer –" a high-towering hoist" into the Red Sox bullpen, hit an estimated 410 feet—gave the Red Sox a 4-3 lead. (*Herald*)

The last pitcher off whom Ted hit two homers in one game was Estrada of the Orioles.

Bob Feller: "You had to throw strikes to him. He would not swing at a ball unless it was over the plate—or he thought it was. He seldom ever took a called third strike that I know if."[117]

Some charged that Williams was too selfish, turning his nose up at balls that were close but not over the plate, taking a pitch for a ball instead of hitting it and maybe driving in a run. "If I were selfish as charged," he said, "I'd swing for home runs all the time, good pitches or bad. I'd end up with more home runs and fewer walks. But you still have to win the game, and whether certain people believe that or not, that is what I am after."[118]

515 (#23) August 20 (first game) at Fenway Park. Pitcher: Chuck Estrada (Baltimore Orioles). RH. Age 22.

Bottom of the sixth. Three-run homer. GAME WINNER.

This was the last multiple home-run game for Ted Williams. This was also the last three-run homer Ted Williams hit—though it was his second one of the game. He drove in six of Boston's eight runs, and they needed them. The final score was 8-6. The second one was the game-winner, and was pegged at 430 feet. It landed "six or eight rows into the bleacher crowd between the end of the bullpen and the flag pole." In center field.

The pair were the only two Ted hit off Estrada. Chuck probably thought that was damage enough.

516 (#24) August 25 at Fenway Park. Pitcher: Don Newcombe (Cleveland Indians). RH. Age 34.

Bottom of the third inning. Two-run homer.

The Sox won, 10-7, on Vic Wertz's fourth-inning grand slam. For Wertz, a grand old man like Ted (Wertz was 35), it was his third grand slam of the season and the ninth of his career. Williams had hit a two-run homer in the third; it was five days until his 42nd birthday. Ted had two singles, besides, driving in three runs in all. His homer "sailed into the right-field seats, several beyond the foul marker." (*Record*)

The former Negro Leaguer and Brooklyn Dodgers star had won 27 games in 1956. His only year in the AL was 1960, and Ted hit just the one home run off him.

A disappointed centenarian was Mrs. Persis Hight of Augusta, Maine. She wasn't happy that the Red Sox were in seventh place. But all would be forgiven, she said, if Ted Williams hit a homer on her 100th birthday, August 27. Ted "can make a home run if anyone can," she said. (*Boston Traveler*) Unfortunately, Williams didn't play in the August 27 game, and the Red Sox lost, 9-6, to Chicago. Two of the White Sox homered, but none of the Red Sox.

517 (#25) September 2 (first game) at Fenway Park. Pitcher: Don Lee (Washington Senators). RH. Age 26.

Bottom of the eighth inning. One-run homer.

It wasn't a good day for Red Sox fans, what with Washington sweeping the doubleheader, 5-1 and then with a come-from-behind 3-2 win in the second game. Jim Lemon homered in each game, a key home run each time. Ted homered, too, accounting for the one and only run in the first game. All in all, not a good day—except for baseball trivia buffs.

Name the only father-and-son combination off which any major league ever homered. Thornton Lee, back in Ted's rookie year, surrendered homer #28 on September 17, 1939. Don Lee coughed up #517 almost exactly 21 years later. The ball landed in the Red Sox bullpen, on the center-field side of the pen.

It was the first complete game of Don's career.

The father/son team of "Lefty" (Thornton) and Don actually combined in another baseball activity as well. Both served as scouts for the St. Louis Cardinals, Don Lee taking the southern part of Arizona and his dad taking Phoenix and north. If one saw a decent prospect, the other would come and check him out.

Don Lee remembers pitching to Ted Williams:

The first time I became aware that there was a trivia question was in Springfield [IL] when they announced during the seventh inning that Ted Williams had hit home runs off a father-son combination, and that one of the people was in the stands tonight. I thought to myself, Gee, I wonder who that could be—and then they announced that it was me!

Dad pitched against a lot of great ballplayers. And so did I, which is one of the things I hold very high. All the people who are in the Hall of Fame on Daddy's side and my side of the game—not too many families get to pitch against so many great ballplayers. I would like to own that lineup if I could put it on the field today.

Daddy told me that Ted Williams was the best left-handed hitter that he'd ever faced. I talked to Ted on numerous occasions my first year in the big leagues. I remember one time when I was in Detroit. We got rained out and I was in the parking lot and we were both waiting for cabs and I talked to him for a good half hour. He was very nice and he was also very complimentary of Daddy. I've read a couple of articles where he said that Daddy was the best left-handed pitcher he ever faced. Of course, he said that a lot [meaning, about a lot of pitchers.]

There was just something about him that when he got into the batter's box he never took his eyes off you. I pitched against him in Washington when I was a Senators that year. The first time I faced him, he hit four balls so hard right at our second baseman that the last time up that kid was in the outfield grass. Of course, Ted had a bit of a temper and he would throw a few choice words out and throw the bat and all this kind of stuff. I never said anything to him. My dad told me, "When you pitch to Ted Williams, you never throw him the same pitch twice." I said, "Well, I'll remember that."

One time I threw him three changeups in a row, which Daddy said never do, and he broke his bat on home plate because he stood and took it. He looked at me and I thought to myself, "Don't you ever throw him another one!"

You tried doing these different little things—in fact, if memory serves me, that was the only hit he ever got off me. He hit this home run, though, and boy, it was a blast. It was in Fenway Park over the bullpen and it was a slider. Two balls and no strikes. I didn't get it in far enough.

He rounded first base and he said to me as he rounded the bag—I was looking right at him—he says, "Take that, you son-of-a-bitch! One off your old man and one off you, and I'm gonna quit." That's what he said. He ran around the bases and I never forgot that. [119]

518 (#26) September 6 at Yankee Stadium, New York. Pitcher: Eli Grba (New York Yankees). RH. Age 25.

Top of the fifth inning. Two-run homer.

Pumpsie Green's inside-the-park homer was more thrilling as homers go, but at this point any home run Ted Williams hit was one to remember. The game was a 7-1 for Boston's Billy Muffett—a three-hitter. The only run scored by New York came with two outs in the bottom of the ninth, when Mickey Mantle crushed a solo homer into the seats in right-center. Pumpsie's homer had come on the very first pitch of the game, scooting around the curving wall in left field. He scored standing up, but staggering—and just barely. With Carroll Hardy on board in the top of the fifth, Williams "lifted a towering shot into the right-field stand." (*New York Times*)

The only Grba in major-league history gave up the last home run Ted Williams hit at Yankee Stadium.

519 (#27) September 8 at Briggs Stadium, Detroit. Pitcher: Jim Bunning (Detroit Tigers). RH. Age 28. Hall of Famer.

Top of the fourth inning. One-run homer.

This was Ted's last home run hit in Detroit. The night before had been "Ted Williams Night" in Detroit, and Ted was 2-for-4 with two RBIs on an eighth-inning two-bagger, but hit no home runs. On this day, September 8, the Red Sox beat Jim Bunning 6-1 and Williams was 3-for-3 with one of the three being HR #519. He also doubled to right center in the first inning, "missing a home run by two feet." It bounced off the top of a screen on the lower deck around the 375-foot mark. The only real difference between the double and the homer—since they were hit to the almost identical spot—is that the fourth-inning four-base hit was "80 feet higher. For a moment, it looked as though it might hit the front of the roof over the high second deck. Instead, it went over an exit — 14 rows up — and crashed against a screen inside the stands which separates the covered right-field grandstand seats from the bleachers." It was hit on a 3-2 pitch and was hit an estimated 450 feet, and it was a hard-hit line drive.

The final one of the eight homers Ted hit off Bunning. The complete list: #383, 439, 440, 455, 472, 498, 504, and 519.

520 (#28) September 17 at Griffith Stadium, Washington. Pitcher: Pedro Ramos (Washington Senators). RH. Age 25. GAME WINNER.

Top of the sixth inning. Two-run homer.

The next-to-last home run Ted Williams ever hit. It was also the fourth game-winner in a row off Pedro Ramos, who was still only 25 years old but had given up six home runs to Williams, with the four game-winners tying him for first place among pitchers who allowed a TSW HR to win a game. The home run provided all the scoring in the game for the Red Sox, the game a 2-1 win for Billy Muffett, who threw a three-hitter just as he had on September 6 in New York.

On a 1-2 pitch, with Willie Tasby on base, Williams "swung at the next pitch and it went on a line toward the top of the right-field fence — 31 feet high, 355 feet away, and 30 feet in from the foul line. The ball was on the rise until it was about 15 feet from the top of the fence. Then it leveled off, and cleared the fence by two or three feet."

The six homers off Ramos: #388, 409, 418, 430, 482, and 520.

521 (#29) September 28 at Fenway Park. Pitcher: Jack Fisher (Baltimore Orioles). RH. Age 21.

Bottom of the eighth inning. One-run homer.

"Everybody quiet now here at Fenway Park after they gave him a standing ovation of two minutes knowing that this is probably his last time at bat. One out, nobody on, last of the eighth inning. Jack Fisher into his windup, here's the pitch. Williams swings and there's a long drive to deep right! The ball is going and it is gone! A home run for Ted Williams in his last time at bat in the major leagues!"—Curt Gowdy's call of Ted's last home run

Perhaps we should reprint John Updike's classic "Hub Fans Bid Ted Adieu" here. We've chosen not to, both because it's been widely reprinted and is readily available and because we'd have to pay a hefty fee for reprint rights. It's recommended.

Updike did advise readers, "Understand that we were a crowd of rational people. We knew that a home run cannot be produced at will; the right pitch must be perfectly met and luck must ride with the ball. Three innings before, we had seen a brave effort fail. The air was soggy, the season was exhausted. Nevertheless, there will always lurk, around the corner in a pocket of our knowledge of the odds, an indefensible hope, and this was one of the times, which you now and then find in sports, when a density of expectation hangs in the air and plucks an event out of the future."[120]

Fifty years after the homer, Ted himself told Jeff Idelson of the National Baseball Hall of Fame:

"I had hunches and could guess good and one of them was the last time at bat. I'd hit two balls good that day and I thought they were going to go, but they didn't. So, here I am my last time at bat, two runs behind, nobody on. He laid a ball right there. I don't think I ever missed like I missed that one. It's the first time in my life I said, 'Oh geez, what happened, why didn't I hit that one?' I couldn't believe it, it was great, not the fastest pitch I'd even seen, good stuff. I missed the swing and…I didn't know what to think…had a hell of a swing and I missed it. I'm still there trying to figure out, what the hell happened. I could see Fisher out there."

Bruce Markusen added, "As Ted observed Fisher, something about his body language tipped off the identity of the next pitch, which would be the same as the last one."[121]

Williams continued: "I saw that and I guess it woke me up, you know. Right away I assumed, he thinks he threw it by me. You know, give me the ball quick, right away I said, I know he's going to go right back with that pitch and sure enough here it goes. I hit that one just a little better than I did the other two. And I got it…There's the lucky part right there. He gave the pitch away practically; he gave it away…and I was right and I must have given it a little something extra."[122]

Sports feature writer Ed Linn was in the clubhouse before the game, and afterwards, and provides perhaps the best objective account of the day and the home run. Had Ted been trying for a home run? Of course. "I was gunning for the big one. I let everything I had go. I really wanted that one." He told the Red Sox batboy to take the bat upstairs for Mr. Yawkey.[123]

The ball was hit through the air, hard enough to slice through whatever stood in its way that day, and landed in the Red Sox bullpen. It was a defining moment, something of a hit of destiny; as John Updike put it, the ball was "in the books while it was still in the sky." It left the field with room to spare, and bounced off the roof over the Boston bench. A home run.

Brooks Robinson was the third baseman for the Orioles that day. The moment was engraved in his memory, and he often sees it on replays. "I see that home run all the time, you know different shots when someone's running some old film. I see that shot and really enjoy telling that story more than anything else. When someone mentions Ted Williams, I say, 'Well, you know I was playing third base when he hit the home run in his last at-bat.' It turned out to be one of the greatest thrills I've ever had of my baseball career."[124]

Though he was only 21, this was the 20th homer Fisher had allowed—and the fourth to a batter named Williams. Baltimore's Dick Williams hit three off him (so had Roy Sievers). But of the 193 homers Fisher allowed in his 11 years in the majors, this is the one for which he is most noted.

After the game

An official Jimmy Fund publication told what Ted did after the game: "But Ted's day wasn't over yet. A public appearance for the Jimmy Fund awaited him in Rhode Island. Although running behind schedule, Ted had no compunction about throwing a curveball into his travel plans: he insisted on visiting a young cancer patient. The thrilled youngster buckled a belt he had made for Ted around his hero's waist.

Ted had come just in time. A few days later, the boy died.[125]

It's not a story we've been able to confirm.

Glenn Stout wrote, "After the game Ted held a party at the Kenmore Hotel, inviting his friends — the bellhops, cops, cabbies, and batboys — as well as his teammates."[126]

What about home run #522? As far as we know, Williams himself was never deprived of a home run by virtue of having hit one in the early innings of a game that was called off before becoming official, nor of suffering a "lost home run" because of umpire error in which a ball that indeed was a home run was ruled something else — a double, a foul ball, etc. On June 27, 1966, Willie Mays hit his 522nd home run (off Bob Gibson), passing Ted Williams on the all-time home run list. Ted congratulated him at the time and then again referenced it during his own speech on induction into the National Baseball Hall of Fame on July 25: "The other day Willie May hit his 522nd home run. He has gone past me, and he's pushing and I say to him, 'Go get 'em, Willie!' Baseball gives every American boy a chance to excel. Not just to be as good as someone else, but to be better. This is the nature of man and the name of the game. I hope that some day Satchel Paige and Josh Gibson will be voted into the Hall of Fame as symbols of the great Negro players who are not here only because they weren't given the chance."

When Ted Williams and Jim Prime later co-authored the book *Ted Williams' Hit List*, Ted again mentioned Gibson, going so far as to rank him #25 on his list of the top hitters of all time, though acknowledging that "because he never played a major-league game, there is no statistical basis for comparison." Also admitting that he faced many pitchers who were probably not of major-league caliber, he did write, "He reportedly hit 75 in 1931 and 69 in 1934…When his barnstorming, Mexican, and Caribbean games are factored in, some estimates of his home runs totals approach the 950 range."[127]

Stan Musial thought Ted Williams might have hit a lot more home runs, himself. "Ted was a once-in-a-generation hitter, the best of our time, without question. He knew his art and knew his pitchers. He had a keen appreciation of the strike zone, a great eye, quick hands — and what power! It's no accident that he hit .400. If he hadn't missed almost five years because of military service in World War II and Korea he might have hit 700 home runs."[128]

How many home runs might Ted have hit had he not devoted most of five seasons to military service?

Any number of people, from Steve Brooks to Keith Woolner, have run projections as to how many homers Ted would have hit had he not lost those years in the Navy and Marines. Just simply looking at the four years preceding World War II and the years from 1946 through 1951, one can project what would have been his totals in 1943, 1944, and 1945. Woolner came up with 40, 41, and 47, respectively—truly his prime years—he turned 25 in 1943. Adding those additional 128 homers to Ted's total and then projecting based on 1939 through 1951 (thus adjusted), he projected 38 homers in 1952 and 29 in 1953. Woolner's overall total would have have brought him to 701. One wonders if Ted had come that close to Babe Ruth's 714, whether he would have stayed on for yet one more year (he had, after all, hit 29 in the year he turned 42.) Brooks' projection came up with figures in the high 600s—672 to 686.

Which pitchers did Ted hit the most home runs off?

The pitchers off whom Ted hit six or more home runs were:

Virgil Trucks — 12
Bob Feller — 10
Ned Garver — 10
Jim Bunning — 8
Fred Hutchinson — 8
Early Wynn — 8
Johnny Rigney — 7
Bob Keegan — 7
Mike Garcia — 6
Allie Reynolds — 6
Art Houtteman — 6
Pedro Ramos — 6
Dizzy Trout — 6
Al Benton — 6
Howie Judson — 6
Bob Muncrief — 6
Steve Gromek — 6
Dick Fowler — 6

Ted Williams' game-winning homers

Based on what research, we do not know, but Williams wrote in *The Science of Hitting*, "I had a higher percentage of game-winning home runs than Babe Ruth."[129]

Ted hit 106 game-winning homers. A little over 20% of the homers he hit won ballgames for Boston.

1939 (9)

May 4—Ted homered in consecutive innings, the second one (off Bob Harris) giving the Sox a 7-4 lead. They ultimately won, 7-6.

May 9—The rookie's three-run homer in the top of the 10th beat Harry Kimberlin and the St. Louis Browns in the team's 14th game of the year.

July 2—Lefty Gomez cost the Yankees the ballgame when Ted Williams broke a 3-3 tie with a three-run homer in the bottom of the seventh and held on to win, 7-3.

July 15—Ted's solo homer off Johnny Broaca gave the Sox their sixth run, on their way to a 9-5 finale.

August 19—Ted's grand slam in the top of the ninth led to an 8-6 final over the Senators. Pete Appleton was the victim.

August 28—Ted hit a three-run homer over Cleveland's right-field screen for the final three of Boston's four runs in the eighth inning. Mel Harder and the Indians lost, 6-5.

August 29—Boston scored six runs in the fifth inning, and Ted drove in the final four with a grand slam off Cleveland's Harry Eisenstat. It was the second game in a row that Ted won with a home run.

September 10—Ted's two-run homer in the top of the fifth (off Philadelphia's Chubby Dean) gave Boston a lead they kept in the first game of the day's doubleheader.

September 10—In the second game, his first-inning homer off Lynn Nelson gave the Sox a lead they only expanded in their 5-1 victory. Ted hit two game-winning homers on the very same day—and he also hit a triple in each game as well.

1940 (2)

June 16—Ted Williams vs. Ted Lyons. Williams won the battle this time, with a 12th-inning solo home run to beat the White Sox in Chicago, 4-3.

July 5—In the top of the fifth, Ted hit a two-run homer to give the Red Sox a 6-1 lead over Walt Masterson and the Washington ballclub; the final was 6-4.

1941 (7)

May 7—Top of the 11th in Chicago. Score tied, 3-3. Johnny Rigney wound up and pitched. Home run, Ted Williams.

May 27—The Sox scored once in the first, once in the second, and one more in the third on Ted's solo homer off Philadelphia's Bump Hadley. 5-2 final.

May 29—Williams broke a 3-3 tie with a two-run homer off Philadelphia's Jack Knott. The final was 6-4.

June 6—Chicago's Johnny Rigney paid for the second time in a month, when Ted hit another homer off him, this time a two-run homer in the third inning giving the Red Sox a 5-0 lead. The score at the end of the game was 6-3.

June 12—Johnny Niggeling of the St. Louis Browns saw Ted bang his pitch out of the park for a two-run homer. The Sox took a 3-1 lead, and only allowed one more run to St. Louis.

August 31—Jack Knott paid for the second time in 1941, a three-run homer that gave the Red Sox a 6-1 lead. The final was 6-3. There was a second game that day, and the Athletics walked Ted intentionally three of the four times he came up to bat.

September 1 (first game)—Ted hit three home runs on the day, two in the first game and one in the second. This was the middle one, hit off Bill Zuber, and provided the runs that won the game.

1942 (6)

May 16—Ted's top of the ninth homer off Bob Muncrief of the Browns turned a 2-2 tie into a 4-2 Red Sox triumph.

May 29—His three-run homer in the first was enough to win the game, but Ted added a grand slam later on for good measure. Russ Christopher of the Athletics took the loss, as Boston won 14-2.

June 24—Virgil Trucks only allowed Ted's solo homer in the seventh, but Charlie Wagner shut out the Tigers in Detroit.

August 15—The two runs that scored on Ted Williams' two-run homer in the third were all it took for Tex Hughson to beat Sid Hudson and the Senators, 2-1.

September 6—Boston scored five runs in the seventh, but Ted's solo homer off Philadelphia's Lum Harris was the run that made all the difference in the 8-7 win.

September 13—The Red Sox scored six runs in the seventh to overcome a 1-0 White Sox lead. The first two came in when Ted drove in Johnny Pesky and himself with a homer off Buck Ross.

1946 (7)

May 2—Bottom of the 10th, and Ted hit a home run off Detroit's Tommy Bridges into the bullpen for a 5-4 walkoff win.

May 22 — After Boston tied it in the ninth, both the Indians and Red Sox scored once in the 11th — but it was Williams' two-run home run in the 12th off Pete Center that gave the Sox the lead for good.

June 6 — Ted's homer off Ox Miller of the Browns plated two runs for the Red Sox for the fourth and fifth runs in a 5-4 game.

July 7 — Ted's second-inning homer scored Dom DiMaggio ahead of him for the first two runs in an 11-1 win over Washington. Sid Hudson served it up.

July 14 — This is the game that inspired the Williams Shift. Ted's three-run homer off Joe Berry in the bottom of the eighth gave Boston an 11-10 lead. It was the third of three homers he hit, driving in eight runs in the process. The shift was never going to help against balls leaving the premises, but Indians manager Lou Boudreau put it on in the second game. Ted doubled and scored two runs.

July 30 — Boo Ferriss threw a three-hit shutout against the Indians. For the third time in 1946, Ted's homer won the game for the Red Sox, this time a solo home run in the fourth off Steve Gromek. 4-0 final.

September 13 — All the Red Sox had needed to clinch the pennant was one more win, but they lost six games in a row. In the very first inning, facing Boudreau's shift, Ted struck a drive into undefended territory in left field and ran all the way around the bases for the only inside-the-park home run of his career. Red Embree didn't know that would be all it took to lose the game but Tex Hughson shut out the Indians on three hits and the Red Sox won the pennant.

1947 (9)

May 6 — Ted's solo homer off St. Louis's Jack Kramer tied the score 3-3 in the ninth. The Red Sox needed all three of the runs his homer in the top of the 11th secured off Frank Sanford for the 6-5 final.

May 16 — St. Louis was visiting Boston, but the Red Sox had a 7-0 lead when Ted's grand slam off Walter Brown made it 11-0. The Browns came back with seven runs of their own, so the slam made the difference in the 12-7 game.

May 19—Boston lost the first game to the visiting Tigers, 3-2 in 12 innings. In the second game, in the bottom of the ninth, Ted's two-run homer overcame a 4-3 Detroit lead and saw Virgil Trucks walk off the field in defeat.

June 4—Another Williams roundtripper did in the Browns, this one a solo home run in the top of the sixth that gave Boston a 3-2 lead. Bob Muncrief lost the game, 5-2.

July 16—Red Ruffing was the first major-league pitcher Ted had ever faced, back when he broke in during 1939. In Chicago, Ted's two-run homer off Ruffing gave the Red Sox a 4-0 lead. The score at game's end was 7-2.

July 26—The Browns were visiting Boston once more. Starting pitcher Cliff Fannin served up a two-run homer to Ted in the first inning. The final score was 12-1.

August 2—Virgil Trucks started for the Tigers. Just as he had a week earlier, Ted hit a two-run homer in the bottom of the first and it held up to win the game. The difference was that the Red Sox never scored again; the score at the end was 2-1.

August 26 (second game)—Ted had only driven in one run in the first game, but five of the nine Red Sox runs in the second game. This one won the game, hit off a Hal White offering.

September 27—His 32nd home run of the season was another first-inning blow, this time a three-run shot off Washington's Walt Masterson. Boston beat the Senators, 6-1.

1948 (3)

August 27—A 400-foot home run into Fenway's right-field bleachers gave the Bosox three more runs, extending their lead to 8-4 in a game that wound up 10-5. The native of Lucca, Italy—Marino Pieretti of the White Sox—served up the ultimately decisive blow.

August 29—Facing starter Karl Drews, the third batter up for the Red Sox—Ted Williams—launched a three-run homer out of Fenway. Birdie Tebbetts hit a grand slam later in the same first frame. Final score, 10-2 over the Browns.

October 2—Another first-inning homer put an end to the pennant hopes of the New York Yankees when the score held up for a 5-1 win over Tommy Byrne.

1949 (8)

May 18—Ted hit another homer off Chicago's Pieretti on the bottom of the third, a two-run homer that gave the Bosox a 5-0 lead. The final total: 7-4.

May 28—Williams broke a 4-4 tie with a solo home run in the bottom of the fifth, the final run scored in the 5-4 win over Washington. Dick Welteroth was Williams' victim.

May 30—A two-run homer off Carl Scheib in the bottom of the eighth gave the Red Sox a 4-3 margin over Philadelphia and a win for the home crowd.

June 24—It was yet another first-inning game-winning homer, this time off Joe Ostrowski, a three-run homer and the first of two by Ted in the game (for a total of seven RBIs) and the Bosox pounded the Browns 21-2.

July 16—In Detroit, Williams hit a two-run homer in the top of the first driving in enough runs to beat Virgil Trucks. The final score was 11-1.

August 9—Ted's two-run homer (courtesy of Vic Raschi) scored the fourth and fifth runs of the 6-3 Sox win over the Yankees.

September 14—There was only one run in the game, a 1-0 win for Boston. It came in the bottom of the sixth on Ted's home run, one of only four Red Sox hits in the game. Hal Newhouser was the losing pitcher. Ellis Kinder (20-5) got the win.

September 21—The Sox beat the Indians 9-6. The solo homer Ted hit off Steve Gromek in the bottom of the seventh provided Boston's seventh run of the game.

1950 (6)

April 19—The only day the Red Sox start their games before noon time is Patriots Day. Ted homered his second time up off Vic Raschi and gave the Sox a 4-0 lead; the final was 6-3.

May 5—On 5/5, Ted hit his fifth home run of the season, giving the Red Sox the lead over Billy Pierce and the White Sox. Boston fans went home happy with the 5-2 win.

May 6—Winning a game two days in a row, Ted's three-run homer off Ken Holcombe was the first of six Sox homers, in an 11-1 win over Chicago.

May 16—Art Houtteman surrendered a home run to Ted with a runner on. The third inning homer gave Boston the lead in a 6-1 game against the Tigers.

June 3—The game was Boston 11, Cleveland 9, and Ted's two-run homer off Jesse Flores was the one that put them over the top.

June 28—Philadelphia and Boston was locked up 2-2 until Williams walloped one off Lou Brissie in the top of the eighth.

1951 (6)

May 6—The Browns had just tied the score 4-4 at the last minute in the bottom of the ninth, but Ted Williams struck in the top of the 10th and won the game for Boston, beating Lou Sleator 5-4

May 21—Even though the Red Sox had scored seven runs in the third inning, they still couldn't beat the Indians until Ted stroked a two-run homer in the bottom of the seventh. Thank you, Gene Bearden.

May 27—Ted hit a grand slam off Julio Moreno in the third inning which beat the Senators, who were further discouraged by Bobby Doerr's three-run homer later in the same inning. Those were all the runs for the Red Sox in the 7-1 ballgame.

June 17—Mel Parnell scattered eight hits in a 3-0 second game shutout; Ted's two-run homer off Al Widmar in the first was all it took to beat the Browns. Boston won the first game, too, 5-4. Ted contributed two of the four, but without an extra-base hit.

September 5—A huge Yankee Stadium crowd of 58,462 saw Ted Williams hammer a Vic Raschi pitch "deep into the right-field stand." The third-inning solo home run gave Boston a 3-0 lead. The final was 4-2.

September 14—In the second inning, Ted drove in a pair against the Browns, increasing Boston's lead to 7-2. It was his second game-winner off Al Widmar in 1951. Ellis Kinder got the win; it was his fifth appearance in five consecutive games.

1952 (1)

April 30—It was "Ted Williams Day" at Fenway Park, the last game before Williams left to report to the Marine Corps for duty in the Korean War. His last time up before leaving baseball for what he thought might be forever, Ted hit a two-run seventh-inning homer off Detroit's Dizzy Trout breaking a 3-3 tie.

1953 (3)

August 19—Capt. T. S. Williams, USMC, completed 39 combat missions over North Korea and had been back less than a month when he smacked out a two-run homer (his third four-bagger since returning) to give the Sox the winning runs in a 6-4 win over Charlie Bishop and the Athletics.

August 31—Mike Garcia saw his pitch delivered into the upper right-field deck of Cleveland's Municipal Stadium, the seventh-inning homer by Ted Williams giving Boston a 5-1 lead—sufficient to hold up for a 6-4 win.

September 17—Boston's Sid Hudson battled Detroit's Ned Garver through 7 ½ innings, with the Tigers holding a 1-0 lead since the top of the second. Then Ted found the pitch he was looking for and hit a two-run homer in the bottom of the eighth some 15 rows up in the right-field grandstand. 2-1 final.

1954 (3)

August 6—Ted's two-run homer in the top of the 10th drove in Jimmy Piersall ahead of him and beat Baltimore and reliever Bob Chakales.

August 11—In the very first inning, with Boston down 1-0, Ted hit a two-run homer off Washington's Connie Marrero. Tommy Brewer only gave up two hits in the rest of the game, and no runs, and Boston won, 10-1. Ted drove in two more runs later in the game.

September 3—The score was 1-1 in the top of the third when Williams touched up Arnie Portocarrero for a two-run shot. Frank Sullivan held the Athletics scoreless for the next seven innings and the Sox won with ease, 11-1. Ted drove in another run in the very next inning.

1955 (6)

June 10—Taking advantage of his favorite ballpark, Ted hit two homers in Briggs Stadium, Detroit—a solo homer in the first and a two-run homer in the third, both off Duke Maas. The final score was 5-2 in favor of the Red Sox.

June 21—This is one Ted felt a little lucky to get ahold of. His three-run eighth-inning homer off Detroit's Ned Garver won the game, 5-4, but afterwards he had nothing but praise for Garver, talking about all the "junk" Garver had thrown him and admitted he didn't even know what kind of pitch it was he'd hit out—rare in Ted's case.

July 29—Willard Nixon threw a four-hit shutout, so Ted's first inning solo homer off Detroit's Jim Bunning was the game-winner, though the final score reads 5-0.

July 31—A little less than six weeks since beating Garver the last time the Tigers had come to Boston, Ted did it again, this time via a fourth-inning grand slam.

August 15—Two runs had already scored, but Williams' 450-foot grand slam completed the six-run second that saw the Sox beat the Senators and Ted Abernathy.

August 27—The third game-winner in a row was yet another grand slam, the fifth time in '55 that Ted had beaten the Tigers with a homer. Two outs in the top of the ninth, BANG! Grand slam off Al Aber. 4-3 final.

1956 (9)

July 8—With the 399th homer of his major league career, Ted Williams gave Boston a 2-0 lead over Ray Moore and the Baltimore Orioles in the first inning of a 9-0 ballgame. In the day's second game, Ted's single drove in his 1,500th run.

July 17 — Homer #400 was a solo homer accounting for the only run of a 1-0 win over Kansas City's Tom Gorman. The ball sailed 15 rows up in the bleachers behind the visitors' bullpen at Fenway Park. It wasn't a great day for KC batters; they were shut out 10-0 in the day's first game.

July 26 — Piersall's double in the eighth scored two to tie the game 3-3. Ted's two-run homer in the top of the 10th beat Bobby Shantz and the Athletics in Kansas City, 5-3.

August 5 — Jackie Jensen's solo homer in the fifth tied the game, 1-1. Ted Williams' solo homer in the sixth beat Bob Lemon and the Indians, 2-1.

August 8 — Though they added four more runs in the bottom of the eighth, it was Williams' solo home run off Baltimore's Connie Johnson in the sixth inning that gave the Red Sox the third run in their 7-2 triumph.

September 1 — The Orioles had just tied the game 2-2 in the top of the eighth. Ted hit a two-run homer off Morrie Martin in the home half of the inning, and won the game, 4-2.

September 8 — Singles by Billy Goodman and Billy Klaus and a three-run homer by Ted Williams gave Boston a quick 3-0 lead in the top of the first. The final score was Boston 6, Baltimore 1. For Ted, it was his third game-winning homer against the O's in a one-month span. This one was hit off Billy Loes.

September 11 — Ted's solo homer into Chicago's center-field bullpen snapped a 3-3 tie in the fifth. Bob Keegan was the White Sox pitcher. The Bosox added an insurance run later on; the Chisox failed to score again.

September 25 — Ted's three-run homer capped a four-run second and gave Boston a lead they never lost, beating Pedro Ramos and the Senators 10-4. The Red Sox played 28 ballgames in September 1956 and Ted Williams won four of them by the home run route.

1957 (8)

May 7 — Williams drove in three of Boston's four runs, the final two coming in the top of the ninth off Chicago's Dick Donovan.

May 8—Boston scored four runs the following day, too—all four thanks to Ted Williams (and Bob Keegan of the White Sox, who surrendered all three homers to The Thumper).

June 2—Washington had a 3-2 lead until Ted hit a three-run homer off Pedro Ramos in the top of the eighth. The final was 5-3.

June 13—A little over a month after Ted hit three homers off Bob Keegan, he hit three homers in another game, this time in Cleveland and this time off two future Hall of Famers: two off Early Wynn and one off Bob Lemon. The three-run homer in the fifth off Wynn led to the loss, for the Indians.

August 14—Hitting against the Yankees' Don Larsen, Ted's three-run homer ended a four-run second inning and gave the Red Sox enough runs to win the game.

August 28—As he had a little more than two years earlier (July 29, 1955), Williams hit a solo home run to beat Jim Bunning. This one came in the seventh, the only run of the ballgame against the Tigers.

September 21—Ted spanked the Yanks at the Stadium again, this time a second-inning grand slam off Bob Turley gave Boston all they needed for an 8-3 win.

September 24—His fourth-inning homer gave the Red Sox a 2-0 lead. Once again, Ted helped Frank Sullivan with a win, 2-1 over Washington at the end. Hal Griggs served it up.

1958 (7)

May 22—The Sox scored once but were still behind by a run, down 3-2. Williams was up with the bases loaded and two outs, acing Jack Urban. He fouled off the first three pitches he saw, then unloaded. Ted's grand slam over Kansas City's 11-foot high wall struck the base of a light tower standing on an embankment about 40 feet beyond the fence. It was good for the final four runs of a five-run fourth.

June 26—Dick Gernert's homer tied it 1-1 for the Red Sox in the seventh but Ted's "towering smash" (UPI) in the top of the ninth won the game, 2-1, beating Cal McLish and the Indians.

June 29—Williams hit one on top of the right-field roof in Detroit, a three-run homer in the eighth off Bill Fischer. A game-winner in the 10-7 game.

July 19—Ted was having a tough day. He misplayed one ball, then grounded out in the bottom of the ninth leaving a runner stranded on third base. To make matters worse, Detroit scored once in the top of the 12th—but Ted came through with a two-run homer off Hank Aguirre for a walkoff win.

July 29—Nine days earlier, Jim Bunning no-hit the Red Sox at Fenway. The Tigers had a 4-0 lead in this day's game in Detroit, but Williams hit a grand slam off Bunning in the third to tie it. Jim was long gone by the top of the 11th, when Ted faced Bill Fischer with two runners on base. Three-run homer. Tom Brewer didn't let the Tigers reach base. Game over.

August 3—Apparently the Indians left Gary Bell in a little too long. He had a 2-1 lead heading into the ninth, but Runnels singled and Williams homered and the game ended 3-2.

September 28—Thanks to a 2-for-4 day, Ted Williams secured the AL batting title against teammate Pete Runnels (0-for-4, and .322 to Ted's .328)—and Ted's second hit of the day was his seventh-inning solo home run off Pedro Ramos, the fifth of Boston's six runs in the 6-4 win in Washington.

1959 (3)

May 30—Ted's two-run homer off Jerry Walker in the second game of a twinbill against the visiting Orioles lifted Boston into the lead and a sweep of the set.

June 27—Ted's two-run homer in the fifth inning gave the Red Sox a 5-1 lead over starter Mudcat Grant. Jensen went back-to-back, and Boston beat Cleveland, 6-4.

August 22—The year 1959 was Ted's worst campaign. He batted just .254 with only 10 home runs, but the third of those 10 won this game. A solo homer off Baltimore's Don Mossi gave the Red Sox a 2-0 lead. Ted drove in another run later, but it was the towering round-tripper that won the 7-1 game.

1960 (3)

June 17—Home run #500! A moment to treasure forever. That the two-run homer hit in the third off Wynn Hawkins won the game and beat Cleveland 3-1 made it all the sweeter.

August 20—Ted hit two three-run homers off Chuck Estrada, one in the fourth and one in the sixth. He also drew his 2,000th walk as a (very patient) major league batter. Baltimore lost the game, 8-6.

September 17—For the fourth time, Ted took Pedro Ramos deep with a game-winning homer, a two-run blow in the top of the sixth in Our Nation's Capitol. And the final score was 2-1, so you know who had the winning hit.

A few thoughts

With nine game-winning homers in 1956, a Williams home run won a little more than 10% of all 83 of Boston's wins in 1956. It was a year in which he only hit 24 homers in all, but he made more than a third of them count for the win.

Overall, some 106 of Ted's 521 homers were game-winners, 20.345%. Williams appeared in 2,292 games — sometimes just briefly as a pinch-hitter. There were times when he hit more than one homer a game, but his homers alone counted for wins in 4.5% of the games in which he appeared.

This section on game-winning homers comes from the book *The Ultimate Red Sox Home Run Guide* by Bill Nowlin and David Vincent, slightly modified here in light of the more detailed research done in preparing this book.

Ted's best months

With most seasons starting only in mid- to late-April during the years when Ted played, it's unsurprising that April was the month in which he hit the fewest home runs. This list shows his most productive months, in each of the six months during the baseball season. His best month of May, for instance, was in 1942.

April—1951 and 1957 (4)
May—1942 (12)
June—1950 (12)
July—1954 (11)
August—1941 and 1949 (10)
September—1939 and 1942 (9)

The other months in which he hit 10 or more home runs:

June 1946 (11), July 1947 (10), August 1949 (10), July 1955 (10), June 1960 (11)

Teams against which Ted hit the most game-winners

Opponents:

Chicago	12	
Cleveland	17	
Detroit	20	
New York	7	
Philadelphia	14	(11 plus 3 more against the Kansas City Athletics after the team relocated)
St. Louis	21	(13 plus 8 more after the franchise relocated to Baltimore)
Washington	15	

Pitchers off whom Ted hit the most game-winners

Virgil Trucks and Pedro Ramos surrendered four each. Ned Garver coughed up three. In the case of Ramos, four of the six homers Ted hit off him were game-winners.

In *Tales from the Red Sox Dugout*, we find this memory of Ramos. The story was one Mel Parnell loved to tell.

Ted Williams was a hero to fans and an idol to fellow hitters, but he was looked on with awe by big league pitchers. Rookie pitcher Pedro Ramos once struck Ted out and then had the gall to enter the Red Sox dugout and ask the Splendid Splinter to autograph the ball used to strike him out. "Get the hell out of here!" roared Terrible Ted. "I'm not signing any ball I struck out on." Ramos, who idolized Williams, was crushed and tears welled in his eyes. Seeing this, the great Williams relented. "Give me the damn ball and I'll sign it," he said.

During the next Red Sox homestand, Ted once again faced Ramos. This time he tore into the pitcher's first offering and drove the ball deep into the right field bleachers. As he trotted around the bases, he turned to the pitcher and shouted, "Go find that SOB and I'll sign it for you, too."

Here is the complete list of the pitchers off whom Williams hit game-winning homers:

Al Aber
Ted Abernathy
Hank Aguirre
Pete Appleton
Gene Bearden
Gary Bell
Joe Berry
Charlie Bishop
Tommy Bridges
Lou Brissie
Johnny Broaca
Walter Brown
Jim Bunning—2
Tommy Byrne
Pete Center
Bob Chakales
Russ Christopher
Chubby Dean
Dick Donovan
Karl Drews
Harry Eisenstat
Red Embree
Chuck Estrada
Cliff Fannin
Bill Fischer—2
Jesse Flores
Mike Garcia
Ned Garver—3

Lefty Gomez
Tom Gorman
Mudcat Grant
Hal Griggs
Steve Gromek—2
Bump Hadley
Bob Harris
Lum Harris
Wynn Hawkins
Ken Holcombe
Art Houtteman
Sid Hudson—2
Connie Johnson
Bob Keegan—2
Harry Kimberlin
Jack Knott—2
Don Larsen
Bob Lemon
Billy Loes
Ted Lyons
Duke Maas
Connie Marrero
Morrie Martin
Walt Masterson—2
Cal McLish
Ox Miller
Ray Moore
Julio Moreno

Don Mossi
Bob Muncrief—2
Lynn Nelson
Hal Newhouser
Johnny Niggeling
Joe Ostrowski
Billy Pierce
Arnie Portocarrero
Marino Pieretti—2
Pedro Ramos—4
Vic Raschi—3
Johnny Rigney—2
Buck Ross
Red Ruffing
Frank Sanford
Carl Scheib
Bobby Shantz
Lou Sleator
Dizzy Trout
Virgil Trucks—4
Bob Turley
Jack Urban
Jerry Walker
Dick Welteroth
Hal White
Al Widmar
Early Wynn
Bill Zuber

Which pitcher gave up the most homers to Ted without even one of them being a game-winner?

The answer is Bob Feller. Ted hit ten homers off Bob Feller but not one of them was a game-winner. That's not to say they didn't help win games, but just that none of the ten was a game-winning hit.

Ted hit eight off Fred Hutchinson and none of those were game-winners, either.

The 17 grand slams of Ted Williams

Date	Pitcher	Inning	Ballpark
August 19, 1939	Pete Appleton	Top 9	Griffith Stadium/Washington DC

Ted's grand slam in the top of the ninth "cleared the right right-field fence" and helped give Boston an 8-6 edge over the Senators in the first game of the day's doubleheader.

Date	Pitcher	Inning	Ballpark
August 29, 1939	Harry Eisenstat	Top 5	League Park/Cleveland

The Kid's homer provided the final four of six runs the Sox scored in the fifth, for a 7-4 win. Just the day before, Ted had hit a three-run homer for another victory, a 6-5 win over the Indians.

Date	Pitcher	Inning	Ballpark
August 15, 1940	Bump Hadley	Top 5	Yankee Stadium/New York

The Sox already held a 6-1 lead, but the Williams grand slam was icing on the cake for Boston's Joe Heving to record an 11-1 win.

Date	Pitcher	Inning	Ballpark
July 31, 1941	George Caster	Btm 7	Fenway Park

Roy Cullenbine hit a grand slam in the first inning and the Browns had a 7-5 lead when the Sox scored six runs in the bottom of the seventh for an 11-7 lead, but St. Louis scored three runs in the eighth and six in the top of the ninth on the way to a 16-11 final. Forgetting that Ted already had three in the books, the Associated Press game story dubbed this the first grand slam of his career.

May 29, 1942   Dick Fowler   Top 8   Shibe Park/Philadelphia
Ted's first homer came with two on in the first inning and was in itself sufficient for the 14-2 margin of victory; his grand slam came in the eighth.

May 18, 1946   Ellis Kinder   Top 5   Sportsman's Park/St. Louis
As with Ted's 1942 slam, the Sox already had a big lead (11-2) when he hit this slam. The first four times up, the Browns had walked him—three times intentionally. With the bases loaded, they foreswore the intentional walk—with disastrous results.

July 14, 1946   Steve Gromek   Btm 3   Fenway Park
In the first game of the day's doubleheader, Ted hit three home runs. The slam came first, followed by a solo homer in the fifth inning and a three-run game-winning homer in the eighth. Boston needed every run—the final was Red Sox 11, Indians 10. They won the second game, too, Ted doubling and scoring two runs.

May 16, 1947   Walter Brown   Btm 5   Fenway Park
The Sox already had a 7-0 lead when Ted smacked a drive about 12 rows up in the bleacher seats in right-center field. It proved decisive; the final score was Red Sox 12, St. Louis 7.

May 1, 1949   Spec Shea   Top 6   Yankee Stadium/New York
Johnny Pesky and Vern Stephens both hit two-run homers; Ted's added the final four runs in an 11-2 romp over the Yankees.

May 11, 1950   Fred Hutchinson   Btm 8   Fenway Park
The Tigers were leading 13-0 so perhaps didn't need to pitch around Williams, but Hutchinson might have had a shutout had Ted not made it 13-4.

May 27, 1951   Julio Moreno   Btm 3   Fenway Park
In the one inning, Williams hit a four-run homer and Doerr followed with a three-run homer; Boston beat the Senators, 7-1, to sweep the double-header. Ted had doubled twice and drove in two in the first game.

July 31, 1955   Ned Garver   Btm 4   Fenway Park
Ted's homer made the difference in the 8-3 twinbill opener. His sacrifice fly helped ensure a 2-2 tie game with the Tigers until Jimmy Piersall won the nightcap in the bottom of the ninth.

August 15, 1955   Ted Abernathy   Btm 2   Fenway Park
It landed about 10 rows up in centerfield bleachers, an estimated 450 feet, part of a six-run second inning that sank the Senators, 8-4. It was Ted's first homer since the slam off Garver a couple of weeks earlier.

August 27, 1955   Al Aber   Top 9   Tiger Stadium/Detroit
The Tigers had a 3-0 lead in the top of the ninth. With two outs, but the bases loaded, starting pitcher Lyn Lary left the game for reliever Al Aber. On a 2-1 count, Aber threw the ball Ted banged high up into Tiger Stadium's upper deck seats. 4-3 final score.

Sept. 21, 1957   Bob Turley   Top 2   Yankee Stadium/New York
The Yankees pitched so carefully around Ted Williams that only one of the 15 pitches he saw was not a ball. The one that was over the plate was pounded out for a grand slam that gave the Red Sox a 5-0 lead in a game that ended 8-3.

May 22, 1958   Jack Urban   Top 4   Municipal Stadium/Kansas City
The fourth-inning grand slam provided the last fours runs of a five-run fourth which left Boston with a 6-3 lead in a game which wound up 8-5.

July 29, 1958   Jim Bunning   Top 3   Tiger Stadium/Detroit
Williams tied Babe Ruth for second place in grand slams at 17 apiece (Gehrig had 23) with his second Tiger Stadium slam. It erased a 4-0 Tigers lead in the third inning. Ted's slam off future U.S. Senator Jim Bunning in July 1958 wasn't enough to win the game, but his three-run homer off Bill Fischer in the top of the 11th was.

Grand slams often win games

Of Ted's 17 slams, nine of them were game-winners: both of the 1939 homers, his 1947 homer, the 1951 homer, all three of the 1955 homers, the one off Turley in 1957, and the May 22 homer in 1958.

Ted hit four of his slams in the fifth inning, three in the third, two each in the second, fourth, eighth, and ninth, one in the sixth and one in the seventh, and none at all in the first inning—he typically batted third.

He never hit a grand slam in April, but hit seven in May. He never hit one in June but hit nine between July 14 and August 29. He hit three in Yankee

Stadium (go, Ted!), two in Detroit, and one each in DC, KC, Philly, and St. Louis. Seven of the 17 were hit in Fenway Park—remarkably, every one of the Fenway homers was hit in the bottom half of the inning!

The White Sox got off scot-free, and the Athletics only got touched up once. Ted hit four of his 17 grand slams against the Tigers (two at home and two in Detroit), and three apiece off the Indians, Senators, and Yankees.

Ted Williams home runs in the minor leagues

Ted never played a rehab game in the minors, though he did have three minor-league seasons—1936 and 1937 with the Pacific Coast League's San Diego Padres and 1938 with the Minneapolis Millers in the American Association.

He was 17 the first year he played with the Padres, joining the team in midseason after finishing school. He appeared in 42 games, batting for a .271 average (29 base hits in 107 at-bats) and recording a slugging percentage of .383. He hit eight doubles and two triples, but not even one home run during the regular season. The Padres made the playoffs, however, and Teddy hit one in the first game, facing Wee Willie Ludolph of the Oakland Oaks, in Oakland. It was in the top of the eighth inning. He "smashed one of Ludolph's fast ones over the right-field fence, scoring [George] Myatt ahead of him."[130] The fence was about 365 feet from the plate. Ludolph led the Coast League in winning percentage that year, with a 21-6 record, and won this playoff game, too. The Oaks won the best-of-seven series in five games.

And then Ted Williams went back to complete his senior year of high school.

Even before going pro, he'd played for the Hoover High School team, achieving some success as both a pitcher and a batter. The story told by childhood friend had Williams—still a Horace Mann Junior High School student in the final days at Mann—turning up for batting practice at Hoover and pestering coach Wos Caldwell for a chance to hit. "Coach, let me hit!" Caldwell didn't pay much attention to him—there were a hundred kids trying out—but he persisted and Caldwell was throwing b.p. himself at the end of the day. Boyhood friend Les Cassie Jr. was there. "It wasn't a ballpark, just a big old open space. In right field was a lunch arbor, a roof over a bunch of benches…The first ball went up on top of that lunch arbor, and no one had ever hit one anywhere near there."[131] In a 1997 interview with the author, Caldwell recalled, "He proceeded to hit two of them on top of a three story school building."[132]

Ted first made the Hoover High School newspaper, the *Cardinal*, on April 20, 1934. In a game against Alhambra, Ted batted seventh in the order (for perhaps the only time in his career) against pitcher John Stocking. In the second inning, he hit a grand slam home run to center field, "a hard-hit line drive over the shortstop's head and between the outfielders." *(San Diego Union)* The *Cardinal* reported, "Ted Williams, sophomore outfielder, started the fireworks with a home run with bases full." And the *San Diego Sun* reported, "Ted Williams started the Cardinals off on the victory road with a home run in the second canto with the bases loaded." It was, as far as we've been able to determine, his only home run at Hoover in 1934.[133]

Ted told of one game against Santa Monica High—which we were never able to locate—where "I once struck out 23—and *homered* in the same game."[134] When he first joined the Padres, he started off well but then opposing pitchers began to get him out. "So Herm Pillette, who pitched for the Detroit Tigers in the 1920s—he was on the Padres, he said, 'What are they throwing you?' I said, 'Some little crappy curve ball.' He said, 'Why don't you go up there and kind of lay for one of those, just kind of lay for it a little bit?' Well, I did—and I got a line drive to right field. I said, 'Hell, if this keeps up…' Pillette got me *thinking* at a young age about having an idea of what the pitcher was throwing. Then once you hit one of them slow curves the pitchers say, 'I can't do that any more.' So you get the pitch *you* want."[135] Williams later hit big-league homers #325 and 347 off Herm's son Duane Pillette.

He hit his first Hoover homers of 1935 in a game against Santa Ana on March 16. Willie 'Emperor' Jones—the "whirlwind Negro pitcher" was regarded as one of the best pitchers in southern California. The *Cardinal* columnist noted, "Coach Wofford Caldwell's team started scoring in the first inning, when Ted Williams, lanky Redbird slugger, connected with one of 'Emperor Jones" fast ones for a long home run over the Saint center fielder's head, bringing in McBurnie, Card center fielder, from second base." In the fourth inning, McBurnie came up again and was hit by a pitch by the "dusky Saint hurler." Ted was up next, batting cleanup. "Williams then took the measure of another of the Saint mound ace's deliveries and sent it over the right field fence for a double, missing the home run marker by only a few feet." Once again, he'd hit one out of the park but it only counted for two bases. Ted faced the 'Emperor' one more time. In the sixth, "Williams layed into one of the 'Emperor's' fast ones and lifted it high over the right field fence for a home run."[136]

In the April 1935 tournament at Pomona, Ted hit a home run in the game on the 24th, a game where he started out as the right fielder, was brought in to pitch and then, when relieved, finished the game in center field. In the final game, on May 11, he hit a "terrific home run" in the sixth inning, reported as a three-run homer by the *San Diego Union*.

The 1936 tournament was the one in which Jackie Robinson also played. Ted's four homers were the most hit by any batter. He hit .529 (9-for-17) and also pitched 17 innings, striking out 21. He allowed three runs and nine hits. In one game, he did something he never did again, as reported by the high school newspaper: "The most novel occurrence of the tournament for Hoover was the situation caused by Ted Williams," *Cardinal* coverage concluded. "Teddy came to bat twice in the same inning of the Monrovia game and got two home runs."[137]

It was actually Herm Pillette who gave up the last homer Ted hit before joining the Padres, in a semipro game. "A long line drive over the right-center-field fence at Golden Hill," Ted told Ed Linn.[138]

In 1937, after more batting practice at the North Park playground and many more milkshakes, he resumed play for the Padres, getting into 138 games.

The playground, a block and a half from his house on Utah Street, is where Ted spent much of his childhood. "I remember my first home run," he wrote. "Came against a guy named Hunt in a Sunday game in North Park. Just a poopy little fly ball to center, but it made it over the fence. There I was, a little 15-year-old standing in against guys 25 to 30 and this guy could really throw hard. I could barely get the ball around on it, and I hit that homer."[139]

Ted also played some semipro ball and Travis Hatfield, his manager for the Texas Liquor House team, told about a game against El Cajon. Down 1-0 in the ninth inning, with two outs and a man on base, fans started to leave. "Ted looked up and waved them back to their seats. 'It's not over yet,' Ted was yelling at them. And it wasn't. He poked one out for a home run and we won, 2-1. Boy, did he have a big grin galloping around the bases."[140]

He'd hit a home run during a preseason exhibition game for the Padres on March 14, hitting it "high on the telephone post in right field" (*San Diego Union*) and seeing the ball carom back onto the field, "but Williams touched all the bases. If the ball hadn't hit the pole, it would have landed on top the Santa Fe freight building." (*San Diego Evening Tribune*)

His first regular-season home run as a professional ballplayer came in the second game of a doubleheader against the San Francisco Mission Reds on April 11, 1937, a two-run homer off a left-hander named Stuart Bolen. He didn't hit his second until April 27, also at Lane Field, a second-inning two-run homer. Ted was 3-for-4 with five RBIs, his "breakout game"—and yet it was almost two months before he hit another homer (June 20).

His homer on June 22 earned him a seven-column headline on the front page of the *San Diego Union* sports section: TED WILLIAMS' HOMER WIN FOR PADRES, 3 to 2. The story was accompanied by a photograph. "Ted Williams, freshman outfielder, is the boy who did the raking. A run behind, one out and one on in the eighth, Williams took matters into his own hands when he delivered victory on a silver platter by smashing a home run deep into center field, scoring George McDonald before him." It was an inside-the-park home run, with Ted "slamming a screaming liner" between two outfielders and "galloping around the bases while they made future efforts to relay it to the plate."

He homered again on the 24th and then once more on the 25th. On June 27, he had his first two-homer day, hitting one in each half of a doubleheader against the Portland Beavers, also at Lane Field; he was dubbed "the hero of both tussles" by the *San Diego Union*. Both home runs were hit over the right-field wall. On July 13, "the sensational sophomore swatsmith" hit two in the same game, helping beat the visiting Mission Reds. On August 31, he had another two-homer game, against the Seals. All four of the homers in the two-homer games were hit over the right-field fence. His 23rd and final home run of the regular season was hit in his last at-bat, on September 19. Again, he pulled the ball and hit it over the right-field fence, this time in San Francisco in a game against the Missions.

Stronger and more accomplished, he hit 23 home runs in 434 at-bats, slugging .504 and batting for a .291 average. Art Hunt of the Seattle Indians led the league, with 39 homers. Only one other Padre reached double digits in homers—Tommy Thompson, with 16. Thompson was 27 years old and played in 169 games (the PCL had a much longer schedule and played 178 games that year—Williams again joined the team after his high school graduation). Thompson had already put in four seasons for the Boston Braves from 1933-36. In all, Thompson played in 397 major-league games and hit nine home runs.

The Padres made the playoffs, and in the clinching Game Four of the first round, "Ted Williams had put the Padres out in front in the fourth by hitting one of Tony Freitas' curveballs over the right-field wall." (*San Diego Evening Tribune*, September 27) The game was tied, 1-1, and the Padres won it in the bottom of the tenth. The Padres won the title in the second, championship round of playoffs, beating the Beavers. Williams was 5-for-16, but without a home run in that final round.[141]

Williams' contract was sold to the Boston Red Sox on December 8, 1937.

In spring training 1938, though disappointed he hadn't made the Boston team, he was assigned to the Millers for a year of seasoning under manager Donie Bush. If there were ever a year in which a player demonstrated he was ready to be called up to the majors the following season, it was 1938 for Ted Williams. He excelled across the board on offense, winning the American Association Triple Crown with a .366 batting average, 142 RBIs, and hitting 43 home runs.[142]

His first home run with Minneapolis was an inside-the-park home run, on the road in Louisville on April 21 in his sixth game of the season. In fact, he hit two inside-the-park jobs in the same game (Parkway Field's center field was expansive, to say the least, the distance 512 feet to straightaway center.)[143] The next time he hit an inside-the-park home run was in 1946, #165—the one that clinched the pennant.

The Millers' home field—Nicollet Park—measured only 279 down the right-field line, though there was a 30-foot high fence. In the 1938 home opener on April 29, he hit one out of the park—and then some. "The fans almost lost sight of the ball as it sailed through the air and landed on the roof of a building on the far side of Nicollet Avenue." (*Minneapolis Tribune*) The short distance to the right-field corner may have helped at times, but some of his homers in the Millers' home park went well over and out. He hit two homers on May 1. One for 400 feet and the other, "driven against a strong wind, cleared the advertising signs atop the right-field wall at about 350 feet from the plate, then sailed the proverbial mile in the air and landed on the far side of Nicollet Avenue. It traveled approximately 450 feet on the fly." (*Minneapolis Star*)

On June 4, he hit two homers in a game at Columbus, said to measure 925 feet *in toto*, with the longer one 500 feet. And on August 27, his 41st home run was "a mighty wallop, the ball clearing the buildings on the far side of Nicollet Avenue, the pellet finally landing in an alley between Nicollet and First avenues. (*Minneapolis Tribune*)

Local Millers fan Dick Durrell, who later founded *People* magazine, said, "The Millers would have problems with the merchants on the street across from the ballpark, Minken's department store, the President Café. The balls Ted hit would frequently go into their windows, and the team had to pay for them."[144]

He ended the season with 43 home runs, with 114 runs batted in, and a .360 batting average. Those totals earned him the Triple Crown in the American Association.

Homers supplied Ted's extended family with boxes of Wheaties

He'd signed endorsement deals with Hillerich & Bradsby, the Louisville Slugger company, and with Wheaties. "After I signed my contract with Wheaties," he said, "I used to get a carton of them when I hit a home run. I used to have a truckload of them going home each year."[145] Cobbler Salvatore Caristo ran Kenmore Shoe Repair a couple of blocks from Fenway Park. He got to know Ted Williams in 1939. Salvy told Tim Horgan, "He came in here and his shoes, both of them, had holes all over. 'So I say, "'Okay, I fix them up." But he say, "Right now. You got to fix them right now." I say, "Why?" And he say, "Because it's the only pair of shoes I got.' In those days, the guy who hits a home run gets a case of Wheaties. And Ted, he send the case of Wheaties to me, for my family. Sometimes I have so much Wheaties I hand them all over the neighborhood in East Boston. Ted don't forget people.'"[146]

The last one Ted hit out at Fenway — 1972

The last time he hit one out at Fenway, it was just foul. But part of an electrifying exhibition on August 25, 1972. He'd been out of the game for a dozen years and was almost 54 years old. There was a home run hitting contest for the Jimmy Fund before the regularly-scheduled Texas Rangers/Red Sox game, featuring some radio personalities and former Red Sox players. Williams was managing the Rangers at the time. He wasn't scheduled to be in the competition, but was drafted by popular acclaim when the event got underway, grabbed a bat and told Lee Stange to "bring it." Texas Ranger Rich Billings said, "He hit line drive after line drive. He hit them everywhere. He hit them off the wall. He hit a home run that was just foul [to right field], everything was a shot. Guys in the dugout were just looking at each other, staring. How old was he? You would have thought he was 22. I never have seen a batting practice exhibition like that from anyone of any age."[147]

Exhibition games

In the era Ted Williams played, it was common to play one or two exhibition games during the course of the then 154-game season. Ted took part in some of these and hit home runs in the first two he played. The first was on May 12, 1939 in Louisville playing against Boston's Triple A farm club, the Louisville Colonels. He had four major-league homers by then. Pitching for Louisville was Rufus Meadows, a 31-year-old career minor leaguer who had appeared in one big-league game, for Cincinnati in 1926, working all of one-third of an inning. In this 1939 exhibition, Meadows pitched a complete game against the visiting Red Sox, losing 7-3. The only home run in the game was Williams', hit in the third inning. He also cracked a 395-foot double in the fifth. Whistling Jake Wade went the distance and won the game for Boston.

The Red Sox played another in-season exhibition game in 1940—the annual Hall of Fame game at Cooperstown on June 13. The Chicago Cubs won the game, 10-9, and Dom DiMaggio was hurt and had to leave the game after he toppled backwards into the center-field bleachers at Doubleday Field, catching a fly ball off the bat of Billy Rogell. Ted Williams starred on offense with two home runs—a solo home run in the second inning and another in the seventh. Rain halted the game after seven innings. The *Boston Globe* reported correctly noted that fences at Doubleday "are quite close in and home runs were easy." That said, there were only three of them, the two by Ted and one by Jim Tabor.

1948 - Boston Red Sox Ted Williams crossing home plate with his head down as Red Sox Johnny Pesky and Dom DiMaggio look on at Braves Field (during an exhibition game).

He didn't play in either of the two in-season exhibitions in 1941, against Indianapolis and Brockton. In 1942, the Sox played an unusual five exhibitions during the season. The first was against the United States Army base team at Fort Devens, Massachusetts on June 12. Some 12,000 soldiers watched the game. Ted had enlisted in the Navy just weeks beforehand, and he came to the plate in the second inning. "Just as a soldier boy was chirruping 'Sailors can't hit,' Ted socked the ball into the heavy foliaged right-field trees." It was a two-run homer, hit with Lou Finney on first base; then Ted "boosted a high home run into the right-field forest...almost over the grove of verdant trees on the deep right-center field embankment." (*Globe* and *Herald*) Boston won. 11-5.

In the September 4 game, played at Camp Edwards' Logan Field in Massachusetts, Ted was unable to hit a home run—but he did pitch four innings, striking out three, allowing six hits. The Sox won, 3-2, in front of 10,000 soldiers. The only homer was hit by a soldier from San Antonio named Muriel Knox, the first batter of the game. The other run came in on Ted's watch.

Between the September 21 game and the final game of the regular season on the 27th, the Red Sox played four exhibition games in New England communities in four New England states. On the 22nd, they played Manchester, New Hampshire (Ted doubled) and on the 24th against the Maine All-Stars in Portland. "Williams socked a long smash to right" his first time up, hitting one of four Red Sox homers which sank the Maine team, 11-4. They played in the 25th at Pawtucket, Rhode Island; Ted tripled in the game. The venue was Lynn, Massachusetts on the 26th—Ted doubled.

The only in-season exhibition game in 1946 was on the 200th anniversary of East Douglas, Massachusetts, celebrated by a Yankees 8, Red Sox 7 game in which Ted was 0-for-2. He didn't homer in 1947 or 1948 and the only homer he hit in 1949 was in the home-run hitting contest before the May 31 game in Scranton.

Ralph Kiner out-hit Williams in a contest before the June 26, 1950 game in Pittsburgh, eight homers to four, but when the Pirates and Red Sox squared off as teams, Kiner was homerless while Ted hit one about 375 feet into the lower deck at Forbes Field.

On June 11 in 1951, Bobby Doerr hit three homers at the Polo Grounds before a game against the New York Giants; Ted only hit one but it cleared the high right-field roof at the 340-foot mark. In the actual game, the only homer hitter was Willie Mays. In a rematch at Fenway on the 25th, Williams was 2-for-5 in the homer-hitting contest, but only played one inning (without out) during the actual game.

He was 5-for-5 in the home run-hitting contest before the June 28, 1954 game against the Giants but 0-for-1 with a walk in the game. In the August 16 contest he failed to hit even one.

There were three exhibition games in 1955. Against the Giants at Fenway on May 23, a "line-drive home run...hit as only Williams hits them" in the third inning and into the right-field seats. His first home run of the 1955 regular season came a few days later. Ted skipped the June 27 game but played in the Hall of Fame game on July 25 and in his one and only at-bat homered over left field off Milwaukee Braves starter Chet Nichols in the first inning. He hit it out over the left-field fence, some 350 feet.

Twenty years after playing for the Minneapolis Millers, Ted Williams came back to town to play against them in a June 16, 1958 exhibition game. First time up, Ted swung at Jack Spring's 3-0 pitch and hit a home run that cleared the park at the 355-foot mark in right field and "with a swarm of urchins in pursuit—reached a light tower 55 feet beyond." Returning to Minneapolis in 1959, he did it again—another first-inning homer, this one a two-run shot on August 17, adding a double and a single later in the game. In his final exhibition game, May 23, 1960, Ted pinch hit but walked.

Spring training games

During Ted's years with the Red Sox, the team played over 500 spring training games—even without counting 1953, 1955, and 1959. We didn't seem it worth the effort to attempt to research each and every one of those spring training games—in large part, because—who cares? Spring training games aren't always real competition, but serve other purposes. On March 14, 2000, the Red Sox won a perfect game in Ft. Myers, 5-0, over the Toronto Blue Jays. It's not a game that goes down in baseball history as meaning much of anything. It was the combined effort of six Red Sox pitchers: Pedro Martinez, Fernando de la Cruz, Dan Smith, Rheal Cormier, Rich Garces, and Rod Beck. After it was over, Beck admitted, "I didn't find out about it until I turned around to shake the guys' hands and I looked up and saw it on the board. I saw 'perfect game' and I said, 'Hey, pretty cool.'" Cormier, who'd pitched the seventh, was out in the parking lot talking to his wife when he heard about it. Smith and Garces both confessed they hadn't known it was a perfecto, either. It just didn't seem worth the effort to see if Ted Williams had hit a homer off a hapless prospect who never even made it to Single A ball. Of course, there's nothing stopping readers of this book from launching an effort to do the research.

His first spring training home run, however, is worthy of note. It came during a lopsided 24-2 game against Boston's Louisville Colonels minor-league affiliate at Arcadia, Florida on March 27, 1939. Jack Malaney described it in the *Boston Post*: "Ted Williams…started away on his 1939 home-run hitting.

He hit the first ball pitched to him in the opening inning over the right-field fence, the barrier being about 300 feet away from the plate."

The first game-winning homer he may have hit came several days later, on April 2. It was the day after the time he'd become so frustrated after he'd let a fly ball fall in front of him that he threw it out of the park in Atlanta (see a brief mention of this in the writeup for HR #3.) Joe Cronin pulled him out of the game and fined him $50. "I'll pay you $50," he told Cronin, "for every one I throw out if you'll pay me $50 for every one I hit out."[148] The very next day, Ted was restored to the lineup. The game was scoreless through the first five innings. Larry Miller was pitching for Atlanta. "Williams was the first batter to face Miller in the sixth. With the count two balls and one strike, Ted unloaded and it was a homer from the instant it left the bat, finally crashing against the third tier of staggered billboards that rise one on top of the other on the right-center-field embankment." The Red Sox won, 3-0. It was a game-winning homer for "Thumping Theodore."

After Ted hit one out in a City Series game against the Boston Braves on April 16, 1950, Braves catcher Del Crandall was asked what it was that Ted had hit to win the game. His response: "A home run!"

Major-league parks where Ted Williams homered

The following list presents the first date in which Ted homered in each of the major-league parks of his day. He never homered at Oriole Park at Camden Yards, or Safeco, or any number of other parks familiar to fans today—because they didn't exist. In fact, of the 30 home fields of major-league teams in 2013, there are only two that existed during the 1939-1960 period: Fenway Park and Wrigley Field.

What follows is a list of the first home runs Ted Williams hit in each major-league ballpark of his day, be it in the regular-season game or an exhibition game.

Baltimore –Memorial Stadium: August 6, 1954 (HR #357)
Boston — Braves Field: April 16, 1948 (exhibition game)
Boston — Fenway Park: April 23, 1939 (HR #1)
Chicago — Comiskey Park I: July 18, 1939 (HR #15)
Chicago — Wrigley Field (none)
Cincinnati — Crosley Field (none)
Cleveland — Cleveland Municipal Stadium: July 15, 1939 (HR #13)
Cleveland — League Park: August 28, 1939 (HR #20)
Detroit — Briggs Stadium: May 4, 1939 (HR #2)
Kansas City — Municipal Stadium: June 4, 1955 (HR #368)
Los Angeles — Los Angeles Coliseum (none)

Milwaukee — County Stadium (none)

New York City / Brooklyn — Ebbets Field (none)

New York City — Polo Grounds: June 11, 1951 (home-run hitting contest)

New York City — Yankee Stadium I: September 30, 1939 (HR #31)

Philadelphia — Shibe Park: July 4, 1949 (HR #12)

Pittsburgh — Forbes Field: June 26, 1950 (exhibition game)

St. Louis — Sportsman's Park: May 9, 1939 (HR #4)

San Francisco — Candlestick Park (none)

Washington DC — Griffith Stadium: August 19, 1939 (HR #18)

One of Ted's biggest hits

World history took another turn when a plot to assassinate Adolf Hitler at Fenway Park in 1939 came to fruition, though it had been planned. This was Ted's first year with the Red Sox and catcher Moe Berg's last. Berg had already carried out a mission earlier in the decade, filming the Tokyo skyline while on a baseball tour of Japan. During a planned visit by Hitler to Fenway Park, a plan was hatched to station a sharpshooter on the roof above the press box during a doubleheader against the Yankees. The plan involved both Williams and Berg. "It was to happen with Ted Williams at bat," explained historians Bill Lee and Jim Prime. "The prearranged signal for the sharpshooter to fire would be a tip of the hat from Williams. At a propitious moment, Berg would relay the sign from the Red Sox dugout, a position that allowed him a clear view [to where the Fuhrer and other visiting officials from the Third Reich were seated near the Yankees' dugout.]" The moment never arrived during the first game, so Ted decided to take matters into his own hand in between games when Hitler was scheduled to throw out the first pitch. Berg was to receive it and Ted was to stand by for a photo op after the pitch.

"Hitler took the ball from the Fenway Park official and rested his right foot on the rubber as he had been coached to do. He went into his version of a pitching windup — right arm extended as in a bizarre Heil Hitler salute, left leg raised as if in a modified goose-step and released the ball. It went slowly but amazingly straight and true toward Berg's waiting glove. As it crossed the middle of the plate, Ted Williams' bat suddenly whipped around at lightning speed. The crack of bat on ball was like a gunshot, and the ball rocketed off the Louisville slugger with the sped of an assassin's bullet, striking the dictator squarely between the eyes. The Hun was stunned. He staggered backward slightly, righted himself momentarily, then pitched face first to the ground, as if poleaxed. He was dead before he hit the ground."

—Bill Lee and Ted Williams, *The Little Red [Sox] Book* (Chicago: Triumph Books, 2003), 81, 88. For any who may doubt the veracity of this tale, the book presents a photograph of the felled Fuhrer laid out on the Fenway Park mound.

Pinch-hit Homers

Pinch hitting is usually much more difficult than hitting during the course of a game. The batter enters cold, without having as much opportunity to become acclimated to the game and without the benefit of having seen pitches from the man on the mound in a first or second at-bat during any given game. All in all, Ted Williams hit for a .344 career batting average, as we know. As a pinch hitter, his average was .297 (33 for 111). He hit seven home runs as a pinch hitter.

July 20, 1941—off Johnny Niggeling in St. Louis (HR #71)

August 9, 1953—off Mike Garcia (Baltimore) in Boston (HR #325)

September 14, 1953—off Mike Fornieles in Chicago (HR #336)

June 25, 1954—off Bob Keegan in Chicago (HB #343)

July 14, 1957—off Stan Pitula in Cleveland (HR #443)

September 17, 1957—off Tom Morgan (Kansas City) in Boston (HR #452)

September 20, 1957—off Whitey Ford in New York (HR #453)

There were some years in which he pinch hit more than others. He didn't pinch hit at all in his rookie year, when he played right field in 149 games. Nor did he pinch hit in 1942, 1946, 1947, or 1949. Ted moved to left field starting in 1940. He pinch hit once in 1940, on August 2, drew a walk, and scored.

In 1941, the year he hit .406, Williams pinch hit in the first five games in which he played, and six of the first seven. And he pinch hit in four games in mid-July. He was 3-for-9 (.333), with a pinch-hit homer in the July 20 game. He had five RBIs in his 10 plate appearances. There was one walk.

Remarkably, the year in which he pinch hit the most often was 1959, his worst year at the plate, the year he was hampered all season long by the pinched nerve in his neck—yet he was 11-for-24 (a .458 batting average). His last year, 1960, he pinch hit 19 times but only got one hit.

His best ratio of homers to pinch hits was in 1957, when he pinch hit seven times, walking twice, and homered in three of his five at-bats.

Though he hit for a .297 average in his pinch-hitting roles, Williams—as always—walked a lot. Once he was hit by a pitch, in 1959. He hit two sacrifice flies. With the bases on balls he drew added in, his on-base percentage as a pinch hitter was .410.

More home runs than strikeouts in a single season

This extremely rare accomplishment is something Ted Williams achieved more than once. He did it four times:

	homers	strikeouts
1941	37	27
1950	28	21
1953	13	10
1955	28	24

Home runs off Hall of Famers

Ted Williams hit 37 of his 521 home runs off eight future Hall of Famers:

Jim Bunning—8
Bob Feller—10
Whitey Ford—1
Lefty Gomez—2
Bob Lemon—4
Ted Lyons—1
Hal Newhouser—3
Red Ruffing—4
Early Wynn—8

Alphabetical listing of pitchers
and the home runs they surrendered
to Ted Williams

Lou Brissie	208, 288
Johnny Broaca	13
Hal Brown	299
Clint Brown	15
Walter Brown	173
Bob Bruce	505
Jim Bunning	383, 439, 440, 451, 472, 498, 504, 519
Wally Burnette	401
Moe Burtschy	289
Bud Byerly	411
Harry Byrd	268, 340, 360, 367, 381
Tommy Byrne	222
Earl Caldwell	212
Paul Calvert	233
Alex Carrasquel	17, 86
George Caster	52, 53, 75
Pete Center	135
Bob Chakales	348, 357, 421
Spud Chandler	117, 125
Russ Christopher	98, 104, 149, 193
Tex Clevenger	476
Jim Coates	494
Ed Cole	4
Joe Coleman	167, 194, 318
Bill Cox	45
Bud Daley	502, 503
Chubby Dean	25, 41, 70
Bill Dietrich	37, 43
Art Ditmar	341, 368, 395, 429
Sonny Dixon	329
Joe Dobson	36
Atley Donald	46, 103
Dick Donovan	424
Fritz Dorish	312
Karl Drews	220
Harry Eisenstat	21, 97
Red Embree	140, 165, 228, 246

Stan Pitula	443
Arnie Portocarrero	362
Nels Potter	10
Pedro Ramos	388, 409, 418, 430, 482, 520
Vic Raschi	250, 266, 292, 293, 321
Allie Reynolds	199, 216, 251, 265, 290, 344
Johnny Rigney	56, 57, 58, 64, 72, 89, 133
Dutch Romberger	345
John Romonosky	475, 481
Buck Ross	66, 123
Schoolboy Rowe	68
Red Ruffing	7, 47, 126, 181
Marius Russo	50, 51
Fred Sanford	170, 188, 202
Bob Savage	166, 178
Ray Scarborough	136
Sid Schacht	281
Carl Scheib	179, 192, 234
Herb Score	373, 382, 389, 415
Bobby Shantz	287, 403
Bob Shaw	509
Spec Shea	198, 224, 309, 326, 328
Ray Shore	241
Dave Sisler	485
Lou Sleater	298, 441
Eddie Smith	172
Gerry Staley	464
Bryan Stephens	215
Chuck Stobbs	408
Dean Stone	377, 410
Tom Sturdivant	419, 455
Steve Sundra	31
Max Surkont	254
Ralph Terry	495
Bud Thomas	1, 67
Forrest Thompson	217
Dick Tomanek	432

Thanks to Steve Gietschier for assistance with the St. Louis papers.

Notes

1   Ted Williams and John Underwood, *The Science of Hitting* (New York: Fireside Books, 1970), 7.

2   Ed Linn, *Hitter: The Life and Turmoils of Ted Williams* (New York: Harcourt Brace, 1993), 4.

3   *Boston Globe,* July 9, 1941.

4   Ted Williams and Jim Prime, *Ted Williams' Hit List* (Chicago: Contemporary Books, 1996), 44

5   *New York Times,* January 9, 1949.

6   Ted Williams, *My Turn at Bat* (NY: Fireside/Simon & Schuster, 1988), 59, 60. Leigh Montville tells the story in more detail in his book *Ted Williams: The Biography of an American Hero* (New York: Doubleday, 2004), 58-59.

7   *My Turn At Bat,* 61.

8   Ed Linn, *Ted Williams: The Eternal Kid* (New York: Thomas Nelson and Sons, 1961), 49.

9   *My Turn at Bat,* 62.

10   This paragraph comes from John Holway's *The Last .400 Hitter,* page 64. When Holway told Ted the story, Ted said, "Naw, Buck Newsom was a good guy. Hell, nothing wrong with Newsom. He threw blooper pitches at me. Couldn't get 'em over. But I would let him think I was a little mad at him."

11   Curt Smith, *The Storytellers* (New York: Macmillan, 1997), 66, 67. Ted's first hit was a single, not a double.

12   John Holway, *The Last .400 Hitter* (Dubuque, Iowa: William C. Brown, 1992), 38.

13   *My Turn at Bat,* 84.

14   *My Turn at Bat*, 114.

15   *The Science of Hitting*, 32.

16   *My Turn at Bat*, 56.

17   Ed Linn, *Hitter*, 146.

18   John Holway, *The Last .400 Hitter*, 99.

19   *The Science of Hitting*, 33.

20   Leigh Montville, 86.

21   *The Sporting News*, July 14, 1941.

22   *My Turn at Bat*, 89.

23   *Boston Globe*, July 9, 1941.

24   Kyle Crichton, *Collier's*, September 28, 1946.

25   John Holway, *The Last .400 Hitter*, 47.

26   Tom Larwin, "Ted's Baseball Return to San Diego in 1941," in Nowlin, ed., *The Kid: Ted Williams in San Diego* (Cambridge, Massachusetts: Rounder Books, 2005), 184-6.

27   *San Diego Union*, October 6, 1941.

28   Michael Seidel, *Ted Williams: A Baseball Life* (Chicago: Contemporary Books, 1991), 89.

29   *The Science of Hitting*, 29.

30   Jim Prime and Bill Nowlin, *Ted Williams: The Pursuit of Perfection*, 103.

31   Bill Nowlin, *Ted Williams at War* (Burlington MA: Rounder Books, 2007), 56, 57.

32   See a detailed account of the full series in Nowlin, *Ted Williams at War*, 68-72.

33   Fred Hatfield, in Danny Peary, ed., *They Played the Game* (New York: Hyperion, 1994), 163.

34   *The Science of Hitting*, 72.

35   Prime and Nowlin, *Ted Williams: The Pursuit of Perfection*, 13.

36   *The Science of Hitting*, 73.

37   Ed Linn, *Hitter*, 194, 195.

38   Ted Williams, with David Pietrusza, *My Life in Pictures* (Kingston NY: Total Sports, 2001), 30.

39   Reprinted in Lawrence Baldassaro, ed., *The Ted Williams Reader* (New York: Fireside Books, 1991),115.

40   Linn, *Ted Williams: The Eternal Kid*, 66.

41   Ibid., 69-70.

42   *My Turn at Bat*, 111.

43   *My Turn at Bat*, 115.

44   *Boston Globe*, March 6, 1947.

45   Author interview with Thomas Seessel on July 1, 1997.

46   *Boston Globe*, March 1, 1949.

47   *The Science of Hitting*, 25.

48   Linn, *Hitter*, 182, 183.

49   Dave Heller, *Facing Ted Williams*, 58-60.

50   *New York Times*, November 20, 1948.

51   Linn, *Hitter*, 185.

52   Dave Heller, *Facing Ted Williams*, 177, 178.

53   *My Turn at Bat*, 154-55.

54   David Cataneo, *I Remember Ted Williams* (Nashville: Cumberland House, 2002), 44.

55   Dave Heller, *Facing Ted Williams*, 197.

56   Linn, *Hitter*, 194.

57   *The Science of Hitting*, 23. The classic case was, of course, home run #521.

58   *My Turn at Bat*, 135.

59   Seidel, *Ted Williams: A Baseball Life*, 218.

60   *The Science of Hitting*, 73.

61   Dave Heller, *Facing Ted Williams*, 67.

62   *My Life in Pictures*, 90.

63   *My Turn at Bat*, 185.

64   *My Life in Pictures*, 98.

65   *My Turn at Bat*, 186.

66   Leigh Montville, 180.

67   Ibid.

68   Dave Heller, *Facing Ted Williams*, 63, 64.

69   Jim Prime and Bill Nowlin, *Ted Williams: The Pursuit of Perfection*, 72.

70   Author interview with Richie Ashburn, August 3, 1997.

71   Author interview with Vince Piazza, May 23, 1997.

72   Seidel, *Ted Williams: A Baseball Life*, 337.

73   Dave Heller, *Facing Ted Williams*, 109, 110.

74   Jim Prime and Bill Nowlin, *Ted Williams: The Pursuit of Perfection*, 56.

75 *My Turn at Bat*, 192-93. The rules have since changed again.

76 Ed Linn, *Hitter*, 191.

77 Ed Linn, *Hitter*, 195.

78 Author interview with Jimmy Piersall, April 20, 1997.

79 Jim Prime and Bill Nowlin, *Ted Williams: The Pursuit of Perfection*, 97.

80 Pedro Ramos, in Danny Peary, ed., *They Played the Game* (New York: Hyperion, 1994), 377.

81 Mickey Mantle, *The Education of a Baseball Player*, quoted in Prime and Nowlin, 101.

82 Dave Heller, *Facing Ted Williams*, 17.

83 *La Prensa* (San Antonio, Texas), September 25, 1955.

84 Ed Linn, *Hitter*, 186, 188.

85 Seidel, *Ted Williams: A Baseball Life*, 225.

86 Mickey Vernon letter to Michael Seidel; see *Ted Williams: A Baseball Life*, 281.

87 *The Science of Hitting*, 49.

88 *My Turn at Bat*, 136.

89 Seidel, *Ted Williams: A Baseball Life*, xiv.

90 *Boston Globe*, March 21, 1951.

91 *Boston Globe*, June 25, 1949.

92 *Boston Globe*, June 20, 1950.

93 Linn, *Hitter*, 183.

94 Author interview with Bob Holbrook, April 23, 1997.

95 *Christian Science Monitor*, September 15, 1956.

96 Linn, *Ted Williams: The Eternal Kid*, 126.

97 *The Science of Hitting*, 31-32.

98 Dave Heller, *Facing Ted Williams*, 46.

99 Dave Heller, *Facing Ted Williams*, 34, 51.

100 *The Science of Hitting*, 16, 18.

101 *My Life in Pictures*, 120, and *My Turn at Bat*, 199.

102 *My Turn at Bat*, 73.

103 *The Science of Hitting*, 31.

104 Montville, 205-206.

105 *My Turn at Bat*, 200.

106 Montville, 207.

107   Ed Linn, *Hitter*, 295.

108   Jim Prime and Bill Nowlin, *Ted Williams: The Pursuit of Perfection*, 195.

109   *My Turn at Bat*, 208.

110   Dave Heller, *Facing Ted Williams*, 96, 97.

111   *My Turn at Bat*, 209.

112   Dave Heller, *Facing Ted Williams*, 32,33.

113   *The Science of Hitting*, 36.

114   Dave Heller, *Facing Ted Williams*, 23, 24.

115   Dave Heller, *Facing Ted Williams*, 78.

116   Dave Heller, *Facing Ted Williams*, 88, 89, 99.

117   Dave Heller, *Facing Ted Williams*, 38.

118   Linn, *Ted Williams: The Eternal Kid*, 130.

119   Jim Prime and Bill Nowlin, *Ted Williams: The Pursuit of Perfection*, 204.

120   John Updike, *Hub Fans Bid Kid Adieu* (New York: The Library of America, 2010), 32.

121   Bruce Markusen, *Ted Williams* (Westport, Connecticut: Greenwood Press, 2004), 89.

122   Interview with Ted Williams, conducted by Jeff Idelson of the National Baseball Hall of Fame, 2000.

123   Linn, *Hitter*, 344, 346.

124   Jim Prime and Bill Nowlin, *Ted Williams: The Pursuit of Perfection*, 121.

125   Christine Paul, "Most Valuable Player," *Paths of Progress*, Spring 1996, 3.

126   Dick Johnson and Glenn Stout, *Ted Williams: A Portrait in Words and Pictures* (New York: Walker and Company, 1991), 117.

127   *Ted Williams' Hit List*, 162.

128   Ibid., 12.

129   *The Science of Hitting*, 25.

130   *San Diego Union*, September 16, 1936.

131   Jim Prime and Bill Nowlin, *Ted Williams: The Pursuit of Perfection* (Champaign IL: Sports Publishing, 2002), 7.

132   Author interview with Wos Caldwell, April 24, 1997.

133   Bill Nowlin, ed., *The Kid: Ted Williams in San Diego*, 52, 53.

134   *My Life in Pictures*, 15.

135   Ibid., 17.

136   Bill Nowlin, ed., *The Kid: Ted Williams in San Diego*, 59.

137 Bill Nowlin, ed., *The Kid: Ted Williams in San Diego*, 76. This book contains more than 70 pages detailing Ted's time at Hoover High School.

138 Ed Linn, *Hitter*, 41.

139 *San Diego Union-Tribune*, July 7, 1988 and undated 1992 article.

140 *Boston American*, December 14, 1950.

141 For details of every game played by the 1937 Padres, see Bill Swank's comprehensive "Ted Williams, Earl Keller, and the 1937 San Diego Padres," in *The Kid: Ted Williams in San Diego* (edited by Bill Nowlin) and published by Rounder Books in 2005.

142 RBI totals per James D. Smith III's article, "The Kid Leaves Home: Ted Williams and the 1938 Minneapolis Millers" in Nowlin, ed., *The Kid: Ted Williams in San Diego* (Rounder, 2005), which is in agreement with Stew Thornley's detailed tabulation in his article for the same volume, "Ted Williams (#19) with the 1938 Minneapolis Millers."

143 The *Minneapolis Journal*'s George Barton estimated the two homers as having gone 470 feet and 512 feet, the second one having rolled right to the base of the fence.

144 Peter Golenbock, *Red Sox Nation* (Chicago: Triumph Books, 2005), 120. See Stew Thornley's detailing of each and every Williams game for Minneapolis, which appears in Nowlin, ed., *The Kid: Ted Williams in San Diego*.

145 *My Life in Pictures*, 30.

146 Tim Horgan, undated newspaper column found in Ted Williams' Hall of Fame player file. Ted also took care of relatives back in Santa Barbara. Danny Venzor recalled, "I remember as kids, we used to get like 1000 little boxes of Wheaties. The whole family grew up—the kids all grew up—with Wheaties coming out of our ears. They'd ship them to us." Interview with author May 7, 2000.

147 Montville, 301-302, and the *Boston Globe*, August 26, 1972.

148 Dick Johnson and Glenn Stout, *Ted Williams: A Portrait in Words and Pictures* (New York: Walker and Company, 1991), 23.

www.ingramcontent.com/pod-product-compliance
Lightning Source LLC
LaVergne TN
LVHW051620080426
835511LV00016B/2083